THE UNIVERSITY OF NORTH CAROLINA PRESS   CHAPEL HILL

EMPTY PLEASURES

THE STORY OF ARTIFICIAL SWEETENERS FROM SACCHARIN TO SPLENDA

CAROLYN DE LA PEÑA

This volume was published with the assistance of the Greensboro Women's Fund of the University of North Carolina Press.

Founding Contributors: Linda Arnold Carlisle, Sally Schindel Cone, Anne Faircloth, Bonnie McElveen Hunter, Linda Bullard Jennings, Janice J. Kerley (in honor of Margaret Supplee Smith), Nancy Rouzer May, and Betty Hughes Nichols.

All rights reserved. Designed by Courtney Leigh Baker and set in Merlo and Unsprit by Rebecca Evans. Manufactured in the United States of America. The paper in this book meets the guidelines for permanence and durability of the Committee on Production Guidelines for Book Longevity of the Council on Library Resources. The University of North Carolina Press has been a member of the Green Press Initiative since 2003.

Library of Congress Cataloging-in-Publication Data
Peña, Carolyn Thomas de la.
Empty pleasures: the story of artificial sweeteners from saccharin to Splenda / by Carolyn de la Peña.—1st ed.
p. cm.   Includes bibliographical references and index.
ISBN 978-0-8078-3409-1 (cloth: alk. paper)
1. Nonnutritive sweeteners—History. I. Title.
TP422.P46 2010   664'.5—dc22   2010006638

14 13 12 11 10   5 4 3 2 1

FOR CATHERINE VADE BON COEUR

CONTENTS

ILLUSTRATIONS

INTRODUCTION

> One cannot simply assume that everyone has an
> infinite desire for sweetness, any more than one can assume
> the same about a desire for comfort or wealth or power.
> —Sidney Mintz, *Sweetness and Power*

In May 2008, I ate breakfast at Café du Monde in New Orleans. It was early in the morning and the café had just opened, but already the tables were filling up with customers ordering the customary cup of house coffee and a heaping plate of beignets. I'd brought a book with me and planned to do a bit of background reading for one of the chapters I was working on. But the scene was too interesting. I was drawn to the sounds of tourists, half American and half foreign, speaking many languages, and the smells of what joined them: mounds of fresh, enormous, heavily sugared donuts.

Next to me was a family of three that I quickly identified by their flowered-print shirts and white tennis shoes as American tourists. Each of them ordered a plate of beignets (three to a serving). I noticed that as the woman ate her first beignet, she looked around the table and, finding something missing, signaled the waiter. She pointed to the white packets of sugar at the table and asked for something. He returned from the kitchen with a small plate of pink, blue, and yellow packets. She opened a yellow one, poured it into her coffee, and drank it as she ate the entire plate of food.

That scene took me back to another in Atlanta, in a small conference room, more than a decade ago, to a moment that was the start of this book (though I did not know that at the time). I was working in corporate branding for a soda client that shall remain nameless. Our assignment was to talk with "diet brand X loyalists," or people who consumed the equivalent of between six and eight diet brand X sodas a day. We were to find out what values they attributed to the product so that we could more effectively market it to people's "aspirations" and thereby sell more soda. I expected the loyalists to talk about how it tasted better or how they were trying to lose weight. They did that. But these women (and they were all women) also talked about the moments when they drank a can of Diet X. They told of working white- and blue-collar jobs that bored them, about their frustration at not being able to control their own tasks and schedules. They talked about taking care of kids and the exhaustion of domestic labor. And they universally characterized the minutes when they consumed a Diet X as distinct from these routines. It was something they did for themselves, a little "treat" that they could have without guilt, a brief period of time when the rest of the world would leave them alone.

I undertook this project to better understand what consumers are looking for when they choose "diet" products sweetened by artificial sweetener. In the process of exploring the history of sweetener invention, production, marketing, regulation, and consumption, I have found that artificial sweeteners have much to tell us about our consumer choices and our vexed relationship with food in the twentieth century. But they also have much to tell us about why individual scientists and business-people within food and pharmaceutical companies were motivated to create these new food products, and why women entrepreneurs and media professionals have been eager to market them as positive goods. Some were motivated by the challenge of technical innovation. Many were eager to distinguish themselves by transcending the limits of what their products—be they foods or pharmaceuticals, cookbooks or columns—could do. When we walk down the grocery store aisle and find hundreds of packaged products claiming that their contents are "low sugar" and "healthy" and "fortified," we are observing the results of neither a rational process designed to serve consumer needs and desires nor a conspiracy to ruin our health by making us dependent on vast quantities of nutritionally bereft foods. What we are looking at are the material results of human desire. The story of artificial sweetener reminds us that real people created the industrial food products many are quick to criticize in American life today. We need to take seriously the motivations of these people and begin to see our food products not as "artificial" or "industrial" constructions that assault us. Rather, our food products embody us.

The transition of artificial sweetener from maligned chemical to praised innovation took place largely between the end of World War II and the early 1980s. The first part of this era saw a new mandate for citizens whereby patriotism should be expressed through consumption. While the effects of this era of plenty have been much studied in the realm of housing (federal loans and the rise of suburbia), material goods (the malling of America), and finance (a new credit culture), we have not thought much about the impact that this relentless push for more has had on the American appetite or our attempts to manage it. It is not a coincidence that the first popular demand for saccharin and cyclamates, the first sweeteners developed for a mass market, occurred in the 1950s as Americans expanded their material consumption at a rate unparalleled in history. Yet need alone might not have been sufficient for many consumers to overcome their initial aversion to sweeteners. It was the pitch people—pharmaceutical salesmen, fruit canners, and diet and beauty experts—who recast artificial sweeteners as health-enabling products. Still, without changes to the nutritional guidelines, sweeteners might not have won over buyers long wary of industrial substitutions and entrepreneurial health claims. What Michael Pollan has characterized as "The Age of Nutritionism," wherein commodity lobbying groups successfully shifted our national dialogue from food quality and portion size to ingredients, calories, and substitutions, ultimately enabled artificial sweetener to realize its potential.[1] As sugar became a high-profile food villain and substitutes shook off their reputation as inferior, artificial sweeteners like aspartame (NutraSweet) and, later, sucralose (Splenda) were successfully branded "healthy" alternatives.

For individuals who have come of age during the eras of sweet substitutions, the results have been mixed. On one hand, many lives have been improved by artificial sweeteners. This is particularly true for those on the promoting end. Cyclamates, saccharin, aspartame, and sucralose were developed in laboratories, but they required nonscientific sensibilities to get from lab to pantry. Local newspaper writers went from writing food columns to lunching with pharmaceutical executives, from passing along well-worn recipes to inventing the art of low-calorie cooking. Product promoters distinguished themselves in industries like canning and weight loss by seeing the possibilities of presenting a chemical as a tool for beauty and health. By working with artificial sweeteners, many gained status, wealth, and power. For consumers, sweeteners have provided a means to enjoy pleasurable foods and drinks while reducing total caloric intake. They have been and continue to be cornerstones in many weight-loss plans and products. As substitutes for sugar and corn syrup in replacement shakes and diet-club meals, sweeteners have enhanced what would otherwise be bland food landscapes. In doing so, they have certainly helped people lose weight. And for diabetics, sweeteners have made the difference between a life with very few sweets and constant sugar vigilance to one where a craving for sweetness can be safely indulged.

On the other hand, one does not have to look long at the positives of artificial sweeteners before the negatives appear. Product promoters, in fact, were frequently left vulnerable in the marketplace because of the uncertain chemical composition of sweeteners and the government's attempts to ban them. The very women who used sweeteners to succeed professionally in food manufacturing and marketing often found themselves promoting a vision of thinness that they themselves found diffiicult to achieve. And consumers have walked a fine line between feeling empowered by the calorie control sweeteners have provided and feeling anxious about sweeteners' safety and possible health risks. Further, it was through artificial sweeteners that pharmaceutical industries made their first major inroads into our food supply. By stripping foods and beverages of troubling calories, they transformed consumer concern about appropriate consumption into profits. They sold more by marketing it as *less*. One is hard pressed to think of a more ingenious system for moving large quantities of product through American bodies in the postwar era.

Since the 1950s, the food industry has promoted eating as an act of pleasure, control, and satisfaction against the backdrop of a general expansion in the importance of material consumption and the proliferation of goods. It has inundated us with "fun foods" for kids and wrapped love in a box of chocolates. It has ingeniously developed ways to toughen the skin of tomatoes and modify the leaves of lettuce to make them cheaper to harvest and easier to transport across vast distances, giving us the "fresh" foods we desire, cheap and year-round.[2] It has found ways to preserve wheat-based products with corn syrups and stabilizers, making snack foods cheap, convenient, and pleasurable. It has created an array of improved tastes—from "home style" cookies to tangy chips—enabling us to indulge our senses with astounding variety. And it has smartly marketed each of these innovations as giving us more of the food sensations we want for less money.

One could draw parallels to a number of industries. Products have diversified across all sectors of the consumer landscape, from cars to clothing. Yet food faced one obstacle that these industries did not: the human body. Nutrition experts recommend that middle-aged people of average weight and height consume no more than 2,000 to 2,600 calories a day to avoid weight gain.[3] As a nation, we can only expand the amount of food purchased—if we stay within those limits—by roughly 2 percent. That is not sufficient for "healthy" market growth. Artificial sweetener has provided the equivalent of buying cars on credit and homes on balloon mortgages—a way to have the pleasure of material consumption while staying within the actual material limits of what we can "afford." It has made appetites that would otherwise be unsustainable possible. And it has enabled us to experience, on the most intimate level, a key promise of postwar American culture, namely, that the continued elevation of consumption levels would create a healthy nation.

As bodies living within this cultural moment, we have a few choices. We can hope to be lucky enough to live in a community where food values are rational.[4] We can simply ignore all food messages from the outside world. We can eat beyond the number of calories recommended for moderately active adults and gain weight.[5] We can commit to rigorous exercise routines to burn extra calories. We can make lists of what we do and do not eat. We can ban certain foods from our diets: animal products, fast foods, nonlocal foods, non–sustainably produced foods, or foods with preservatives. Or we can attempt to buy what we desire but strip those desired foods of their "bad" qualities. This last option is a form of socially acceptable bulimia, a way that the food itself can be "eaten" but not digested. And, thanks to artificial sweeteners, it has been the most popular way of dealing with our national eating disorder over the last fifty years.[6]

At the start of the twenty-first century, we are left wondering whether there are consequences to pursuing what one NutraSweet executive once referred to as "the free lunch." The rise of old-fashioned "original formula" sodas points to a new desire, particularly among young consumers, to return to a sugar-sweetened past. New variations on stevia, a sweet leaf, have recently been approved for inclusion in manufactured foods and beverages and are proving popular with people who want "diet" sweets that are more natural.[7] Websites attest that conspiracy theories are still popular, decades after they emerged, accusing manufacturers of artificial sweetener of obscuring evidence that their products are harmful to human health. At least one recent study has suggested that artificial sweetener may in fact actually contribute to weight gain by increasing users' postconsumption desire for carbohydrates.

As compelling as these questions of current definitions of "natural" sweetening and possible negative physical impacts of sweetener may be, this book is a cultural history. My focus is on the values and beliefs that produced these commodities and enabled their popularity. I leave chemical compositions and physiological effects to other researchers. Exploring the complex past of sweetener leaves me convinced that we are asking the wrong question when we wonder whether artificial sweeteners are physically "bad" for us or if other substitutions might be better. Decades of scientific inquiry, by competing industry researchers and consumer groups, have yet to find that artificial sweeteners make us sick, even at high levels of daily consumption, unless we are in a very small minority of people who have severe reactions to particular chemical combinations. If we shift our view a bit and ask whether artificial sweeteners are culturally "bad" for us, however, the discussion becomes more interesting.

The promise of artificial sweeteners is that consumer pleasure can be stripped of its negative consequences. Since their arrival on the market in the 1950s as products for the well (as opposed to the diabetic or dangerously obese), saccharin, cyclamates, aspartame, and sucralose have been marketed as guilt-free sites of indulgence. Advertisements for diet sodas have long featured slim, attractive, mostly white women in states of digestive ecstasy holding cans of diet soda or spoonfuls of "sugar-free" puddings. Diet organizations like Jenny Craig, NutraSystem, and Weight Watchers have made artificial sweeteners "free" or "legal" for their followers and the basis for enormous profits for themselves. Yet there are, as most of us suspect, consequences to consumption—all forms of consumption. It is within this context that we should ponder the last century's rapid, thorough, and "sweet" uncoupling of indulgence and restraint.

CHAPTER OUTLINE

It is easy, when writing a study of a commodity, to focus on consumer manipulation. Marketing and advertising materials are plentiful, and they offer cohesive narratives wherein individuals choose one object over another because they are persuaded to do so by those who profit from the purchase. I think it more interesting and accurate, however, to look at how consumers make their own meanings, how producers and marketers amplify and alter these meanings, and how both groups are frequently steered by larger cultural forces. Thus, *Empty Pleasures* relies on archives, personal correspondence, biographies, and photographs, as well as successful and failed promotional campaigns. These are the places where complex and contradictory motivations can be found, where the march of progress slows to allow for accidents, imperfections, and sometimes just dumb luck. Artificial sweeteners have always been co-creations. As a result, chapters here alternate between producers' and consumers' points of view. The first three explore the rise of artificial sweetener prior to its mass marketing and unified messaging that would come with the mainstreaming of "diet" sweet products between 1955 and 1965. The first chapter explains why American consumers in the Progressive Era rejected saccharin. Here the story links inextricably to sugar, and specifically to the historical association between sweet taste, "healthy" calories, and labor. Unbeknownst to drinkers, carbonated beverage manufacturers had begun to substitute the new chemical sweetener for more-expensive sugar. When the press revealed this practice, consumers' outrage rivaled that incited by contaminated sausage. Sugar-sweetened soda, many argued, was good because it delivered calories to the body. Saccharin, on the other hand, offered nothing of value. Quickly labeled an "adulterant" and "false scarlet," the sweetener became a symbol of dishonest manufacturing practice and sparked a cry for regulatory reform. The debate reveals the initial value of sweet calories and suggests the dramatic differences between that era and our own.

In the second chapter I consider the period between this early twentieth-century consumer rejection and the early 1950s, when many consumers came to see saccharin and the newly discovered sweetener cyclamate as desirable commodities for many of the very same reasons saccharin was rejected a generation earlier. I place these substances in the context of women's relationship to sugar in the mid-twentieth century, particularly during World War II, when sugar rationing emphasized their responsibility to nurture others by restraining themselves. Through this lens, we can understand the dramatic recasting of artificial sweetener from negative to positive in many American women's lives. Because saccharin and cyclamate were chemicals produced in a lab, and not natural substances for "good health," they enabled female consumers to create an experience of sweet more focused on indulgence than service. Some bought miniature, jeweled containers for displaying and using sweeteners. Others undertook their own kitchen experiments in low-calorie cooking. Imagining this early era of pills and powders, before the mass marketing of "diet" foods, uncovers the visual and tactile experiences that connected chemical sweets to power, creativity, and self-indulgence. At the same time, the fact that early users were predominantly white women suggests that not everyone had the same invitation to "redefine" sweet.

In chapter 3 I look at the role of men through a case study of the development and early marketing of canned "diet" fruits. Using archival documents spanning the twenty-year relationship between a canning chemist and pharmaceutical sales agents, I argue that the first artificially sweetened products were created for two reasons, and both have to be understood if we want to know why diet products have so proliferated in the postwar United States. First, the rise in popularity of dieting suggested a new market for manufacturers who could take products known to be high in sugar calories (like canned fruit) and render them low calorie. Second, the men assigned to product innovation in fruit canning and in pharmaceuticals found they could enhance their own status by joining forces. The history of sweeteners and dieting, then, is as much about masculinity through scientific expertise as it is about a rising feminine imperative to be thin. This assertion is especially germane for those who seek to change the way Americans eat today. Often our emphasis is on the point of sale, where we try to influence consumers to make "good" choices. It is also important to look at the motivations of our food makers.

In chapter 4, attention shifts to the mass marketing of saccharin- and cyclamate-sweetened food and beverage products between 1955 and the late 1970s. Female manufacturers, marketers, and newspaper writers encouraged American consumers to accept chemical substitutes for sugar by casting substitute-sweetened products as a "modern" means of calorie control. They bridged laboratory and pantry by perfecting the message that artificially sweetened drinks and desserts could help users lose weight and gain pleasure.

Consumers would eventually fight for saccharin, and this is the story told in Chapter 5. Its focus is on a six-month period in 1977 when a threat by the Food and Drug Administration (FDA) to ban saccharin and all saccharin-sweetened products (after a ban of cyclamates in 1969) motivated hundreds of thousands of individuals to put pen to paper to explain exactly what made saccharin so important in their lives. A sample of the roughly 1 million letters received by the FDA and Congress illustrates that while consumers recognized the scientific evidence that saccharin could be dangerous, many felt they had more to gain by consuming it than they had to lose. Letter writers sought to educate the FDA about what risk looked like from where they lived. In doing so, they presented a worldview in which dangerous external risks were offset by the chosen, pleasurable risk of saccharin. Their arguments suggest that, by the 1970s, saccharin had two primary meanings in American culture. It was a way to cut calories *and* it was a way to heighten the sensation of control in a society where consumption posed substantial risks.

Chapter 6 explores the highly orchestrated debut and promotion of NutraSweet beginning in 1982 and extending through the decade. Embedded in playful gumball packs that landed without warning in millions of American mailboxes, NutraSweet ultimately usurped sugar as the nation's "healthy sweet" and birthed a billion-dollar business. Its promoters drew from and improved upon techniques used by saccharin and cyclamate innovators. NutraSweet's materials taught prospective users to understand its chemistry as natural, encouraged them to see it as an empowering choice, and emphasized its ability to deliver pleasurable weight loss. At the same time, changes in U.S. nutritional regulations made it easier for consumers to see health as achieved through control of ingredients rather than physical exercise or overall food choice. Within a vacuum of unbiased nutritional advice, sugar was vilified in popular culture, the number of artificially sweetened products increased exponentially, and NutraSweet became a "good" choice for sweetened drinks, desserts, and packaged foods. At the same time, its success, combined with a new set of superconsumers who drank gallons of aspartame-sweetened soda and coffee a day, made NutraSweet a lightning rod for controversy among consumer health advocates. The term "NutraSweet syndrome" emerged to describe physical ailments ranging from headaches to brain cancer. A close look at this rhetoric, in light of NutraSweet's claims, suggests the intensity of the hopes and fears we have placed on the chemical decalorization of pleasure in the American diet.

The Conclusion takes stock of where roughly 100 years of artificial-sweetener production, promotion, consumption, and protest have gotten us. It considers the recent lawsuit brought by Equal, a maker of aspartame, against Splenda, a maker of sucralose. There is great irony in the former's claim that the latter has lied in declaring it is "made from sugar," given NutraSweet's own claims in the 1980s that it was "just like nature."

CODA

The most common question I've been asked by friends, acquaintances, and students over the several years I have spent working on this book is whether artificial sweeteners are "unhealthy." For a long time I avoided answering. Like a good historian, I tried to assert that the answer was complicated, that artificial sweeteners had multiple meanings, that at certain moments they were good for consumers or that they had been good for business, or that in small doses they were not bad for anyone, as long as you didn't have one of a handful of rare genetic conditions. I still think these things are true. But they no longer add up to a sufficient answer to that basic question. I am now ready to say that artificial sweeteners have been unhealthy for us as a society. They do not appear to facilitate long-term weight loss for the majority of users. In fact, recent studies suggest they may actually leave us hungrier, and more likely to consume after ingesting them.[8] They have enabled pharmaceutical companies to enter our food supply and promoted new systems of nutritional information that encourage decision making based on a confusing array of ever-changing numbers and substitution strategies rather than on the origins, preparation, and taste of food. They have discouraged us from accurately noting and evaluating our own food desires. And they have ultimately made it very difficult for us to ever be *full* of sweets.

I say this with some trepidation, and a caveat. Certainly for diabetics or the sucrose intolerant, artificial sweeteners have made sweetness possible, increasing the palatability of daily diets and providing an important source of gustatory pleasure. And even for those who can consume sugar, artificial sweetener has provided more food and drink pleasure more often because of its noncaloric properties. This is something I have heard directly and found in the archives. Back in Atlanta, many diet "loyalists" described diet drinks as tools that make their lives better by giving them sweetness without guilt—a "healthy choice" for pleasure that offered a break from a day spent worrying about others and feeling out of control. I hear in their words echoes of the women who experimented at home with cyclamates in the 1940s and 1950s, exercising control over families and innovating faster than the food industry. I also have deep appreciation for the ways in which developing and promoting artificial sweetener have enabled many men and women to acquire expertise, control industries, and transcend barriers of gender, class, and profession entrenched within the food, pharmaceutical, and marketing industries.

But from where we sit today—in the midst of a $45 billion annual expenditure on weight-loss products, a continuing state of confusion about sweeteners (something, ironically, corn syrup manufacturers are taking advantage of with their "What's wrong with corn syrup?" campaign), and obesity rates that seem to stubbornly resist stabilization—these stories of artificial sweeteners as agents of consumer choice and smart substitutions for the calorie conscious seem more fairy tale than fact.[9] If we want to understand how we could, as a society, simultaneously support a massive increase in low-calorie food and beverage sales and a relentlessly rising "average" American weight over the last sixty years, we need to look more closely at what low-calorie foods have actually been designed to do. History reveals that the answer is sell products not create thin people.

After World War II, pharmaceutical companies needed to find markets for accidental creations, fruit canners had to combat sagging sales, owners of women's magazines needed to increase ad revenue, and food and beverage manufacturers needed to expand product lines. Food promoters from multiple sectors found in artificially sweetened, calorie-reduced foods a tool similar to consumer credit for nonfood commodities. Both were ways to move products through consumers by removing barriers of capacity. The impact on our culinary landscape has been profound. Consider the total market for Diet Coke and regular Coke, or "sugar-free" and regular Dannon yogurt. Look closely at the total ad space occupied by light and sugar-free product variations in a mainstream "family" magazine. The ability of the low-calorie market to expand the total market for American foods is surely proof of the ingenuity of capitalism, whether you admire or decry the results.

We live in a culture that urges us to buy, to load our 2,500-square-foot houses with overstuffed furniture, and to park our gas-guzzling vehicles in the three-car garage. An ever-more-sophisticated manufacturing and marketing sector does its best to convince us that we can, in fact, consume our way to the American dream. But on the terrain of our bodies, these visible signs of acquisition are largely unacceptable. As a host of fat-studies scholars and tabloid headlines have announced, valued American bodies tend to be thin bodies. And therein lines the dilemma: we can overstuff our couches and our houses and our cars but we are not permitted to overstuff ourselves. Artificial sweeteners allow us to try to have it both ways. We can hyperconsume while "working" to be thin. We put more into our bodies in order to end up with less body overall. And so one of the paradoxes central to contemporary capitalism is resolved: un-fettered consumption can lead to fiscal—and physical—health. Or not.

As we reconsider so many of the false promises of "supply-side eco-nomics" promoted over the last decades, the moment is right to look suspiciously at those pink packets, "sugarless" yogurts, twenty-four-can cases of diet soda, and guiltless Frappuccinos that have come to seem such a normal part of our foodscape. Artificial sweetener has enabled us to have sweets, lots of sweets, whenever we want them. And it is, of course, far more enjoyable to live in a world in which "diet" means sweet beverage or tasty dessert rather than the absence of something we desire. Still, in a century where our key challenge as Americans is to find a way to limit our desires to what our markets, our planet, and our bodies can hold, it may be time to reassess what artificial sweeteners and the low-calorie industry they have enabled have actually done.

FALSE SCARLET

HEALTHFUL SUGAR VS. ADULTEROUS SACCHARIN IN THE EARLY TWENTIETH CENTURY

> Saccharin is as false a scarlet as the glow of health trans-
> ferred from the rouge pot to the cheek of a bawd.
> —Alfred McCann, late 1920s

In the twenty-first century, few of us are shocked to find artificial sweeteners on our supermarket shelves. We rarely gasp in horror when we see
a can of soda sweetened with aspartame (Equal/NutraSweet) in a fellow
shopper's cart. We do not complain to the manager when we find a bag of
sucralose (Splenda) next to the sugar in the baking section, advertising
its ability to facilitate sugar-free cakes for the "health-conscious" family.
We may reach for a little pink packet to sweeten a restaurant-ordered
iced tea simply because saccharin dissolves easier than sugar. We sometimes answer "diet" when asked on the airplane if we would like a com-
plimentary beverage, perhaps calculating missed time at the gym and
the number of hours we will spend sedentary. Consumption of artificial sweeteners is normal, accepted. While some people use an artificial
sweetener because of diabetes, most consumers use it because they want
to. They actually prefer it to sugar.

This preference would have seemed strange, if not dangerous, to our
great-grandparents. In the 1910s, Americans actively campaigned against
saccharin, the first artificial sweetener to be used in processed foods and
beverages. The early years of saccharin's introduction in the United States

reveal that the sweetener entered the marketplace an unknown good, something without precedent and therefore not clearly defined as a positive or negative commodity. Very quickly, however, in a climate where sugar reigned king, home baking was admired, and industrial food processing was distrusted, it became associated with duplicity, impurity, and poor nutritional practice. The initial assessment of saccharin by Americans was deeply embedded in their cultural moment. Because health was wed to calories and the home was a more trusted place for sweet production than the market, sugar was deemed an appropriate, and saccharin an inappropriate, sweet.

In the intervening century, we have learned to see artificial sweeteners in a very different light. Whereas they were once dismissed as detrimental to Americans' diets, today they have become synonymous with the very term "diet." This shift represents a profound reevaluation of sweetness in American life. It also reflects a change in the way we define the proper relationship between sweetness and calories. We have, in a relatively short time, gone from promoting the healthfulness of calorie-rich sweets to deeming them a significant cause of ill health. The result has been, since World War II, a growing acceptance of what health reformers once insisted were inferior, dishonest products. We now find little dissonance in ingesting noncaloric chemicals in pursuit of health.

Our attitudes have not changed merely because of calories. While shifts in nutritional science and postwar consumer practices have encouraged a new emphasis on low-calorie eating and drinking, other factors have also been influential. Chief among them are early- to midcentury redefinitions of the trustworthiness of industrial food manufacturers and the proper place of chemicals in everyday life. Much of the early critique of saccharin depended on a view of industry that drew a strong line between "natural" and "artificial." Advanced technologies, in fact, produced both sugar and saccharin. Yet because sugar contained calories and saccharin did not and sugar had its origins in plantation fields while saccharin had its origins in coal tar, individuals saw the former as natural, or connected to nature, and the latter as artificial, a product of the chemist's lab. The very taste of saccharin, slightly chemical and intensely sweet, was understood as a further sign of its true nature as an inferior substitute. Preferring sugar to saccharin was not merely about preferring a kind of sweet or privileging calories; it was also an assessment of the proper place of technology in everyday life. In the early twentieth century, sugar was as much the product of the field as it was of the factory, and therefore it represented an important stasis between past and future so important to modern life. This view would shift with the chemical revolution produced by World War II and its immediate aftermath.

The following pages explore the antisweetener, prosugar value systems of our grandparents. They illuminate the process by which artificial sweetener was introduced into the American food supply and its subsequent popular reputation as a symbol for all that was wrong with industrial food and beverages. There was, in the early twentieth century, nothing inevitable about the negative characterization of saccharin any more than there is something inevitable about the positive characterization of sucralose (Splenda) today. Much of the negativity was produced by the sugar industry and sugar-using soda companies through antisaccharin advertisements that publicized problems identified by the Department of Agriculture to American consumers. Nutrition reformers also urged Americans, particularly members of the working class and immigrants, to see sugar as the more virtuous sweet because of its quick, cheap carbohydrates. Cookbook writers and women's advice columnists on the wartime home front also elevated sugar to an essential "fuel" that could win the war, a message that enhanced its prestige and status as a precious commodity.

By 1950, this close affiliation between sugar, nature, labor, and women's domestic roles would have the opposite effect. Sugar's preciousness, suddenly a liability, would provide just the opening needed for a positive reassessment of artificial sweetener.

SACCHARIN AT THE FAIR

Saccharin made its U.S. debut at the 1893 World's Fair. This is not surprising. The fair was the occasion to promote new innovations, especially those that represented significant advances in a nation's industrial, agricultural, and consumer technologies of production and distribution. Saccharin appeared in the agricultural building, where it would have been positioned between farm implements and transport machinery used in food production and finished goods more familiar to consumers from market shelves. While photographs of the saccharin booth do not appear to have survived, one can assume that the arrangement mirrored other displays of canned goods during period consumer expositions: impressive stacks of product stretching toward the ceiling, sometimes placed next to descriptions or installations of factory production or distribution processes. Product promoters in the rapidly expanding canned goods market often arranged their product against backdrops of industrial efficiency to appeal to consumers who, according to one historian, were "often frightened" by what he terms the "scale, power, and remoteness" of industrial food production.[1] Combining playful pyramid displays for consumers to peruse with helpful agents who could describe the production process enabled manufacturers to infuse their products with large-scale quality and direct-sale trustworthiness.

Curiously, though, and despite the best efforts of its promoters, saccharin appears not to have appealed to consumers in Chicago. Like other commodities, it was on display for the public during the length of the exhibition. Its placement in the agricultural building suggests that people should have associated it with food production and realized that it was an important modern advance. Existing copies of the pamphlet that was distributed to fairgoers suggest that the product's inventor and booth manager, Constantin Fahlberg, aimed to communicate the virtues of his new substance directly to consumers (fig. 1.1). Visitors who opened the pamphlet would have learned that saccharin was developed by Dr. Fahlberg about twenty years earlier, made of something called coal tar, and described only as "a perfectly harmless spice" that was 500 times sweeter than "the best sugar" and had already come into general use in "numerous industries."[2] It was telling that Fahlberg focused on a description of saccharin as a "spice" rather than defining coal tar, the material from which it was distilled, a brown or black liquid produced by the carbonization of coal.[3]

If few fairgoers familiarized themselves with saccharin in Chicago, it was not because the pamphlet was inaccessible, as it was printed in German, English, French, and Spanish. Nor was it because Fahlberg failed to reach out to individual consumers, as the booklet explicitly explains that his goal was to make saccharin "of use and service to everybody." It may be that the booth was located in an inauspicious spot in the building or that its unfamiliar name failed to attract sufficient attention. It is possible that there was some concerted effort to prevent Fahlberg from receiving attention, given what he characterizes in the booklet as "violent opposition" by the sugar interests, who would have been represented in the same agricultural building, possibly in a neighboring exhibit.

It remains a mystery as to why Fahlberg's attempt to pitch saccharin to the general public failed. But fail it did. According to one historian, most U.S. world's fairs have been designed, in fact, to "advance the mate-

FIG. 1.1 *Saccharin*, brochure distributed for free at the 1893 Columbian Exposition, Chicago. Warshaw Collection of Business Americana—Sugar, #60, box 1, folder 12, Archives Center, National Museum of American History, Smithsonian Institution.

rial growth of the country at large," rather than to promote individual products to visiting consumer tourists.[4] As part of the agriculture exhibits, saccharin would have been in the midst of inventions meant for large-scale industrial applications, such as seed technologies, irrigation tools, and harvesting machinery. Within this environment it seems likely that manufacturers, rather than consumers, comprised the majority of visitors to Fahlberg's booth. In fact, the material form of the commodity, packed in large tins rather than small packets or prepackaged food products that consumers could taste, further emphasized its industrial applicability. The first time most American consumers would hear about saccharin was nearly two decades later when they learned it had long been inserted, without their knowledge or consent, into carbonated beverages and packaged food products. In spite of Fahlberg's initial efforts, saccharin quickly became affiliated with the worst of American food industry practices. Unlike sugar, which had for a century been promoted as a healthful sweet with clear origins on plantations in Mexico, Cuba, and the Caribbean, saccharin emerged from a laboratory as the refinement of a substance that offered no calories and seemed to have nothing to do with food. It was deemed a false scarlet, a sweet masquerading as something it was not, a coal-tar derivative, and a product of unsafe chemical origins. The result of saccharin's debut was indeed "excitement," but not the kind Fahlberg intended.[5]

SACCHARIN'S INVENTORS AND INDUSTRIAL BIRTH

Saccharin's initial consumer reception was in many ways a logical consequence of the promotion tactics used by its early entrepreneurs. Constantin Fahlberg first discovered the substance when working with coal-tar derivatives with the hope of discovering a new food preservative in 1879. He was, at the time, a chemist working in Professor Ira Remsen's laboratory at Johns Hopkins University. The research was part of a project overseen by Remsen. After unintentionally licking his finger (so the story goes) after a day's experiments, however, Fahlberg's perspective on their partnership shifted. Convinced that he had found something of far greater value than a mere food preservative, Fahlberg began secretly working to refine and replicate the substance that he called, because of its intense sweetness, saccharin.[6]

Remsen was dismayed when, several years later, papers appeared in U.S. and German chemistry journals declaring Fahlberg the sole inventor of saccharin. Likely motivated by this struggle over who the rightful progenitor of saccharin was, Fahlberg worked tirelessly to promote the product, find industrial buyers, and produce publications. Much of this activity appears driven by his desire to fend off Remsen's claims by associating his name with saccharin in as many venues as possible in the shortest amount of time. At an 1885 taste demonstration at a London exposition, Fahlberg attracted the attention of several beverage manufacturers from New York. He appears shortly thereafter to have begun working with a six-member business cartel in Westhusen, Germany, to increase the production of saccharin and facilitate the discovery of other coal-tar derivatives. With saccharin as their prized commodity, the cartel and Fahlberg embarked on a fifteen-year monopoly over production of the product. Eager to maximize profits, the cartel actively courted executives and chemists from the rapidly expanding canned food and soda manufacturing industries. By prioritizing rapid expansion and industrial partnerships over direct-to-consumer marketing, Fahlberg had succeeded by the time he arrived at the fair. Visitors who thought they were encountering saccharin for the first time were probably already drinking it in their sodas.

Saccharin continued to be a tool for industrial food manufacturing and corporate expansion in the hands of John Queeney, who established its first manufacturing facility in the United States. After several years of carrying saccharin as one of his products as an independent sales agent working with the Westhusen cartel, Queeney saw an opportunity in 1901 to open his own shop in St. Louis.[7] The company would eventually come to be known as Monsanto Chemical. Queeney's decision to base his company on saccharin was predicated on upticks he had noticed in saccharin consumption among soda manufacturers who found it easily soluble in carbonated beverages and far cheaper per unit of sweetness than sugar (one report from 1906 claimed that sugar was approximately thirteen times as expensive as the amount of saccharin that yielded a similarly sweet taste). Further, because saccharin was produced in the lab from organic materials, rather than in countries with political instability, it was not subject to the market fluctuations that frequently surrounded sugar. Sugar became even less attractive after the passage of the Dingley Tariff in 1897, an action designed to protect the fledgling domestic sugar industry that effectively asked industries reliant upon sugar to take a loss in profits for an uncertain period of years.[8]

By 1903, Monsanto Chemical Company was producing caffeine, vanillin, and saccharin, the three chemical components of soda. That same year, Queeney's investment paid off when he signed an exclusive contract with the Liquid Carbonic Acid Manufacturing Company, the largest seller of soda fountain supplies. By 1906, soda manufacturers were increasingly looking to saccharin as a low-cost alternative, and Monsanto was busy expanding its production to fill demand.

SACCHARIN CONSUMERS DISCOVER THE FALSE SCARLET

In many ways, saccharin embodied the efficiency and scientific rationality desired in the late nineteenth century. Because it was a highly concentrated substance, it delivered more from less. Because it was a sweetener as well as a preservative, it could enhance the flavor of food and keep it on the shelves longer. Because it was cheaper than sugar, it offered a chance to further democratize sweetness, a flavor that had been becoming more accessible to the masses since sugar's arrival in Europe in the sixteenth century.[9] One can easily imagine saccharin as one of the "inventions" featured in Edward Bellamy's best-selling *Looking Backward*, an 1888 novel that described a future world of efficient inventions, where pneumatic tubes delivered products automatically and universal "umbrellas" appeared at the first drop of rain.[10]

That saccharin did not enjoy widespread support has much to do with Fahlberg and Queeney's decision to develop and market the substance for an industrial food system without informing consumers. In spite of the fact that New York was home to many of the soda manufacturers in the early twentieth century, a survey of contemporary *New York Times* coverage yields only two articles (one in 1896 and one in 1901) that mention saccharin. Neither discusses saccharin as something that an ordinary consumer would choose in order to sweeten a product. Nor do they suggest that saccharin was, in fact, something that many were already ingesting. Instead, the articles feature individuals who are consuming saccharin for strategic ends, such as deployed soldiers and athletes "entering an important contest."[11] Because soda was often served at soda fountains, where ingredients lists were not available, and labeling of bottled soda was not then mandated by law, consumers were equally unprompted by their own consumption habits to think of saccharin as an everyday product.[12]

The first large-scale discussion of saccharin appears to have begun as part of Harvey Wiley's well-publicized crusades against impure foods as part of the Food and Drug (FDA) legislation during the Progressive Era. In 1911, Wiley, who as the head of the FDA had undertaken recent studies into food additives and impurities, made specific recommendations against what came to be known as "adulterants." Among these were additives such as alum, benzoate of soda, and sulfate of copper that provided color, flavor, and filler with deleterious nutritional effects. Wiley had sought to have saccharin included on this list, and discussions of saccharin had accompanied those of other additives and fillers that would eventually be banned through FDA regulations. Saccharin's status as a clear danger to public health appears to have been difficult to determine under these studies. The laws authorized the Department of Agriculture to remove known poisons and valueless fillers from processed foods, but saccharin was not clearly classified as either of those things.

Ultimately, it was President Theodore Roosevelt's actions that prevented saccharin from being banned. When Wiley asked Roosevelt directly to ban the substance in 1908, Roosevelt instead established a five-member panel that found no evidence that saccharin was harmful when ingested in small amounts.[13] The panel's objectivity remains unclear, however, given Roosevelt's own doctor-recommended daily use of saccharin and his public declaration that anyone who would consider saccharin to be harmful was "an idiot." Although the panel did not ban saccharin, it did provide an assessment of the substance that would prove damning. Because saccharin had no food value, they concluded, substituting it for sugar in any product did in fact lessen the quality of the product.[14] They advised that saccharin be recommended for use only by those with medical conditions, such as diabetes, that required abstaining from sugar. In the end, the panel left saccharin in the food supply but simultaneously declared that anything that contained it was not a quality food.[15]

This declaration was all that competing soda manufacturers needed to bring the panel's opinion to the American public. While the FDA undertook its investigations into these substances, soda manufacturers launched their own wars of reputation based on additives that were used by their competitors and not yet banned by the Department of Agriculture. In 1906, the New York Bottling Company ran an advertisement in the *New York Times* characterizing its ginger ale as "always pure, made from cane sugar exclusively, without preservatives of any kind, free from aniline colors or saccharin."[16] Sugar-using manufacturers amplified the message after 1908. The same year of the findings of "lessened quality," Leggett's Premier Foods developed an advertising campaign that portrayed consumers as unsafe unless they took direct action against saccharin and other impurities. Over the past three years, claimed one advertisement from 1911, there had been "eight hundred prosecutions of adulterated and misbranded foods." Readers found a list of substances called "legalized impurities," with special attention given to saccharin. It was time for consumers to take action: only by buying Leggett's products could they avoid this substance lurking within items labeled "pure food," a claim Leggett's described as "legal" and "farcical."[17] Even those likely to dismiss the accuracy of advertisements critical of competitors whose demise offered clear profits for the copywriters were hard pressed to ignore indictments of saccharin. Reporters at the *New York Times* also contributed copy that affirmed saccharin's fraudulent nature. One story from May 1911, titled "Saccharin Lowers the Quality of Food," noted the unauthorized substitutions of some manufacturers and urged consumers to beware. Many, the anonymous piece explained, had long been "deceived" by the "popular belief that it is a form of sugar or chemically related to it."[18]

Leggett's was only one of several soda and canning companies to attempt to profit on their colleagues' use of saccharin. Clicquot Club, makers of club soda and ginger ale, also produced advertisements between 1911 and 1914 designed to disturb. Not only had consumers probably ingested saccharin, these allegories revealed, but it was likely making them sick. One 1911 advertisement asked, "Did you ever taste saccharin?" before insisting that most consumers had, since it was a common ingredient in competitors' products. Another ad, from 1913, showed children reaching for a safe "treat" of soda at home. The accompanying text warned vulnerable readers that only by purchasing sugar-containing Clicquot could they be certain that their children were not spending their "nickels" on drinks containing "saccharin, glucose, coal tar products and dangerous adulterants" (fig. 1.2). By 1914, Clicquot's technique had shifted from the shock of recognition to the specter of immediate threat. Readers drawn into one particularly compelling advertisement saw Clicquot associated with a fantasy of relaxation: a man lounges on a ship, watching the waves, with a bottle of Clicquot next to him. The text, however, points out the peril of sipping a competitor's brand. "Saccharin, the chemical that's used instead of sugar in cheap ginger ale, has such concentrated sweetening power that a tiny pill of it on your tongue will almost sicken you. There is no saccharin in Clicquot Club Ginger Ale."[19]

Here in one phrase were the era's three primary objections to saccha-

FIG. 1.2 "Let the Children 'Treat' at Home," Clicquot Club Ginger Ale advertisement, *New York Times*, July 25, 1913, 3.

rin: it was cheap, it was a chemical, and it had no place on the palate. The first objection was not unique to saccharin. Cheap in these executions would have been understood as pointing to a variety of dishonest practices well documented in the American food industry. The Clicquot ads followed only a few years after the 1906 publication of Upton Sinclair's *The Jungle*, an indictment of the labor practices in meatpacking plants that also illuminated the impurity of meat and cast suspicion on industrial foods, in general. They also appeared in the midst of Harvey Wiley's public crusades against aesthetic additives in canned goods, such as the alum used to render canned greens "green." In this climate, anxiety about saccharin echoed the concerns of Progressive activists and informed consumers for whom it was yet further proof that food manufacturers damaged the health of consumers in order to increase their own profits. Further, like many of the "adulterants" highlighted by Wiley's campaign, saccharin was added to make a canned or bottled food more palatable. Alum, for instance, hid the browning effects of oxidation. It is difficult to imagine, however, a similarly evocative campaign against alum. Oxidation was a process, not a product. But saccharin was a chemical substituting for sugar. Instead of providing consumers with something regarded as valuable, nutritive, and pleasurable, manufacturers were giving them dangerous pills, chemical substances that, as Clicquot reminded readers, would make a person sick if taken on the tongue. By alerting consumers to the fact that what had tasted to them like sugar was, in fact, at the very least a drug and perhaps even a poison, the campaign effectively elevated the threat of saccharin's dishonesty to a level well beyond that of its competing "impurities."

Saccharin, then, made its debut as the wrong kind of domestic technology. Rather than producing more goods for more people, as Ford had with the Model T, or revealing the hidden mechanisms of the natural body, as had the photographs of Eadweard Muybridge, or heightening one's sense of control, as did Edward Bellamy's fiction, saccharin brought less to more people, in that it removed calories and used chemical technology to pretend to be natural when it was not. Furthermore, it failed the test of purity and economy so important to domestic reformers involved in the popular "scientific cookery" movement.[20]

Saccharin might have been a scientific product, but it was clearly not nutritive. This was abundantly clear from the myriad comparisons with sugar that emerged. It is difficult to understand, from a twenty-first-century perspective, the high regard for sugar that existed in the twentieth-century American mind. We hear much today about sugar's link to hyperactivity and tooth decay; we are admonished to avoid the "empty calories" of sugar-laden foods. Many schools now ban sugar snacks from lunch boxes and vending machines and proactively work to educate children about the importance of a low-sugar diet. In 1911, however, sugar was a health food. Considered essential for energy, sugar was an important part of the American diet. It was the removal of sugar as much as the presence of saccharin that angered U.S. consumers.

THE PLEASURE OF SUGAR AND THE INAPPROPRIATENESS OF SACCHARIN

At the same time that consumers felt deceived by the collusion of saccharin manufacturers and food and beverage manufacturers, they also reacted strongly against the replacement of sugar with saccharin. Whereas sugar was primarily treated as a means for sweetness, and a volatile one at that, among contemporary producers, it had quite a different meaning among consumers. The history of the attitudes of American consumers toward artificial sweetener cannot be considered apart from a history of attitudes toward sugar. In an early twentieth-century climate of "sugar value," saccharin could not help but appear an interloper, an "adulterant," and an undesirable. Certainly the method manufacturers used to introduce saccharin to Americans hurt its reputation. It is difficult to imagine, however, that Americans would have accepted saccharin even if they had known it was in their food. There could be no early twentieth-century "diet soda." Sugar, as compound and symbol, was too important to American social, industrial, and domestic life.

During the nineteenth century, according to one historian, in the United States sugar was transformed from being a "rare and precious good" to one of "prolific consumption."[21] The shift can be explained by a number of forces: reduced costs resulting from increased competition among U.S. sugar producers, technological improvements in sugar production and distribution, and the active marketing of sugared commodities by manufacturers and promoters. Equally, if not more important, however, were advances in nutrition science and their attendant impact on the domestic habits of American women. Thanks largely to the work of pioneer nutritionist W. O. Atwater, sugar was rendered a late nineteenth-century health food. Chief among its attributes, it was reported, was its generous "fuel value" when compared with other carbohydrates. Atwater spent much of the 1890s researching and publishing the energy value of various common foods. Taste and people's eating habits were not his priorities. Rather, Atwater wanted Americans to learn to decode food options with an eye toward requisite amounts of protein, carbohydrates, and fats. All foods were not equal, he argued. This was particularly important for the working class, whose limited budgets and large energy expenditures, he believed, made abundant calories essential. In *Foods: Nutritive Value and Cost*, published by the Department of Agriculture in 1894, Atwater charted the importance of sugar; given a fixed amount of money, he demonstrated, consumers could purchase a higher amount of "fuel value" from sugar than from beans, mutton, salmon, or cheese. A mere twenty-five cents, according to Atwater's calculations, could purchase nearly 10,000 calories of carbohydrates.[22] These findings influenced early nutrition reformers, particularly the first graduates of departments of domestic science in the early twentieth century. According to Laura Shapiro, these women often "admired the way fats and sugars packed a large number of calories into a small amount of food."[23] Sugar was cheap, easy to digest, and palatable, all reasons why it was commonly praised as a quick source of energy essential for working-class productivity.

If nutrition experts actively promoted the caloric importance of sugar, the sugar industry elevated it to the level of indispensability. One must always read promotional materials with a built-in corrective for the hyperbolic. Certainly American consumers did not believe everything the sugar industry told them about the wonders of sugar. Nor, for that matter, can we assume that the ideas of nutrition reformers accurately reflected the attitudes and practices of actual consumers. The stories of immigrants in the Lower East Side of New York City during this period, in fact, suggest that many working-class Americans resisted the mandates of nutrition experts.[24] Yet the particularly lengthy period of sugar promotion, as well as the fact that the same rhetoric appears in antisaccharin advertisements, suggests that Americans had many opportunities to learn about a specific set of sugar virtues. Chief among these was sugar's strong correlation with the nurturing figure of the mother, who was, through her baking, the alchemic force that transformed the nutritive properties of sugar into bonds of domestic affection.

Similar to the boosterism practiced by saccharin's first entrepreneurs, sugar executives eagerly cast theirs as *the* American industry, one that had produced an essential commodity by improving upon the bounty of nature. Typical was the assessment of Earl Babst, an American Sugar

Refining Company executive, in 1915. "By reason of its great food value and comparative cheapness," he explained, "sugar is attracting probably greater attention . . . than in any period of its long history." In a 1918 annual report for which his audience was fellow sugar executives, Babst summarized his opinion of their shared product: "Before the European war, sugar, like air and sunshine, was taken rather as a matter of course. While its food value was recognized to a certain extent, the war has shown its indispensability to the world's cuisine."[25]

Declaring sugar as important as air and sunshine was a self-serving strategy designed to increase sales. Yet Babst's remarks appear to have echoed consumers' own opinions. These bubbled to the surface in newspaper letters to the editor written by individuals protesting the industrial use of saccharin as a sugar replacement. One disgruntled, unwitting saccharin consumer from Stonington, Connecticut, wrote the *New York Times* to suggest prison terms for soda makers who used saccharin instead of sugar. "It ought to be a penal offense," explained "Junius," "to put it on the market under its present name and to dole it out to the public in soda water, beguiling them with the idea that they are being regaled with drinks sweetened with cane syrups."[26]

Using saccharin did not land American soda manufacturers in jail. Nonetheless, most seem to have abandoned it for mass-marketed products after several years of bad press. By 1912, readers of the *New York Times* were told that saccharin did have one redeeming value. "In some diseases the consumption of sugar is injurious," the reporter explained, "and the use of saccharin in limited quantities is indicated."[27] Official recognition of saccharin's inappropriateness for the well came in the form of new federal food and drug regulations that allowed pharmaceutical companies to produce saccharin as long as it was labeled and sold for medical purposes. Evidence from manufacturers suggests that they took these public admonishments and new restrictions seriously. "Saccharine [*sic*] must be made under Government supervision," explained one British manual used by chemists in the United States and Europe, "and it is sold by apothecaries to diabetic patients as a substitute for sugar." Its "chemicals possess no food value at all, while sugar," the manual explained, "is a valuable food."[28]

Until and during World War I, saccharin use within the United States remained limited outside the diabetic market. This was true even in the face of wartime sugar rationing. Whereas in Europe consumers had turned to saccharin as a viable replacement for the increasingly hard-to-find sugar, Americans continued to avoid the substance, suggesting the antisaccharin and prosugar messages of the preceding years had a profound impact on producer behavior and consumer preference.[29] From the vantage point of carbonated beverage industries, the risk of using saccharin was sufficiently high such that substituting it for sugar during wartime was not a viable option in spite of the dwindling supply of sugar. This perspective continued well into World War II. "In our opinion its use will hurt the industry as it has done in the past," explained H. G. Pfafflin in *Suggested Bottlers Syrup Formulas Using Other Than Cane or Beet Sugar*, a text written in response to the pressure sugar rationing had placed on the industry. It might seem expedient to reach for an artificial sweetener, but manufacturers should keep in mind the price they might have to pay. "When the war is over the soda bottlers will have to live down the deficiencies," he explained.[30] What had once been deemed a modern marvel had become a danger to consumers and a liability for producers.

WOMEN AND THE SUGAR BOWL

We cannot know the precise amount of saccharin consumed before 1940, largely because of the secrecy with which pharmaceutical concerns guard their records and the fact that saccharin does not show up on census-based surveys of commodity consumption. Yet in spite of this official story that saccharin dropped from view, evidence suggests that the possibilities of saccharin continued to be a topic of interest for nondiabetic consumers. On the west coast, especially, this emerged in the form of experimentation with saccharin as an aid to weight loss, much in line with President Roosevelt's own use in 1908. On both coasts, it appeared after an intensifying affiliation between women and sugar sweetness, particularly in the form of domestic service. Ultimately, both strains provided entry points for women, who would begin to articulate a new set of positive values for saccharin after World War II.

California emerged as the region most likely to discuss saccharin, at least in the popular press, prior to World War II. In the 1920s, the *Los Angeles Times* "Diet and Health" column, written by physician and dietbook author Lulu Hunt Peters, addressed saccharin directly. It was a product for diabetics, she explained, and if it was used, "the quantity should be strictly limited."[31] Her description of its properties and health effects remains similar to those declared a decade earlier: It is a coal-tar product, a chemical, and one that adulterates rather than enhances food and beverages because it has no caloric value. Some physicians (like Roosevelt's) advised nondiabetic patients to take up to two grains a day for weight reduction, the equivalent of eight quarter-grain tablets, each of which was equal to the sweetness of a teaspoon of sugar. Health reformers like John Harvey Kellogg of the Battle Creek Sanitarium and radio show host Alfred McCann were less enthusiastic. Kellogg advised followers to avoid saccharin because it could adversely affect the heart. McCann objected to saccharin as a poor substitute for sugar and a ploy by industry to adulterate the food supply. Comparing saccharin to an actor in the 1920s, McCann declared it "as false a scarlet as the glow of health transferred from the rouge pot to the cheek of a bawd."[32] Peters's own cautiously positive tone may have foreshadowed the embrace of saccharin soon to follow in California. It would be on the west coast, with its growing ranks of dieters, where the first mainstream artificially sweetened products would emerge.

By the late 1920s, with saccharin still relegated to diabetics and the medically obese and with the rise of corn syrup still on the horizon, sugar reigned king. Largely owing to the research funding provided by the American Sugar Refining Company, chemists and food scientists had undertaken new inquires into sugar's nutritive qualities and overcome processing difficulties to ensure its place in the burgeoning market of packaged goods. There were new pamphlets and nutrition guides produced by the new Sugar Institute, founded by industry executives and charged with passing "on to the general public scientifically authenticated facts concerning the value and effects of sugar on the diet."[33] At the same time, increasingly sophisticated marketing techniques carried positive sugar messages to consumers.

Herbert Hoover, as head of the FDA, could declare in 1927 that sugar had grown "into our culinary and dietetic life to act as a sort of minding material on which our cuisine so largely resolves."[34] The assertion that sugar was at the base of American "cuisine" may have raised eyebrows among the culinary elite, but there was no doubt that sugar was an important part of a "healthy" American diet. For no segment of the population was this truer than for children. Women's magazines featured numerous advertisements touting the importance of sugared foods for children's healthy development. A typical ad, promoting Minute Tapioca, appeared in 1927 in *Good Housekeeping*. It argued that children needed sugar for strong physical and psychological development. "Desserts are an essential part of your child's diet because they satisfy his craving for sweets," a craving the ad claimed was "the natural expression of the child's need for energy-producing foods." The specific endorsement of tapioca as the best means by which to ensure that children received this essential sugar energy encouraged visions of tiny tapioca balls facilitating a quick-energy release system. "Tapioca is one of the most easily digested of all carbohydrates," the ad explained, distinguishing tapioca sugar from sugar in general, because the former "affords an immediate supply of energy with very little tax on the digestive system."[35] Women rarely appear in these advertisements, but they are nearly always the intended viewer whose job is to keep the sugar-eating man or child well-supplied with the essential product. "He'll eat half his weight in SUGAR this year," read an advertisement for Domino in 1938 that featured a young boy biting into a sweet treat with a smile on his face; "Be sure it's pure!" (fig. 1.3). It was simply assumed that women would understand that the exclamation point was aimed at them as shoppers, providers, and purveyors of sweet.

Sugar, however, was not an automatic delivery system. In fact, the "delivery" of sugar depended on two separate labor systems, that of the fieldworkers in the producing regions of Hawaii, Cuba, and Puerto Rico, primarily, and that of U.S. women in their home kitchens. As early as 1910, every American consumed roughly eighty-three pounds of sugar a year, a portion of which came in the form of prepared candies, cakes, chocolates, and ice creams available from regional and national vendors. But sweets were not exclusively mass-produced products. The profusion of confectionary cookbooks for women from the late nineteenth and early twentieth centuries serves as a marker, according to historian Wendy Woloson, of the "degree to which Americans had accepted sugar into their lives both physically and psychically." It also suggests that women working in the home produced a significant portion of these sugar-sweetened products themselves.[36]

In her history of confectionary, Woloson argues that sugar has been as much a "repository of sentiments" as a source of nutrition in American life. These sentiments are particularly complicated among women. At the same time that sugar has served as a site of pleasure and indulgence, particularly in the forms of fancy cakes and bonbons, it has also been embedded in notions of women's service within the home. Sugar faced, but overcame, critiques similar to those of saccharin in the early twentieth century. Many domestic reformers and cooking school experts questioned the purity of sugar and the manufacturing processes

FIG. 1.3 "He'll eat half his weight in SUGAR this year," Domino Sugar advertisement. N W Ayer Advertising Agency Records, #59, box 7, folder 1, spring campaign 1938, Archives Center, National Museum of American History, Smithsonian Institution.

involved in its inclusion in all sorts of sweets. Within these critiques, cheap candy was frequently mentioned as something easily accessed by children, who, away from supervising adults, could freely consume concoctions of unknown origin from general stores and street vendors. The solution, according to many domestic experts, was for women to produce confections themselves. Thus, sugar was not merely a "necessity in every household," as Paul Vogt, author of *The Sugar Refining Industry in the United States*, remarked in 1908.[37] Close inspection reveals that sugar was also a necessity in the daily labors of women.

Mothers were confronted with double duty with regard to sugar. On one hand, they were advised to ensure the purity of confections by making them at home. Confectionary cookbook authors frequently admonished women to beware of the dangers posed to children by "adulterated candies." On the other hand, they had to carefully regulate their children's consumption of sweets to prevent overindulgence. One article in the *Ladies' Home Journal* from 1906 called sugar consumption a "dietetic sin" craved only because of the "ravings" of "a deranged" stomach.[38] It was the mother's job to keep that stomach in a state just shy of such derangement. Thus, the front lines of sugar control became the kitchens of the American middle and working classes, whose children were thought particularly susceptible to the evils of adulterated sweets.[39] Baking cakes, making taffies and ice cream, and setting chocolates were acts loaded with competing cultural meanings: they were nutritious energy items, they were protections against market impurities, and they were potential sites for dangerous overindulgence.

The intense connection between women and the sugar bowl is illuminated in a cartoon from the *New York World* in 1929. Likely commissioned to protest the successive tariffs on Cuban sugar in 1922 and proposed again for 1930, it also suggests that readers would have understood sugar prices and sugar supply as a woman's issue (fig. 1.4). Here a dark, portly man wearing a top hat, tails, and the insignia "sugar high tariff baron" accosts a woman in her kitchen. Leaning on the window, gun in one hand and a decree outlining the tariffs' $80 million price tag in the other, he takes aim at a female figure labeled "housewife." The image merges the woman's body and the sugar bowl, clearly connecting her status and power with her ability to guard it. Her facial expression, with chin set and eyes narrowed, suggests that she might, in fact, sacrifice her life for that sugar bowl. Her posture suggests that if the tariff baron wants that sugar, he had better be prepared to use his weapon.[40]

Rollin Kirby in the New York World
April, 14th

THE HOLD-UP IN THE KITCHEN

FIG. 1.4 "The Hold-Up in the Kitchen," *New York World*, April 14, 1929, reprinted in Bottlers of Carbonated Beverages, *What Price Sugar* (Washington, D.C., 1929).

WORLD WAR II AND WOMEN'S SUGAR SERVICE

Sugar was one of the earliest products to be regulated by the Office of Price Administration (OPA) and one of the last to be released.[41] A product that had been pushed by nutritionists, politicians, food advertisers, and sugar manufacturers as a cheap, efficient, essential carbohydrate was, between 1942 and 1946, rare, precious, and tightly controlled. It continued to be regarded as an essential source of physical energy for individuals. At the same time, that importance was elevated by a new emphasis on the importance of sugar as a fuel for soldiers on the battlefield.

The close affiliation between sugar power and soldier power created an environment at home between 1943 and 1945 in which every ounce of sugar consumed by an American woman was evidence of something not done for the cause of victory. Wartime descriptions of the importance of sugar leave little doubt that Atwater's lessons, namely that sugar delivered efficient, cheap energy for effective labor, were absorbed by the military. Soldiers were provided with nearly unlimited access to sugar. In chocolate bars, Coca-Cola (whose sugar was not rationed in recognition of its significance to the troops), sugar bowls on mess hall tables, and meals that typically included at least two desserts a day, soldiers were pumped full of sugar, thanks to a partnership between the military and American food and candy manufacturers. The economic motivations were downplayed in favor of a public message that sugar had entered the battlefield as a public service and its energy-producing power would win the war.[42]

Women were told that they could contribute to the vitality of the soldiering force (a force constituted of their husbands and sons) by making sure that sugar bypassed their lips in order to reach those of fighting men. For women raising children, this created a perplexing conflict of duties. At the same time that the OPA told them, as citizens, that "we must get along with less sugar this year," as mothers they still had to meet the health needs of their children, who were productively fueled by the carbohydrates of sugar.[43] In spite of the fact that rationing dramatically decreased the available supply of sugar, children's nutritional needs were unchanged. In deciding where to make the cuts in sugar intake demanded by the new levels of sugar supplied, a patriotic woman committed to her mothering responsibilities could hardly suggest that soldiers do without or that children sacrifice the sugar-rich carbohydrates so important for growth and development. The only sacrifice she could effectively make was her own. The "sugar energy" connection thus turned, during wartime, into a system that encouraged women to deprive themselves of pleasure in order to nurture the nation's future.

"Are you sure that you really need two large lumps in your breakfast coffee, or are you just thoughtlessly following a long-established habit?" asked Margot Murphy in her popular *War Time Meals* cookbook of 1942. Her wagging finger nearly points off the page, suggesting that women are stuffing themselves with sugar pleasure as their men struggle on the front.[44] It was not new to associate sugar with women's service; such connections had been established since the 1890s, when sugar was first regarded as an essential carbohydrate for productive work. Yet there had previously been a balance between service and pleasure. As historian Amy Bentley explains, "Women who baked at home (with sugar as a primary ingredient) received important recognition from their families for this 'special' contribution to the family."[45] What had once been a "pleasurable activity" that brought "deep personal satisfaction" had become a substantial burden.

It was enough to inspire Mrs. H. C. Jons of New Market, Alabama, to write to her senator when she did not receive her allotted sugar ration. "My 79 year old mother drinks coffee for breakfast—my son eats cereal," she explained. "I do neither, trying to make the sugar allowance stretch. We don't have desserts and if sugar is an energy food we just don't have any."[46] On the surface, she is frustrated with the lack of sugar and the impossible stretching she must do with her limited supply. Yet on a deeper level, Jons is also frustrated with her service, the thankless sacrifices she endures every day as she spreads sweetness around to people in her life and does without it herself.

Women like Mrs. Jons complied willingly with the OPA, doing without sugar, replacing it with honey and maple syrup in baked goods, and eliminating the pleasure of sweetness almost entirely from foods such as coffee, where it served no one but themselves. Through the act of rationing, many women came to redefine consumption as a political rather than a private act. Set against a backdrop of tunes like the "Consumer's Pledge" (sung to the "Battle Hymn of the Republic") and popular tributes to patriotic consumers who fought the war through wise pantry choices, sugar-sparing women had ample opportunity to see their own consumption habits as a battlefield parallel to the one on which U.S. soldiers were fighting.[47]

This sacrifice came at a cost. In 1945, the most stringent year of domestic rationing, American women were asked what one product they found it hardest to cut down on or do without. Twenty percent, the majority, named sugar.[48] Like Mrs. Jons, they came to experience a world of sweetness associated nearly exclusively with service, anxiety, and duty. No longer could they easily balance the labor of cake baking with the pleasure of cake eating or the feeding of tapioca for nourishment with a stolen moment and a sweetened cup of coffee. Sugar became a symbol for what American women had to give out and give up during the war. And as they began to search for alternatives, there was room, for the first time, to desire a taste of pleasure removed from the burden of caloric sweet.

SARCASTIC SHAM? TURNING TO SACCHARIN

Saccharin entered the American pantry during World War II out of necessity. Severe sugar restrictions forced women to seek alternative sweeteners. Food experts conspicuously avoided mentioning saccharin in their lists of alternative sweeteners and ration-friendly recipes, preferring instead to recommend corn syrup, molasses, maple sugar, and maple syrup.[49] When they did mention saccharin, they typically had little good to say about it. Jane Holt, food reporter for the *New York Times*, provided one of the few direct admonitions regarding saccharin's domestic use in her 1943 column "News on Food." "Don't use saccharin in canning because it's bitter," she proclaimed.[50] Holt's characterization of saccharin as inferior echoed those of male critics who reported on the substance during the war years. Henry J. Taylor, also of the *New York Times*, used saccharin to illustrate the extreme deprivations experienced by Germans in 1942. In "Cheerful London; Sullen Berlin," the tiny pellets revealed the hardship of German life. "Saccharin is used there entirely, and in the best cafes when your coffee is served the waiter comes around with little pellets of saccharin arranged in orderly rows on a flat plate."[51] Four months later, Howard E. Kershner used saccharin cakes as a symbol of France's defeat. Things labeled "cakes" in this once culinary-proud nation were now "made without flour, sugar, or eggs, probably from ground birdseed, almonds, and saccharin," he explained, calling them both "unappetizing" and "not very nourishing."[52]

In spite of such associations between saccharin, deprivation, and poor taste, American women began to use it. Helen Griffin, a twenty-six-year-old secretary from St. Louis, submitted her first poem to the *St. Louis Globe Democrat* in December 1942. Set to the meter of "The Night before

Christmas," it parodies the difficulties of cooking during wartime rationing, complete with a description of saccharin-sweetened canned goods. The poem was popular enough to catch the ear of President Franklin D. and Eleanor Roosevelt, who reportedly heard it read and requested a copy.[53] As early as 1942, *Business Week* reported that the substance, previously desired only by "the diabetic and unhappily obese," was now "being eyed by the slim and healthy as a possible supplement to their half-pound-per-week sugar ration."[54] The article hints at two ways that saccharin was becoming part of the domestic diet. Manufacturers like E. R. Squibb and Sons, realizing a possible market expansion among the sugar-deprived, were producing display pieces for pharmacies and department stores specifically designed for use "by the unaffected." These small packets, often mounted in neat rows on cardboard for easy removal, used phrases like "don't miss your sweet" or "all the sweetness of sugar" to catch consumer eyes and inspire impulse purchases. The article, however, suggests that women did not wait for special displays to appear in stores inviting them to try the alternative sweetener. They went straight to the "diabetic" supplies, experimenting on their own before advertisers and marketers offered them official sanction. This turn to the diabetic aisle is reflected in the author's observation that there was, at the moment, "no law, of course, to prevent the public from picking up a few saccharin tablets at the corner drug store and using them to help up the sweetness of home-concocted brews."[55]

We can assume that the *Business Week* reporter was not the first to observe the practice. Women began as early as the first year of sugar rationing to bring bottles of saccharin from pharmacies and "household drug" sections of department stores into their kitchens. By July 1942, only a few months after rationing had begun, Monsanto, the leading producer of domestic saccharin, reported that output had fallen behind demand, and Park, David, and Co., a leading saccharin distributor, cited a thirtyfold increase in demand for domestic consumption.[56] The fact that saccharin use occurred so early after the start of rationing suggests that American women did not share the aversion of "food experts" to the product. Perhaps they read some of the brief articles that began to revise saccharin's wartime reputation. "Experiments made on animals leave no doubt that saccharin is safe," reported the *New York Times* in 1940.[57] Three months later, another brief article explained that in Germany, out of necessity, saccharin had gone from being "medically branded a poison, so that even diabetics were afraid of it" to a product whose "curse is removed."[58] And in 1942, science seemed to reverse itself in an article from the same newspaper, explaining that while testing remained "far from adequate," a new pamphlet on saccharin produced by the Cornell University School of Nutrition concluded that there was, as of yet, "no sound evidence . . . presented" to say that saccharin has an "injurious effect when used in moderate amounts by a well person."[59]

By 1945, saccharin's reputation was undergoing revision. While some critics continued to view it, as had their Progressive predecessors, as the commodity of greedy businesses, chemical adulteration, and lax government regulation, many more perfectly "well" consumers were clamoring to add it to their food and drinks.

ALCHEMIC ALLY

WOMEN'S CREATIVITY AND CONTROL IN SACCHARIN AND CYCLAMATES

> [It] is possible through the new sweet-
> eners to satisfy both needs and wants.
> —Poppy Cannon, *Unforbidden Sweets*, 1958

Before the pink packets, before the Tab, before NutraSweet and Splenda were embedded in our "light" prepackaged desserts, women had to open pill bottles and empty the contents into their food. This era of experimentation, extending roughly from 1945 to 1958, has been largely forgotten today. The years after World War II, however, are an important "alchemic era" in artificial sweetener's history, a time when the user had to discern the possibilities and delineate the limitations of chemical sweets.

By 1958, artificial sweeteners were commodified. Canned fruits, jellies, and salad dressings sweetened with saccharin and the new cyclamates (or a blend of both) would appear in supermarkets in special dietetic sections. The first diet sodas would be available in a variety of flavors. At this point, the majority of artificial sweetener consumed in the United States would be embedded in products clearly marked as diet and sold as aids for weight loss. For the first time, consumers would be able to purchase full lines of alternative products whose calories were reduced by the substitution of artificial sweetener for sugar or corn sweeteners. Before that, however, consumers who wanted foods sweetened by low-calorie substitutes had to buy a sweetener in pill, powder, or liquid form and add it themselves. Still dispensed in medicinal bottles from pharmaceutical companies such as Abbott and St. John's Laboratories, saccharin and cyclamates originally lacked clever marketing slogans and user-friendly packaging. As a result, consumers had to make meanings for them, a process that involved new materials and new methods. Exploring this early period of adaptation reveals that women initially had complex experiences with sweeteners. While much of their motivation was expressly to control and limit sugar calories, their interactions with the substances prior to the point of ingestion provided other positive experiences, such as creativity, control, and self-care.

Today, we tend to accept as inevitable the fact that people trying to lose weight will drink diet soda. But what has made diet soda their preferred beverage? After all, water is a better beverage choice. It has no calories, and it contains no sweetness that can stimulate rather than satiate the appetite. Is diet soda something we choose to help us lose weight, or is that simply what advertisements have told us about ourselves? By establishing some critical distance from the phenomenal success of diet products today, we gain the ability to look for other meanings given to artificial sweeteners and to see how those meanings, particularly among early consumers, might have influenced an affection for what was once an "adulterating" chemical.

Early experimenters with saccharin and cyclamates created an intensely self-focused, empowering relationship with sweetness. By working closely with these new substances to transfer them from pill bottles to delicate containers, by manipulating them as pills and powders that had to be attentively added to foods, and by subsequently altering, undetected, their family's food supply, women were able to heighten both their experience of control and their actual control through their labor as preparers and servers of food and drink. This provided a powerful counterpoint to sugar.

During the first decades of America's diet culture, limiting calories by using artificial sweeteners was both a positive expression of self-determination and a means for women to pursue unrealistic beauty norms. Many of the women in this chapter clearly took pleasure in buying beautiful containers and filling them with pills of precious sweetness. Others found creative expression in their ability to master new sweetener-based recipes and make resulting dishes that tasted "just like sugar." And some certainly went so far as to use sweetener-based cooking as a means to manipulate their husbands and children. At the same time, all of these practices mark the beginning of what Kathleen LeBesco has called the production of "bodily forms of highest value."[1] These women, most of whom were white and middle to upper class, were the first to invest time and money in caloric control. And thanks to saccharin and cyclamates, it was a project they could undertake with reasonable expectations of success. Much about these early years of sweetener use was empowering for women. Yet ultimately, this narcissistic emphasis on self-fashioning through calorie sparing would feed a diet market more oppressive than the sugar bowl.

THE BACKDROP OF "DIET" IN THE 1950S

As early as the 1930s, many white middle-class American women had begun to characterize themselves as dieters. In the language of the time, "reducing" was a national phenomenon. This decade saw the publication of the first best-selling diet book and the popularization of nationwide "diet parties." So interested were people, particularly women, in successful strategies for losing weight and maintaining weight control that radio broadcasts for products advertised as diet aids frequently incited thousands of interested listeners to write personal letters in response.[2] The vogue of slimness had been on the rise for a decade, thanks to the stylistic changes that arrived with the figure of the young, carefree, female "flapper." Women's bodies were far more visible with the flapper's short hair, short sleeves, and short hems. Corsets, common elements in the nineteenth-century woman's wardrobe, were now frowned upon. The result was the ascendance of the tall, thin female body type. Given that this was not an average physique, many American women developed a keen interest in slimming suits, diet plans, and weight-loss pills. Not all, it should be noted, were equally interested in dieting. According to one historian, the "craze for slimness" in the 1930s had so many women embarking on crash diets that one physician had to write a popular article reminding them that it was, in fact, "better to be fat than dead."[3] "Women" here, however, should be clearly defined. There does not appear to have been a corresponding diet craze among African American or Latina women. The beauty business for women of color during this period was, in fact, more focused on hair products and skin creams than on weight-loss tools.[4]

Histories of eating and nutrition do not pay sufficient attention to racial differences. Arguably, there was no universal category of "American" eater after the immigration waves of the 1890s, if in fact there ever was. It is particularly problematic to make generalizations about women's body ideals, eating practices, and culinary techniques. During the 1920s, for instance, major newspapers and magazines had racially segregated readerships. One cannot quote the *Los Angeles Times* and the *New York Times* or popular books on food and nutrition without noting that such publications targeted a white readership. Stories were certainly written by white reporters. Advertisements were aimed primarily at white consumers. Similarly, diet books and diet products were sold to consumers who had enough money to discover that excess consumption was a problem and who came from cultural backgrounds that had begun to equate thinness with beauty. Such consumers most often were white. Therefore, while much of the language in popular media claimed that women used artificial sweetener, it should be noted that until the late 1960s these women were assumed to be white.[5] Cookbooks with tips on cyclamate use and advertisements for pills and liquid substitutes were created by white advertisers and publishers for white readers. Still today, there are few low-calorie cookbooks aimed at nonwhite women that advocate using artificial sweetener or chemical substitutes of any sort. This is not to say that women (or men, for that matter) of color did not purchase saccharin and cyclamates in the 1950s and 1960s. Certainly some did, given that these products were available in pharmacies and grocery stores without a prescription. But nonwhites were not urged to do so by popular culture or, evidence suggests, their own culinary traditions.

A small number of women appear to have experimented with saccharin as a direct means to lose weight prior to World War II. Well-known author and physician Lulu Hunt Peters's columns in the *Los Angeles Times* of the 1920s, for example, suggest that at least some readers were getting tips on substituting saccharin for sugar to get slim. While weight-watching guides from this era do not generally advocate saccharin substitution to cut calories, some nutritionists and "health gurus," especially those in and around Southern California, were beginning to consider the possibilities. In 1939, William Brady, a physician based in Los Angeles and author of the regular *Los Angeles Times* column "Here's to Health," revealed his own discovery of saccharin. "I use saccharin because I'm too fond of sugar," he explained, and "the sweetening effect of a bit of saccharin in coffee or tea is as satisfactory as a lot of sugar." The column is particularly interesting as a bridge between old and new ideas of the substance. On one hand, Brady's description resembles Leggett's thirty-year-old antisaccharin campaign, minus the conspiratorial tone. Saccharin was "a chemical substance made from coal tar (toluene)" that was "very much used for sweetening tea, coffee, or various fruit or other dishes, by patients with diabetes who have to limit their intake of sugar." And yet, the chemical coal-tar description is lightened by saccharin's reported usefulness as a diet aid. Not coincidentally, the column appeared in July, when Southern Californians may have been particularly motivated to minimize their weight. The column recommended saccharin as a viable substitute for "stout people who are trying to reduce and those who wish to avoid accumulating more slacker flesh."[6] Brady appears to have grown only more enthusiastic about saccharin over the next few years. By 1946, after several years of sugar rationing, his column offered a more robust endorsement. There was, he explained, "ample scientific evidence" to suggest that anyone could use up to five grains a day "with impunity." "Saccharin is saccharine," he alliterated, playing on the dual meaning of the term as a chemical and an adjective to describe something exceptionally sweet; further, since it was a common ingredient in "canned goods, chewing gum, soda water, pop, ginger ale, and chewing tobacco," there was no reason to avoid it if one wanted "to reduce . . . painlessly."[7]

Still, "with impunity" and "no reason to avoid it" were not ringing endorsements. For diet pundits and their readers, saccharin's calorie-free sweetening was a new positive attribute. The new cultural codes of slimness, by which stoutness was no longer merely an adjective but instead a condition to be ameliorated, required new tools and techniques for calorie reduction. Yet this assessment was not, in itself, sufficient to cast off sweetener's previous negative reputation. For Brady and Peters, saccharin might not be injurious in small amounts, but it was still a medicinal product, one that you reached for when you had a problem (weight gain) and used until you achieved the solution (weight loss). Their efforts began saccharin's rehabilitation, but there was still a ways to go.

CONTAINING SACCHARIN IN THE 1950S

Anthropologist Sidney Mintz has argued, in the case of sugar, that "one needs to understand just what makes demand work: how and why it increases under what conditions." In this sense, saccharin, in particular, and cyclamates, by association, can be understood through a process he refers to in *Sweetness and Power* as "extensification." In the case of sugar, extensification occurred when it became a treat for the masses rather than a commodity under the purview of the few. When they bought sugar rather than other, carbohydrate-rich staple foods, English working-class consumers asserted the importance of pleasure in the midst of monotony. In the case of saccharin and cyclamates, the extensification was dramatic. As substances that tasted similar to, but were not, sugar and contained none or few of sugar's calories, artificial sweeteners could not merely present themselves as "like" sugar. Sweeteners demanded a new set of rituals, rituals that, as Mintz has noted with sugar, were "specific to the social and cultural position of the users."[8] But they also demanded rituals that contended with the commodities' obvious chemical origins and their divorce from the domestic roles traditionally connected to caloric sweet. As opposed to sugar, there was no "natural" reason to consume artificial sweetener. It did not enable productive labor. It did not cover the taste of bland starches. It did not preserve foods in more efficient ways.

In the immediate postwar era, artificial sweetener was, visually and practically, an unfinished commodity. It required consumers to act upon it in order to have meaning, because without marketing or package branding, it failed to deliver a cohesive message about what it meant and what it could do. This was unusual some twenty years after the psychologically oriented advertising techniques of industry innovators like Ernest Elmo Calkins (the "Arrow Shirt Man") and Bruce Barton ("Betty Crocker") had become ubiquitous.[9] The emergence of saccharin and cyclamates not from professional product pitchers but, rather, directly from pharmaceutical companies and druggists meant that artificial sweeteners lacked specific instructions as to how they should be used or affiliations that would provide particular emotional values. By storing, serving, embedding, cooking, and feeding, consumers made meanings for themselves.

In the early 1950s, Dan Kasoff, a jewelry maker based in Brooklyn, realized that many women were carrying saccharin pills in their purses but seemed uncomfortable, given the unattractiveness of the medicinal bottles, with taking them out in public. They would, he recalled, reach into their purses and remove the pills first, or cup the bottles in their hands to keep them out of view. Kasoff, founder of Florenza, a leading maker of costume jewelry and metal novelty items, saw a business opportunity in their discomfort. He designed a metal bird, hollowed out on the interior with a removable lid, that could double as a container. In order to prevent the saccharin from changing its chemical structure, Kasoff coated the interior with an antioxidant; then he sold the metal bird to depart-

FIG. 2.1 Saccharin containers, circa 1955 (author photograph).

ment store buyers, who put it on shelves across the country. By 1952 his line had expanded to include a number of models. Women no longer had to settle for pill bottles to carry their saccharin; instead, they chose from saccharin sparrows, peacocks, poodles, and gilt boxes (see fig. 2.1).

Kasoff's containers were popular throughout the 1950s and 1960s. Larry Kasoff, Dan's son, recalled that the company discovered their popularity as gift items early and began to sell them wrapped, so people could go directly from the store to a social event.[10] "If you went to somebody's house," he explained, "if you needed to bring something you knew they didn't have this."[11] Because company records were destroyed in the 1980s, it is difficult to determine precisely how many Florenza containers were sold and whether they were purchased wrapped as gifts. Kasoff recalled "everyone" having a sparrow in his Brooklyn social circle and estimates the number of sparrows alone sold in the United States through the

1960s as 50,000.[12] Certainly the price of the Florenza containers, $2.00 in the 1950s, put them in reach of most consumers. Contemporary advertisements suggest that consumers had ample opportunity to encounter these containers and to understand that they were designed to hold artificial sweetener. Newspaper advertisements often included illustrations of saccharin pellets placed inside and special offers for installment purchasing plans for the more expensive designs.

While containers like the sparrow have all but disappeared from the historical record, they are at least as important as the first can of diet soda to our understanding of what sweetener meant to consumers who chose it. Anecdotal evidence suggests that the majority of women who added saccharin to foods and beverages during the "pre–diet product" era used some sort of container for display and dispensing. This makes sense, given saccharin's standard packaging in small, medium, and large medicine bottles, depending on the size of the grain. Saccharin was sold nearly exclusively in pill form during these early decades, likely because that made it easy to carry and add to hot beverages (it dissolved quickly) and because its target market continued to be diabetics, who used it for medicinal purposes. "Well" consumers, however, appear not to have wanted people to see them sweetening with a pill.

The chemical composition of saccharin changes when it is heated for long periods of time. As a result, it did not easily lend itself to baking or cooking. It did, on the other hand, dissolve in hot water and, in pill form, was simple to equate with a teaspoon of sugar (a quarter-grain pill equals roughly one teaspoon). Thus it was frequently added to hot tea and coffee. It is notable, in this context, that women did not simply keep the saccharin pills in their bottles. What women did instead was far more complicated. When decorative containers were used as dispensers, there was a greater chance for error and awkwardness. The transfer of the pellets from their bottles to these decorative objects, then, provides a unique opportunity to see what kind of attention many women first paid to themselves *through* sweetener.

The sparrow, Florenza's first container developed especially for saccharin, gestures to nature rather than science. One might expect a pharmaceutical product to be in a more modern container, especially given its well-known chemical origin. It would also be sensible for a diet product to be placed in an inconspicuous container, something simple, geometric, and perhaps flat and easily put out of view. The sparrow, however, is exuberant. Its lifelike qualities (the striped lines along the feet look

FIG. 2.2 Saccharin sparrow (author photograph).

like actual skin folds, the feature lines etched over the surface create an illusion of depth, and the gemstone eyes appear to glimmer) draw the viewer's attention toward the object, encouraging close observation before opening the lid to retrieve the contents. The sparrow does not resemble sugar bowls from the era, which still had round shapes and neutral colors or floral patterns that had changed little from the nineteenth century. The sparrow bore a closer resemblance to costume jewelry than to a food or condiment container. According to historian Deanna Cera, animal designs were particularly popular in costume jewelry in the 1950s; chief among those were renderings of birds and domestic pets.[13] The popularity of the sparrow and its jeweled, gilded presence suggest at the very least that these were considered attractive objects that encouraged rather than discouraged attention.

And this only intensified when it was used. At three inches long and one and a half inches tall, it is quite small (see fig. 2.2). At first glance, one is compelled to pick it up, and in fact, it fits neatly within a cupped hand. Yet although the bird seems in some sense made for holding, doing so actually prevents its operation, as the lid has to be separated from the base in order to reveal the saccharin. If one holds the bird in one hand and lifts the lid with the other, however, one needs yet a third hand to actually extract the pellets. It is easy to see how a user would have to interact with the bird and figure out its operation on its own terms.

Removing the pellets is a similarly demanding process. The lid detaches easily, yet the tiny tongs are more difficult to manipulate. Attached by a magnet on the underside of the lid, they have to be tugged for removal; once removed, they nearly disappear into one's hand. Since approximately twenty quarter-grain pellets are designed to fit comfortably within the sparrow's body base, it takes skill to use the tongs to pick up one pellet without disturbing the rest. Whereas sugar required using a spoon to scoop—familiar equipment and motions—saccharin dispensing required a new process, one more closely associated with beauty procedures than with food preparation. The tongs look like tweezers, and grabbing the pellet suggests intricate sewing or perhaps even laboratory work. The user's body is on display here, since this delicate reach, grab, and lift operation would have to be performed in front of others to sweeten one's coffee or tea at women's social gatherings. The motion encourages close attention to the fingers and hands; it requires, at least initially, the user to focus on herself and the sense of herself being observed by those around her. This experience was very different from dropping a teaspoon or two of sugar into one's beverage and moving on.

In fact, this close attention to the two fingers, evocative of the process of grabbing tongs and placing the saccharin pellets in a beverage, was emphasized in the first advertisements for Sucaryl, the brand name for cyclamates, a new form of artificial sweetener that entered the market in the early 1950s. In 1951 promotional material to be used in initial product marketing, two well-manicured female fingers hover over a hot dish of what appear to be stewing tomatoes (fig. 2.3). The image is more fiction than fact, as surely a woman would not put her fingers so close to the top of what must have been a steaming brew. Thus we can assume that rather than providing instructions as to how one should add Sucaryl tablets, the image was likely meant to associate this new commodity with something known and attractive. Similarly, direct-to-consumer advertising for Sucaryl in the late 1950s featured women dispensing the sweetener with two delicate fingers. An example from *Good Housekeeping* in 1960 (fig. 2.4) is particularly telling, as there was no reason, given the new technology of direct dispensing, why a woman would have to hold the product between the thumb and forefinger as she once had to extract saccharin from a container.

This continued evocation of the two-fingered "sweetener drop" suggests that there was something powerful in the image of women holding small pills of sweetener between delicate thumbs and forefingers. When we put this in the context of other commodities that surrounded saccharin and cyclamates, the cultural appeal of this image becomes clearer.

FIG. 2.3 "Two-fingered" sweetening as featured in Sucaryl promotional materials. William D. Pratt, *The Abbott Almanac: One Hundred Years of Commitment to Quality Health Care* (New York: Benjamin Company, 1987), 140.

FIG. 2.4 Sucaryl "No thanks!" *Good Housekeeping*, April 1960, 141.

"Sugar is sugar," stated Walter Landor, president of the advertising and marketing firm Walter Landor and Associates, in 1956.[14] The packaging specialist had been brought in by the Spreckles sugar company to increase its market share and, in the process, had discovered that sugar had no distinctive image in the mind of the average American consumer. Much of sugar's promotion throughout the early twentieth century had been in pursuit of just such nondistinctiveness. The 1923 Havermeyer sugar company's publicity pamphlet, for example, uses prominent photographs to show sugar being grown in fields, processed by large machines, and carried home by children in fifty-pound sacks.[15] In contrast, little emphasis is put on brand distinctiveness or the enjoyment of sweets in the form of finished goods. The only image of an actual user is that of a middle-aged white woman scooping sugar directly out of a huge opened bag that sits on a kitchen chair; presumably she will make a dessert for the children who wait nearby.

By the 1940s, sugar's appeal to female consumers was on the decline. In addition to the difficulties of obtaining sugar because of the depression and rationing, women faced social criticism if they indulged in its consumption. Sugar had become so closely affiliated with women by the early twentieth century that women, in fact, had come to be called "saccharine." Women and sweets were often described with this same adjective, meaning "nonessential, decorative, sweet, ethereal, and generally lacking in substance."[16] When children and fighting soldiers enjoyed sugar sweets, they were building strong bodies and protecting the nation. When women consumed them, however, they were selfish and indulgent. The result was a mixed message: sugar was good for women, but only if they gave it away.

The two-fingered sweet of saccharin, ironically nearly the same word used to criticize overly indulgent female sugar eaters, would have been a powerful icon of restrained indulgence against such a cultural critique. Equally important was how the two fingers neatly distanced saccharin users from any sort of sugar labor.

Early twentieth-century manufacturers had consistently marketed sugar to consumers (largely female) by emphasizing its production on faraway plantations. Havermeyer's 1923 pamphlet was typical. It features photographs of dark-skinned plantation laborers loading donkey carts with sugarcane, along with the explanation, "Sugar is raised so far away from its place of ultimate consumption" that only the "last lap of the journey from plantation to sugar bowl is in the hands of the consumer himself." Another description from 1924 explains that "the sugar in the carton . . . is only the last chapter in a business romance that starts in the tropics, spreads out over thousands of miles, involves vast agricultural enterprises, mills, refineries, railroads, fleets of steamships, and a great army of workers."[17]

It is quite possible that what had originally been an effective "romance" between brown labor, Western technology, and white consumers (at least as far as marketers were concerned) had become more complicated by the late 1940s. Not only did the linkages "from plantation to sugar bowl" intensify the connection between sugar and labor that many women had come to find tedious during World War II; those connections might also have seemed distinctly unmodern. In the midst of the dramatic scientific and technological mobilization required to shift the nation from domestic to wartime production, visions of commodities such as sugar locked into bucolic scenes evocative of the eighteenth century may have seemed particularly distant—and unappealing.

Monsanto Chemical produced a number of wartime advertisements, aimed at homebound consumers, touting its technological prowess. These were designed expressly to instruct readers about the dramatic advances in chemistry that were changing the material realities of war and to preview how these advances would soon change domestic life. In one ad, a soldier uses a portable phone on the battlefield, with the question "How Much Chemistry Per Soldier?" asked squarely over his shoulder. A list, on the left, divides Monsanto products by wartime category: metals, plastics, ammunition, textiles. On the right, a large M lets us know that Monsanto chemicals and plastics will bring this soldier safely home.[18] Once the battle was won, Monsanto switched gears. Instead of depicting its role in facilitating the soldier's work, these ads highlighted the power of scientists to shape the future. "Monsanto Chemistry is Ready for 1946 . . ." the copy boldly proclaims. The text makes clear the origin of Monsanto's postwar readiness: "almost without exception," it tells prospective industrial consumers who hope to "cash in on the pent-up buying demands of 1946," "these are the same chemicals and plastics that we made during the war years."[19] This advertisement invites the consumer to identify with the scientist; one looks through the chemistry equipment to take in the surroundings, as does the man in the white coat. As historian Roland Marchand argued, this sort of "master of all he surveys" visual cliché was commonly used in period advertisements to entice readers to try on the privilege of a particular actor as if it were their own.[20]

It is notable that whiteness dominates these images. The laboratory interiors are white, the lab coats are white, the reflection in the light of the glasses of the scientists is white, and the male scientists are white.[21] This scene, multiplied hundreds of times in popular magazines, television programming, and newspaper coverage of military advancements, created an environment in which commodities were shown to be not "born" in fields via brown-skinned labor but engineered in laboratories via the minds of white-skinned, white-suited professionals. This is not to say that consumers who purchased saccharin during this era did so because they consciously wanted to affiliate with chemists, or that they even understood that saccharin was directly related to wartime chemical companies (though it was).[22] It is to say, however, that they had ample opportunity to affiliate modernity with scientific progress and the latest innovations, divorced from the labor and geography-bound manufacturing reminiscent of the nineteenth century.

If substitutions had won the war, they could hardly be regarded as "sarcastic shams." And it was likely difficult to continue to regard pills as dangerous or chemicals as things that can "sicken you" in an era when tranquilizers like Miltown, Valium, and Librium were becoming household names. According to one historian, these pills "were everywhere in the popular media" in the 1950s and 1960s.[23] Educational material provided to physicians encouraged them to see young women, particularly young mothers, and those adjusting to suburban lifestyles as likely to benefit from prescriptions. It could not have gone unnoticed that saccharin and cyclamates bore a close resemblance to these new "happy pills." In this context, sweeteners may have been particularly attractive as precious substances that could alter one's relationship to the domestic sphere.

FROM BAKING TO ALCHEMY: COOKING WITH CYCLAMATES

Women could use "saccharin" containers to hide artificial sweeteners' medicinal origins and turn sweetening into a festive act. Thanks to the invention of cyclamates, they could also find in sweeteners a tool for creative cooking. Cyclamates appeared on the U.S. market in the 1950s and offered many of the same advantages as saccharin. They were thirty to fifty times sweeter per unit than sugar. They were noncaloric. They were produced in a laboratory and thus not subject to market fluctuations. In addition, the substance had two important advantages over saccharin. First, it produced sweet tastes without the bitter "chemical" aftertaste that many consumers found in saccharin. Second, it could be baked or boiled for long periods of time without losing its sweet flavor.

Once Sucaryl, Abbott Laboratories' liquid version of sodium cyclamate, entered the market, artificial sweetener shifted from a product used to sweeten an individual cup of coffee or tea to a substance for cooking dishes that could be used to feed others. Part of this shift appears to have been Abbott's doing. The company provided cookbooks to consumers, informing them how its liquid form of cyclamate could be used to sweeten drinks, entrées, and desserts. It also encouraged cookbook and women's magazine writers to experiment with Sucaryl, apparently by providing the product free of charge. But the shift was also, in part, driven by consumers' desire to experiment, especially in search of "decalorized" food.

Early "diet" cookbook authors celebrated cyclamates' (and on occasion saccharin's) ability to magically remove calories, rendering unhealthy high-sugar desserts and sweetened vegetable dishes healthy by contemporary nutrition standards. In this sense, sweetener cooking appears to be an early means of producing "diet" dishes that facilitated weight loss, primarily, for those who used it. Below the surface, however, these cookbooks suggest that cleansing food of calories was not the only goal of cooking with sweetener. Equally important was the creativity of the cook, who by achieving an artificially sweetened dish that pleased, could prove her culinary skills and control her family.

The postwar food landscape was no place for the weak palate. Women's magazines aimed at both white and black readers actively stretched the standard staples of the dinner table. Recipes frequently encouraged readers to experiment with fare far afield from the standard American meat and potatoes. In the 1950s, *Life* magazine ran a decade-long series featuring exotic recipes. Menu recommendations included Szechuan noodles, pressed duck, bouillabaisse, and kidney-liver kebabs. According to one historian, the 1950s should be understood as an era in which magazines were "teeming with recipes."[24] And while the increasing importance of food-related advertising revenue explains much of the magazines' motivation to recommend dishes with new, packaged ingredients, the persistence of such recipes suggests that they also found appreciative readers. Certainly the opportunity to distinguish oneself as a creative cook through a bake-off or to present dishes associated with travel and wealth were important factors. But through these products, there was also an opportunity to influence the symbolic world of the table and those who sat around it. It is here that cyclamates made their chief contribution.[25]

Postwar cooks faced an important, and oft-overlooked, culinary challenge. Most traditional American recipes were high in calories. And calories were increasingly recognized by experts as something that had to be cut to ensure health. The situation presented a conundrum for household cooks, the majority of whom were women. They were responsible, on one hand, for creating the food pleasure that brought children and men to the table. On the other hand, they were to blame if too much pleasure resulted in poor habits and health.

White women were told, repeatedly, that it was their job to control their own appetites in the 1950s. Yet just as audible—if buried deeper in the historical record—were messages that held them responsible for the eating habits of their husbands and children. The challenge facing postwar wives was how to deliver traditional, appealing dishes without saturating the family with more calories than "modern living" could effectively endorse. In other words, the table was not merely a site of creative expression. It was a microcosm of aspirations and identity for the middle class. As such, worldly dishes were not merely creative; they symbolically broadened the world through taste even as that world was increasingly restricted due to the spatial segregation of suburbanization. Reconciling the symbolic "health" of dinner with the physical health of its eaters became a chief responsibility of postwar cooks.

CREATIVITY AND EXPERIMENTATION

Early users of artificial sweetener did not gather in groups to share information. Nor do they appear to have often written down and passed on their motivations to use sweetener or their experiences in the kitchen. As a result, during the first years saccharin and cyclamate were used by the well, consumers turned to cookbooks for information on where to find the products and what to do with them. These texts offer a glimpse of the past that is otherwise difficult to reconstruct.[26] Their authors nearly always included substantial introductions, since readers were likely to be unfamiliar with cyclamates, in general, and their use in cooking, specifically. These commentaries, along with the recipes, suggest that achieving success with sweeteners required resourceful thinking and creative license. They also suggest that cooking with artificial sweetener, at least in its early years, offered cooks a way to fool their families.

Sodium cyclamate, along with calcium cyclamate, is an artificially prepared salt of cyclamaic acid made through the sulfonation of cyclohexylamine. It was discovered by accident in 1937 by chemistry graduate student Michael Sveda at the University of Illinois, who was looking for a way to mask bitterness in medicines. It was patented, purchased by DuPont, and sold to Abbott Laboratories in 1947. Abbott stabilized the product, branded its form of sodium cyclamate as Sucaryl, and received approval from the Food and Drug Administration for its general consumption in 1951.[27] Cyclamate was superior to saccharin in many ways. Its success, however, was not automatic. Consumers had to be convinced that cooking with sweetener was a good idea, and they had to learn to see value in dietetic lines of food. For the first goal, Abbott turned to a cookbook, produced in 1952 and distributed free through doctors, pharmacists, and nutritionists to potential Sucaryl consumers. That cookbook quickly found itself in the company of several others, as female entrepreneurs produced their own guides to recipe invention and modification using the new chemical substitute.

Authors of cyclamate cookbooks assumed that readers were not familiar with Sucaryl as a product and sodium cyclamate as a material. Many of these cookbooks begin with declarations of safety. In Abbott's own publication, *Calorie Saving Recipes for Foods Sweetened without Sugar Using Sucaryl*, readers are informed that cyclamates had undergone "long and successful clinical trials" overseen by Abbott, "manufacturers of fine pharmaceuticals since 1888."[28] Competing cookbooks made similar declarations, even those that appeared a decade after the first period of postwar experimentation. Ruth West's *Stop Dieting! Start Losing!* published in 1956, features both cyclamates and saccharin and begins with an admonition to readers to regard the latter as an "indispensable stand by" and to overlook what she characterized as the "stern phrase" printed on its containers that warned that the product was only for use in sugar-restricted diets. The warning was only there, she explained, because of "one of those legal Donnybrooks" and should be disregarded by those who wanted to shed pounds easily. Far from a dangerous substance, saccharin was "pure gold" with "infinite" possibilities.[29]

Abbott and West's cookbooks, like others, explain what these substances are, assure readers that they are safe, and suggest that they open up new alchemical possibilities in the kitchen. They do not minimize the artificiality of these substances or obscure their laboratory origins. On the contrary, most encourage women to embrace the fact that these products were scientific and not yet standardized. One of the most surprising things about these texts, taken as a whole, is how little they stress weight loss and deprivation and how much they stress creativity, innovation, and experimentation.

Recipes found in these cookbooks suggest that creating an artificially sweetened dish was no casual affair. At first glance they appear straightforward. Poppy Cannon's *Unforbidden Sweets*, a collection of cyclamate-sweetened dessert recipes from 1958, has fairly consistent recommendations for how much Sucaryl should be added. Both the Sugarless Sponge Cake and the Low-Calorie Nesselrode Pudding are sweetened with three tablespoons of Sucaryl, though the pudding also requires a can of "dietetic fruit cocktail."[30] Ruth West's guide, published two years earlier, clearly explains that some dishes, such as Apple Betty, require four times as much cyclamate as the cranberry sauce. Bernard Koten's *Low-Calory Cookbook*, from 1951, suggests using saccharin in chili sauce, specifying that the cook should make sure that it is "tiny grain."[31] One does not have to read far within these books to get a sense of how little certainty and how much contradiction there was among early writers of sweetener recipes. Whereas Cannon recommends using the liquid Sucaryl, West recommends using cyclamate in tablet form. Koten prefers saccharin tablets but fails to mention whether cooks should use quarter-, half-, or one-grain tablets. Some authors, in fact, urged cooks to eschew purchased liquid blends or easily added tablets and instead create their own home brew. According to Llewellyn Miller, author of the *Reducing Cookbook and Diet Guide*, published in 1951, the proper approach would be to "make the liquid form yourself." To do this, one need only dissolve forty-eight tablets in a cupful of hot water and then measure out one teaspoon of liquid for the equivalent of one teaspoon of sugar.[32]

Dissolving forty-eight tablets in a cup of hot water was not terribly difficult. And cooks could, with a little trial and error, figure out what grain saccharin tablets worked best in their chili. All of this, however, required effort and offered a real possibility of failure on the first try. If forty-eight tablets were needed, not forty-seven or forty-nine, women had to concentrate on the task at hand. Imagining the process enables us to see an exercise more suiting a pharmacist than a cook. Further, there was no guarantee that simply counting one's tablets was sufficient to ensure success. As Cannon admitted, "Writing recipes that include non-nutritive sweeteners has its difficulties." Because formulas still seemed to vary from batch to batch and between competing pharmaceutical companies, it was, she explained to readers, "impossible to say that so much of the sweetener is equal to so much sugar." The only way to guarantee success was to taste the results and anticipate a certain amount of trial and error.[33] A professional food writer who frequently worked with food industries to develop recipes for convenience products, Cannon had a good amount of experience in test kitchens. For her to admit that she had difficulty writing recipes for a product was significant.

Experimenting with artificial sweeteners in cooking was reminiscent of the work of domestic scientists generations earlier. In 1895, home economist Mary Wade gave the following advice to readers of the *New England Kitchen Magazine*: "There is no reason why the cook should not be as sure of her results as is a chemist. When the druggist has a prescription to fill he does not mix his ingredients in a haphazard manner . . . but everything is carefully weighed and measured and put together in just the right way, and then he knows exactly what the result will be."[34] The shift here is in experimentation. Whereas the turn-of-the-century domestic scientists had stressed precision in cooking and the careful anticipation of taste outcomes, early adopters of cyclamates instead stressed the connection between chemistry and creativity. Cannon explained to her readers in her cookbook's introduction that "the emphasis all through the book is on glamour."[35] She was, of course, referring to the Nesselrode Pudding. But one can also appreciate how the art of creating the recipe, measuring just the right amount of liquid sweetener, never reaching for the sugar bowl, and whipping up creams and cakes that were (after some trial and error) beautiful and nearly calorie free could spread the glamour from product to producer.

The experimental work of cooking with sweetener went beyond achieving a dish that tasted appropriately sweet. The cook also had the responsibility of saving Americans from their own cuisine. In 1956 Ruth West coined a verb for this process. Decalorizing was what the nation's foods needed, and sweetener was just the product to do it. "America's traditional recipes were not handed down from The Mount," she explained. "They were compounded, not in laboratories by white-coated technicians, but by ordinary women in gingham aprons with no help but that of their taste buds and imaginations." This, she explained, was the core of American cooking: the creative cook who took the lead in the kitchen by using her own senses. Yet, while praising the ingenuity of the traditional American housewife, West urged readers to experience the best of both worlds by joining kitchen and laboratory. "We need this kind of creative cook to modernize and de-calorize the old anachronistic recipes," she asserted, a feat that could only be achieved by "using the de-calorized new ingredients food chemists have perfected for us."[36] She urged women to use her "six twentieth-century master recipes" to create a new flavor base for old American favorite dishes. Her "Hollandaise for moderns," for instance, calls for Sucaryl and low-fat milk, instead of sugar and full-fat milk. West urged readers to think of these substitutions as a "game" that challenged "those creative instincts that are the making of a good cook."[37]

Not all women were interested in chemical creativity in the kitchen. It is perhaps significant that none of these cookbooks feature African American recipes, where heavily sweetened desserts and drinks were common. If we consider these messages in cultural context, it becomes clearer why the evocations of laboratories, pills, and scientific advances in these early promotions of artificial sweetener would likely not have appealed to African American women, who had few reasons to look favorably upon products from the laboratory, even less so if they came from mainstream chemical industries and pharmaceutical companies. While it was true that wartime technology had benefited all Americans, in the sense that innovations were often credited for the victory, the segregation of African Americans during the war combined with the lack of recognition for African American soldiers after the war made it clear that whites and blacks were not equal beneficiaries of "the march of science." Further, by the 1950s, black Americans had ample evidence that science and technology could easily do more harm than good. Colonial policies frequently gave Native lands to whites, based on the Indians' "inferior" technical knowledge; systems of racial segregation were upheld by nineteenth-century pseudosciences like phrenology, which declared whites intellectually superior to other races because of their cranial measurements; and medical professionals used African Americans in experiments designed to further scientific knowledge by putting their bodies in peril.[38] From the beginning, then, the very presentation of artificial sweeteners as agents of scientific progress may have encouraged nonwhite consumers to view such products with suspicion.

For white consumers, suspicions may have been focused more on unhealthy foods than on untrustworthy science. By the 1940s, thanks to nutritional research prompted by World War I, most Americans were aware of the importance of vitamins B, C, and D and had reason to suspect that they were missing from their diets. World War II intensified this concern as health experts publicized the "hidden hunger" found among recruits deemed nutritionally deficient. Specific vitamins were often cited as causing soldiers' poor performance in the field. In one case, missing thiamine was discussed as the direct cause of low morale, and increased quantities were urged in the diets of fighting men.[39] And in response to what Washington's health experts deemed a "hungerless vitamin famine," in 1941 bread was first enriched with vitamins B1, iron, and nicotinic acid.

This was the context in which Cannon and West urged women to become "good cooks" by altering an essential ingredient in order to render foods more appropriate for the modern age.[40] When we consider artificial sweetener from either end of the twentieth century, it hardly seems an ingredient indicative of culinary excellence. For midcentury advocates, however, the material was no longer a dangerous adulterant. Nor was it a substitute for an essential nutrient. Cyclamates and saccharin in the kitchen allowed women to join in the important work of improving American bodies by altering the nutritional composition of their food.

REDUCING THE FAMILY

As commodities that increased women's control over their surroundings and promised to make difficult tasks easier, saccharin and cyclamates were not unique. It is, in fact, tempting to see them as an edible example of what American studies scholar Jeffrey Meikle has termed an "era of damp-cloth utopianism," referring to a recurring trope during the 1950s and 1960s wherein products' internal technologies made hard work obsolete.[41] Probably the best-known example was the Home of the Future, installed in Disneyland in 1957 by Monsanto as a means of advertising recent advances in chemical manufacturing, particularly plastics, that could free women from onerous domestic chores.[42] According to promotional material, visitors learned that postwar chemicals had created a world where kitchens and bathrooms had a permanent "showroom freshness and sparkle," and among all interior elements "hardly a natural material appears in anything like its original state." By the time it was removed in 1959, the Monsanto Home had drawn an unprecedented 20 million visitors.[43] Two important differences, however, distinguished saccharin and cyclamates from other modern domestic products. First, they harkened back to the past as much as they looked forward to the future. Second, their technology alone was not enough to guarantee their success. Women had to master the art of cooking with sweetener and then they had to fool their families.

The majority of artificial-sweetener recipes in cookbooks were not new. Sponge cake, puddings, pies, chili, and stewed tomatoes had been culinary standards since the nineteenth century. One might expect women like Poppy Cannon, known for her ability to innovate with new food products, to create entirely new dishes that used liquid sweetener as a base. The persistence of the American culinary canon seems, at least in part, to have been motivated by the fact that the majority of the dishes in these cookbooks were not meant to be consumed by women alone. On the contrary, they were designed to be served to family members whose tastes were not terribly adventurous. Cooks experimented with sweeteners and cooking processes to create new dishes that tasted familiar.

Myra Waldo's best-selling *Slenderella Cook Book*, which formed the basis of the well-known Slenderella "slimming system," was aimed at women who were responsible for the family meal and who were, as she put it, ready for "an entirely new concept in cook books." Waldo's success, arguably, relied on her ability to present palatable Sucaryl recipes *and* instruct women on how those recipes could be used to painlessly "reduce" their family members. What Waldo termed her "new concept" in cooking was based on the principle that there was nothing natural about diets that deprived people of good tastes. Nor was there anything virtuous in eating foods recognized primarily as health foods. The problem, as she saw it, was not that people were eating bad food but, rather, that they were living lives that had gotten out of balance with what they were eating.[44]

"Fifty years ago," explained Waldo, "the modern woman of her day arose at dawn, cleaned her home, prepared three meals a day, baked bread and cakes, washed laundry by hand, took care of several children, and was physically active all day." Thankfully, those days had passed because of "the genius of American engineers" who had eliminated "much of the heavy drudgery" from the lives of busy suburban housewives. The problem, however, was that regardless of how busy those housewives were, they were not using what she characterized as their "larger muscles . . . that burn up energy." At the same time, they continued to indulge in food patterns that were "inherited" from those hard-laboring grandparents. The resulting weight problems, she believed, could only be combated by changing the foods people were eating.[45]

It is telling that Waldo spent a good amount of time explaining the history of American industrialization and her own version of the evolutionary changes brought about in those bodies lucky enough to enjoy the pleasures of modern ease. Several cookbook writers seem to have understood that readers would be interested not just in how they could remove sugar to save themselves calories but in how removing the calories from food was, in part, a modern evolution in itself, one that was essential for the health and well-being of the American family. For Ruth West, the real audience for decalorized food was the oblivious husband and children. She distinguished between the women who cooked and their family members when it came to adapting to the changes of modern eating. Because a woman's family members "are often more conservative in their eating habits than she," West explained, it was impossible to make them begin to eat "a whole strange new way" without losing "her happy home." Women could not just introduce unsweetened salads, unsauced meats, and fruit-limited desserts. Thanks in large part to "the new sugarless sweeteners" as well as the "new ways for short-cutting on fats and starches," West insisted, "a modern cook can recreate the family's favorite dishes with the greatest of ease."[46]

American women had long been responsible for balancing their families' desires for sweet with productive calorie intake. This is what domestic scientist Mary Elizabeth Hall was doing with her 1912 recipe for "lima bean taffy." Sugar, she conceded, was a "laudable element" but one that could easily result in the "temptation to overeat." Mothers with culinary skills, however, could use what was fundamentally good about sweetness, the compulsion people had to consume it, to get their families to eat more of the nutritious food they needed. By mashing the lima beans and adding them to a sweet taffy base, one could enjoy the taste and even desire to continue to eat beyond satiation, but "because of the bulk" of "nutritious vegetable bases," one would be unable to overeat.[47]

Forty years later, this occasional attempt to make healthy food more palatable through sweetness became a preoccupation. Part of this had to do with a shift in cultural values. Whereas the domestic science movement preached that food consumption was a rational process best governed by measurements and precision, psychoanalysis had revealed that people were far from rational in their desires, gustatory or otherwise.[48] There were still plenty of messages available to women that dietary health was a personal project to be achieved through eternal vigilance. One 1941 article in the *Ladies' Home Journal*, for example, admonished readers, "Don't say you are dieting for a week or a month or three months, say you are adjusting your food to your circumstances forever."[49] Such advice remained consistent through the rise of diet organizations like Weight Watchers in the 1960s and 1970s, where gaining control over food emerged as the primary goal for members. With saccharin and cyclamates, however, the cook had a weapon to use to control people other than herself. Because she could not get her family to eat what they should, she could change the contents of what they would eat. The sneaky two-fingered drop placed caloric control in the mother's hands.

At least one cookbook author seems to have recognized that women desired to change more than caloric intake through the modification of foods with sweetener. Ruth West explained to her readers that what she termed "alcohol calories" were particularly "sneaky to cope with." For those women who had husbands who frequently engaged in "two-fisted drinking," removing sugar from the diet and replacing it with sweetener at least repaired some of the damage done.[50] Certainly West realized that removing a few hundred calories from sweetened desserts was not going to solve the problems of alcoholism. Yet she did not suggest that women discuss drinking problems with their husbands, even from a nutritional perspective. Instead, she advised women to be "sneaky." Dropping powder into the sponge cake mix may have offered physical and psychological remedies in domestic situations in which women had little control. It removed calories, helping the family achieve a desired slim look associated with good health. It also deceived others, something that may have enhanced a woman's sense of control.

These cookbooks do not mention that cyclamates failed to produce the same taste and texture as sugar, or that there were numerous failures along the trial-and-error process leading to "creative success." It is hard to imagine that husbands and children would not have guessed that women were using a substitute. Some may have adjusted and accepted the change; others may have pushed back, insisting that sugar be returned. For most, the increase in eating outside the home was a larger factor in weight gain, making "sneaky" changes in the kitchen less and less relevant to achieving overall familial dietary health.

We cannot know if women who adopted Sucaryl did, in fact, reduce the amount of sugar calories consumed by families, thereby recalibrating their bodies and their cuisines. It seems likely, given the difficulty of mastering these substitutions, that many husbands and children did, in fact, reject mom's "sugarless sponge cake" out of hand. By the 1960s, prepackaged, artificially sweetened "diet" foods would appear on the market, effectively removing the impetus for women to create their own low-calorie dishes at home. Along with such products would come diet plans that increasingly targeted women only as the appropriate weight-losers, and a modern age of feminine "diet sweet" would emerge.

Still, women who learned to contain these new commodities and use them in cooking developed specialized skills that emphasized their bodies as they were and the abilities they were newly acquiring. Through words, touch, and taste, many connected cyclamates and saccharin to creative expression, beauty, control, and alchemic intelligence. Through new processes of self-focus and food fashioning, they developed a world of sweetness set apart from sugar and the service of others. Saccharin and cyclamates remained a means to feed families but also emerged as powerful deliverers of a woman's will.

THREE

DIET MEN

THE FOOD–PHARMA ORIGINS OF
ARTIFICIALLY SWEETENED PRODUCTS

Obviously, the food industry and the pharmaceutical industry
have become partners in the new field of therapeutic dietetics.
—*Drug and Cosmetics Industry*, 1953

In November 1970, executives from the California Canners and Growers (CCG) were thinking about Guatemala. Having been informed by the
Food and Drug Administration (FDA) that their cyclamate-sweetened
canned fruit would be banned in the United States, the CCG had a mountain of product with no place to go. Warehouses sat filled with cases of
chemically sweetened apple sauce, apricots, apricot nectar, cherries, figs,
fruit cocktail, fruit salad, grapefruit sections, mandarin oranges, peaches,
pears, pineapple chunks, and plums—all of it rejected by alarmed wholesalers and consumers. Diet Delight, a brand of cyclamate-sweetened dietetic fruits that had just a year earlier been the market leader in diet fruit,
had become, in the words of one company insider, primarily "a problem
of disposal." With enough fruit remaining to give a can to each person
in the United States over five years old, the canners faced a staggering
loss. It was uncharted territory for the cooperative, a loose network of
1,200 fruit "ranchers" who had for more than a decade pooled resources
and equipment to can their own product at a profit. For several consecu-
tive years, CCG farmers had found that the demand for their cyclamate-
sweetened fruit easily exceeded the supply. Suddenly they could not give

it away. After a failed, yearlong attempt to relabel and remarket the fruits as drugs under the new FDA rules, company executives looked to dematerialization strategies. They even considered burying the cans, but that would have required sixty-four trenches, each measuring 500′ × 5′ × 1′, across forty acres. After determining that burying was prohibitively expensive, the CCG vice president urged the president to consider the benefits of a charitable donation abroad, where the FDA had no jurisdiction. Perhaps, he suggested, they should consider Guatemala or northeastern Brazil, where the need for food was "so vast" that cyclamate-sweetened fruits "would vanish like a snowball in the desert."[1]

Few in 1968 would have imagined such an ignoble death for Diet Delight. Between 1960 and 1968, its market share was 30 to 40 percent; from 1960 to 1965, case sales went from $7 million to $16 million, leading to a 125 percent increase in profit.[2] It was an industry David and Goliath story: Diet Delight, produced by a regional co-op, outsold the low-calorie fruit products of national giants Dole and Libby. Today, Diet Delight has been all but forgotten, and the idea of diet fruit seems strange, a historical oddity. At the time, however, it fulfilled several unique desires of canning and pharmaceutical executives, a fact that explains both its success and its failure.

Industry executives had many reasons to collaborate on diet products in the early 1950s. Unlike soda manufacturers, fruit canners believed the future of their industry lay in scientific advance. One could only sell so many canned fruits, particularly in an era when fresh fruits were increasingly available and cheap year-round due to advances in international trade and refrigeration and transport technologies.[3] By collaborating with Abbott Laboratories, makers of artificial sweeteners, early on Richmond Chase (which would become the CCG in the 1960s) was in many ways doing nothing new. The company was simply looking for ways to innovate in order to protect its market share. The same is true of Abbott, which, by partnering with Richmond Chase, sought a way to open the door between the chemical industry and the food industry, one that could potentially increase consumer trust of Abbott's own brand name and sway regulatory agencies that might look askance at a chemical company entering the food supply.

Much of the motivation for these two companies, each with its own form of scientific production and business culture, to come together was market driven. Yet it is not possible to get from 1951, when the partnership began, to 1969, when the CCG found itself with a football stadium of fruit to be buried, without some detour into psychology and culture. Written exchanges between the chief food technologist at Richmond Chase and the sales and research staff at Abbott Laboratories provide a unique opportunity to probe the ways in which human relationships and individual aspirations shaped artificially sweetened products. Most of the scientists and technologists involved in the first successful mass marketing of diet fruits were driven by a desire to perfect the absorption of cyclamates in canned fruit syrups and expand their respective market shares through increased commodity sales. Letters that remain from the years of this "rational" collaboration, however, reveal that both sides were also driven by very personal desires to expand their knowledge, affiliate with scientific and technological expertise, and form social bonds that provided class distinction. The development of diet fruit was driven, on a very personal level, by the desires of individual men. As a result, the CCG's executives had, in fact, developed two products by 1969: Diet Delight and a partnership with knowledge producers at Abbott Laboratories. And the second undid the first.

The lobby of Abbott's Chicago headquarters contained a mural by Weimer Pursell. It was the first one painted by the artist who was better known for his posters, including several for the Chicago "Century of Progress" World's Fair held in 1933. The floor-to-ceiling painting, completed in 1938, was called *The Abbott Tree* (fig. 3.1).[4] It presents a powerful allegory of nature's promise fully realized through man's technology. Following the image from the base to the top, the basic chemical elements of life appear as root nourishment for the tree. They are rendered usable by white men in white coats whose intellectual status is indicated by spectacles and their location surrounded by laboratory equipment. The tree that emerges from these elements is large and imposing. It is also unmistakably phallic. From out of its branches, located roughly where genitals would be, emerges a muscular, naked male body. The underlying narrative is one of nature producing raw materials that are taken by scientists and turned back into more powerful forms of nature that ultimately produce a superman. Indeed, the company brochure from that year describes the figure as "heroic." It is one of the more striking examples of a common midcentury trope of scientific expertise: white males, through their ingenuity, improve upon nature to bring about the modern age.[5]

The origins of the mural's narrative are unclear. There are no public records of the corporate decision to employ this particular image or artist. One can assume, given the fact that this was a work of art intended

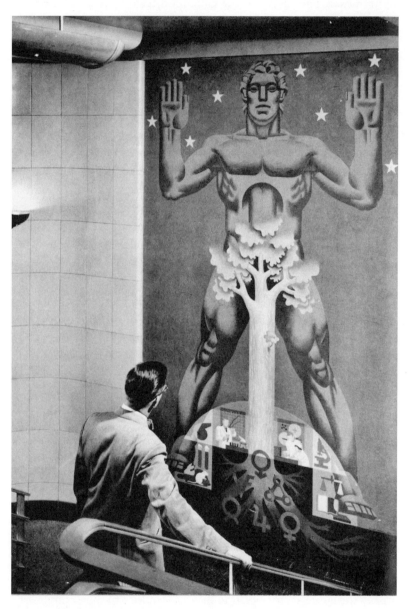

FIG. 3.1 Abbott Laboratories "tree" mural, in Abbott Laboratories, *The Abbott Tree* (North Chicago, 1955), 5.

for a public entry hall and that it was featured prominently in corporate materials, that executives at Abbott approved of the choice. Its placement guaranteed that it would remind Abbott employees of the larger context in which their individual work, be it research and development or marketing, was done. It also would have been the first image to greet visitors from the outside. As they ascended from the lobby to the stairs, they literally climbed up the image from the elementary level to the muscular half-man half-tree figure of chemical progress. One imagines it was a powerful experience, and not just for members of the public. It was also the first image to greet men like Edwin Mitchell, Raymond Chase's chief technologist, when they came to discuss Sucaryl, Abbott's brand of sodium cyclamate.

In 1951, Abbott Laboratories was a dramatically different place from the Richmond Chase canning operations in San Jose, California. Between 1939 and 1959, domestic sales of pharmaceuticals increased from $300 million to $2.3 billion. In 1947, roughly fifty cents of every dollar in industry profit was from a product that had not existed a decade earlier.[6] This context, combined with the imagery represented in the mural, set the stage for Mitchell as he established a relationship between the two businesses. Whereas canners had made a relatively stable product with stable technology for a century, Abbott was the new frontier of scientific innovation. Chemical companies in postwar America were changing the very landscape of everyday life. They were, quite literally, growing new materials and new bodies. By creating, promoting, and defending Diet Delight, the men of Richmond Chase/CCG joined their ranks.

VANISHING FRUIT

Diet Delight was, in many ways, an improbable success. The CCG was a network of small to medium-sized fruit ranches, many of which were farmed by second- and third-generation growers. As a co-op, it used a "single pool" structure to determine profits and losses. Members sent their apples, apricots, cherries, figs, grapefruit, mandarin oranges, peaches, and pears to be combined, processed, canned, stored, marketed, and ultimately shipped to grocery outlets across the country. Profits (or lack thereof) were determined by dividing the total sales by the amount of raw fruit contributed. "Rancher" members had ample reason to use conservative, proven technologies in the process of converting raw fruit to finished commodity. For many, the fruit provided for a year's canning represented 35 to 40 percent of a total year's yield. It was a significant amount of money to tie up every summer and could only be repaid when consumers chose CCG products over Libby's, Tillie Lewis's, or Dole's.[7]

The significant up-front investment required on the part of member ranchers should have discouraged executives from developing new brands with uncertain futures. The limited funds for research and development and the minimal internal technical expertise should have prohibited the CCG from undertaking the extensive experiments and adjustments required for early innovations with artificial sweeteners. The co-op structure itself should have provided ample opportunities for individual farmers to object to bathing a near-majority of their crop in a controversial chemical sold by a pharmaceutical company. That such barriers were not sufficient suggests that there was a unique relationship cultivated between pharmaceutical companies and canners in the early development of diet food.

On the surface, the "problem of disposal" was caused by government regulation. The FDA had approved cyclamates for general consumption in the early 1950s and designated them GRAS, or Generally Recognized as Safe, in 1958. Yet in 1965, as increasing numbers of nondiabetic consumers began using cyclamate-sweetened diet foods, the agency began to look more closely. The ruling in 1969 came as little surprise to those well versed in the Delaney Clause, a 1958 amendment to the 1938 Food, Drug, and Cosmetic Act that prohibited the use of carcinogenic substances in the U.S. food supply. Once laboratory investigations definitively revealed an increased risk of cancers in rats fed diets heavy in cyclamates, the FDA had little choice.

Below the surface, misplaced faith, as much as regulatory fickleness, was the cause of the canners' loss. Between 1951, when Abbott first began regular communication with Richmond Chase, and just days before the FDA's 1969 "ban" announcement, the fruit canners relied on their cyclamate supplier, Abbott Laboratories, for assurances of the safety and marketability of cyclamates. Abbott carefully cultivated the canners' trust through years of professional alliances and personal connections. Without accounting for the faith-tinged science adopted by male food technologists within these early diet companies, it is impossible to comprehend the meteorlike rise and fall of Diet Delight.[8]

There was no natural market for diet foods. As previous chapters have argued, consumers initially used artificial sweetener when they could control it. The material confrontation was important; Americans had once seen saccharin as an industrial adulterant because it showed up unannounced and replaced a "vital" food. By discovering it, placing it in containers, and experimenting with it in their own kitchens, many users developed alternative meanings. Still, they were a minority. The majority continued to use sugar after wartime restrictions eased. For these prospective consumers a cautious marketing strategy would be required, one that infused a chemical with a still-uncertain reputation with an essence of trust and safety. To achieve this, manufacturers of artificial sweetener (Monsanto and Charles Pfizer also would produce sodium cyclamate) needed companies like Richmond Chase/CCG to use their products.

Fruit, packed in cans and sweetened by Sucaryl, helped legitimate cyclamates, generally, and artificially sweetened consumer products, specifically. In doing so, the CCG provided a precedent for pharmaceutical interventions in American foods. The relationship of one food technologist and several pharmaceutical agents cannot entirely explain artificial sweetener's success in the postwar era. But it can demonstrate that female consumers were not alone in discovering a new need for diet products. Men also needed diet foods, though not always for the reasons we might imagine.

Cyclamates, it turns out, posed no significant health risks for average consumers. Subsequent research found them no worse than saccharin (currently on the market in spite of attempts to ban it in 1977). Nor are they less healthful than aspartame (Equal/NutraSweet) or sucralose (Splenda). In massive doses they did cause cancer in laboratory animals, but equal doses of sodium would likely have the same result. They did, however, pose a business risk for early entrepreneurs. This was particularly true for men like Edwin Mitchell who were deeply invested in creating what one historian has termed the era's "evolutionary and transformative" products for their industries and for themselves.[9]

CYCLAMATES AND ABBOTT LABORATORIES

Recalling the early days of cyclamates from the vantage point of 1970, former FDA commissioner Herbert Ley Jr. remembered their consumption during the 1950s as having "little commercial significance." Most artificial sweeteners were then used for what he termed "special dietary purposes," particularly as alternative sweeteners for diabetics.[10] By 1970, the landscape dramatically changed: roughly 75 percent of the U.S. population were consuming some artificial sweetener.[11] And before October 1969 most of it came in the form of cyclamates produced by Abbott Laboratories. Although only one of three cyclamate producers, Abbott successfully created a market among both manufacturers and consumers. Abbott's two-pronged approach was arguably more important than the actual "innovation" of the substance itself. The company sought success by courting consumers with its individual Sucaryl bottles and manufacturers through bulk sales.

According to Abbott's own company history, *The Abbott Almanac* (1987), cyclamate was, quite simply, predestined to succeed. "Almost by osmosis," it explains, "news of the remarkable sweetener gravitates to the brand-new world of dietetic beverages." The metaphor was followed by another suggestive of military operations. "By next year," it continued, "no fewer than 400 food manufacturers will have invaded grocery stores with canned fruits, jellies and jams, frozen desserts, and baked goods—all saving precious calories because of Sucaryl." It was a period glowingly referred to as the Sucaryl "honeymoon."[12]

Here Abbott's writing team suggests that the chemical moved of its own volition, magnetically drawn to commodities within which it could rest. Food manufacturers appear to have little choice in the matter. While the piece was clearly unapologetic self-promotion (and perhaps written tongue-in-cheek), in fact, little about cyclamates, or Sucaryl, was inevitable.

Because cyclamates were banned in the United States in 1969, few people are familiar with them today. In fact, they were essential to building the modern American market for artificially sweetened products. Their superior flavor in comparison with saccharin made it possible to replace sugar with artificial sweetener in foods that lacked the carbonation necessary to cover up a slightly metallic taste. Their ability to withstand heat made it possible to use them in processes that required high temperatures. Most importantly, cyclamates came in the form of a branded, patented commodity: Sucaryl. And they were accompanied by a very well funded marketing campaign. Without cyclamates, and specifically Sucaryl, it is difficult to imagine the widespread use of artificial sweeteners that occurred in the mid- to late 1960s.

Abbott gained FDA approval for cyclamate in 1951 and maintained the sole right to sell cyclamates through the mid-1960s. The result was the right product at the right time: between 1963 and 1967 the estimated U.S. consumption of cyclamates increased from 6 million to 18 million pounds.[13] One government official anticipated in 1969 that by 1970 that number would reach 25 million (a figure that the ban on cyclamates ultimately shrank).[14] Abbott's internal reference to this era as the honeymoon phase of cyclamate's life span reflects the intense demand for the substance from both manufacturers and consumers. "Arranged marriage," however, is perhaps a more apt metaphor than "honeymoon" when one considers Abbott's heavy promotion. Abbott carefully cultivated both message and messenger by courting food technologists and priming consumers for the products their companies would create.

THE ATTRACTION OF CYCLAMATES

Abbott Laboratories' motivation to acquire, develop, and market cyclamates is easily understood. Founded in 1888 as Abbott Alkaloid, the Chicago-based company had long specialized in granule drug production before entering the manufacture of synthetic drugs based on coal-tar organic chemistry. During World War II, Abbott expanded into the lucrative areas of sedative, antibiotic, and antiseizure drug production. By the 1950s, it was a company skilled in product improvement and marketing rather than initial research and development. By acquiring cyclamates, Abbott played to its strengths.

The trajectory from canned peaches with sugar to canned peaches with cyclamate, however, is less intuitive. In fact, Richmond Chase already had a diet line of fruit well before Abbott introduced Sucaryl. Relying on water only, the canning company's line was originally a response to sugar shortages during World War II. Suggesting an early marketing savvy, the company turned a negative (no sugar) into a positive (fewer calories) by calling its water-pack fruit Diet Delight.[15] It is difficult to determine from company records just when and why Richmond Chase turned to cyclamates. Evidence suggests that the water-pack fruits failed to gain a significant market share or build a brand reputation. What is clear is that after 1951, the company did not have to look hard to find cyclamates. Richmond Chase was ground zero for Abbott Laboratories' concerted efforts to gain a market among food manufacturers for Sucaryl.

In 1951, the audience at the Institute of Food Technologists convention heard a keynote address by Ernest Volwiler, the new president at Abbott Laboratories. Volwiler appears to have used most of his speaking time to announce the arrival of cyclamates, which Abbott marketed in powder and liquid form under the brand name Sucaryl. Volwiler encouraged them to begin experimenting with this "non-nutritive sweetener" in their packaged and canned goods.[16] For Edwin Mitchell, this was in fact old news. Earlier in the year, he had received a personal invitation to visit Abbott's Chicago laboratory for a hands-on introduction to sodium cyclamate. Records suggest that the trip involved conversations with Abbott research scientists about cyclamate properties and safety. Mitchell returned from his Chicago trip with an Abbott-published "recipe" book and a sample of cyclamates sufficient to begin product testing. Over the next months, Mitchell experimented with the substance in canning. By April, a month before Abbott would debut the product, Mitchell was able to report limited success back to Abbott, along with a request for additional information to solve a problem with bitterness in canning and to assure him that calcium and sodium were safe for human consumption.

After discussions with others at Richmond Chase, Mitchell concluded that it would be "better if the compound were used at the point of consumption, and in this manner a person could control his daily intake." He appears to have been working with Abbott's guidelines of cyclamate levels commensurate with a safe daily dose of eight tablets. Yet, Mitchell wondered, was it not possible that a person using cyclamates in coffee, desserts, and dietetic fruit would exceed such a dose, perhaps without realizing how much he or she had consumed? Mitchell closely connected these concerns about consumer health to his company's health by noting that if consumers were harmed using Sucaryl in Diet Delight, "it would do irreparable damage to our label." The conflict was clear for Mitchell even at this early point. It might be safer to allow consumers to select their own dosage, but this would not create sales for Diet Delight. Mitchell's letter suggests that ultimately he was looking more for reassurance than technical advice. He appears to have been also convincing himself that Sucaryl was safe and desired by consumers. "On the other hand," he said, following his statement about safety concerns, "if we can use the compound safely and the public wishes dietetic fruits with Sucaryl added, we do want to be the first ones to offer these products."[17]

Richmond Chase was one of the smaller canning operations in the marketplace. Local competitor Tillie Lewis, founder of Flotill, based in Stockton, fought for shelf space in California along with nationally known brands like Libby and Dole. If Mitchell could turn Diet Delight into a true diet first, Raymond Chase could poach consumers from the better-known brands. This may have been particularly important given the precarious position of the canning industry in the 1950s. Canned fruits had been available since the 1820s, when canning technologies were first patented and used in mass distribution. Not until the late nineteenth century, however, did the industry provide inexpensive canned fruits to the majority of urban Americans. By the 1920s, canned goods were marketed by the industry as especially suitable for consumers "in cities and factory towns" who could, thanks to technology, have from a can "a kitchen garden where all good things grow, and where it is always harvest time."[18] Nutritionists agreed. "Research has shown conclusively that commercially canned foods have the same food value as similar foods prepared in home kitchens," explained W. O. Atwater's daughter Ruth, herself a nutritionist. In fact, canned foods were better than fresh foods, she explained, given the "added energy value due to the presence of sugar syrups in many canned fruits and a few canned vegetables."[19] So fused was the link between nutritional health and canned goods that the daughter of the first calorie codifier would go on to work for the National Association of Canners.

After World War II, advances in technology and increases in production, thanks to the ending of soldier rations, gave Americans easy access to cheap and diverse canned fruits and vegetables. Yet the sheer amount of canned fruit to move from wartime to peacetime consumption proved challenging for producers. According to one longtime industry supervisor, California canners typically had inventory levels that exceeded demand in the late 1940s.[20] Compounding the problem was the fact that the very sugar Ruth Atwater had, in the 1920s, praised as adding energy value was increasingly seen as also adding excessive calories. Smart canning executives had reason to look for new methods of diversifying their products, especially if they could bring traditional staple products like peaches, apricots, and tomatoes closer to the "fresh" standards of the new American consumer. Diet products may have been particularly appealing in this context, given the fruit juice industry's successful, if short-lived, advertising campaigns in the 1930s for grape- and grapefruit-juice-only diet plans. Fruit canners sought similar opportunities to boost sales by promoting self-proclaimed slimming virtues of fruit.[21]

Within this industry context, Mitchell had ample cause to adopt cyclamates, regardless of Abbott's promotions. Yet his early letter reveals doubts about safety and fears of possible "irreparable" damage to the Richmond Chase label. Abbott, whether through luck or keen intuition, appears to have been adroitly poised to address these concerns. Throughout 1951, it provided a skillful one-two punch, sending a steady stream of scientific safety assurances and suggesting that there was little time to dawdle, should Richmond Chase really want to be first.

Mitchell's April letter was immediately forwarded to someone with the expertise to answer his safety concerns. Four days later, he received a reprint of a paper by the chief pharmacologist of the FDA, along with a letter directing Mitchell to take a look at page 87, which stated specifically that Sucaryl was "considered safe for food and drug use." In this case, Abbott's representative explained that they could not yet reveal the results of studies on "radioactive-tagged Sucaryl" to determine if it was absorbed into the body at high levels of consumption. But they could disclose that there was "some very important data" coming in a few months and that, so far, "no ill effects whatever" were seen in participating subjects.[22]

Letters sent by Abbott executives cultivated Mitchell's trust, professionally and personally. In addition to bringing him to Chicago, providing free products, sending two recipe books (after the original was lost), giving regular updates on research progress and reprints of selectively culled government documents, and responding immediately to his questions, Abbott policed his silence. In June, after receiving no response from Mitchell, Floyd Thayer, director of Abbott's Chemical Sales Division wrote, asking, "Have you sufficient material to conduct all of your experimental work of incorporating Sucaryl Sodium and Sucaryl Calcium in your diabetic food line?" To be sure that Mitchell understood this was not merely an inventory inquiry, Thayer also implied that Mitchell's silence was making it difficult for Abbott to determine proper production levels. "Can you at this time indicate your requirements?" he concluded.[23]

Mitchell, still concerned about safety, spent the summer running cyclamate experiments and investigating FDA research on the substance. In July he responded to Thayer's inquiry with news that while they were "still working with sodium cyclamate in our dietetic products," it appeared that it would "be impossible" to obtain "the Seal of the Council on Foods and Nutrition on any foods in which we incorporate Sucaryl." He noted that he had also written directly to the FDA to ask if it would find Richmond Chase's use of cyclamates "objectionable," but as of yet he had not received a reply.[24] Abbott executives appear not to have waited for Mitchell to finish his tests and hear back from the FDA. In October, Edgar Carter wrote to Richmond Chase's J. R. Braden to follow up on a recent visit. The Council on Foods and Nutrition of the American Medical Society had just met, Carter reported, and "accepted the Sucaryl sodium and calcium on an equal basis with saccharin." Although he did not yet have "an exact account of just what they did," Carter was confident that Sucaryl would be deemed safe. He sent along the results of an Abbott-funded study at the University of Illinois that found no harmful effects on individuals ingesting large doses of cyclamates. Perhaps intuiting that Richmond Chase was at a critical juncture in its decision-making process, he reminded Braden, "As I told you when I was in your office, I would hate to see you wait until the procession has passed by."[25] Braden appears to have agreed. Although Richmond Chase was ultimately beaten to the punch by No-Cal soda of Brooklyn, by 1953 it was the first non-soda food company mass-producing cyclamate diet products.

THE MUTUAL BENEFITS OF PARTNERSHIP

In the early twentieth century, Leo Baekeland, inventor of the first plastic made from synthetic compounds, expressed frustration with his new role of instructor. "People do not know the technique of Bakelite and I have to teach them," he lamented.[26] With imperfect products emerging labeled as "Bakelite," the inventor found it necessary to provide not only the raw material for the process but the equipment and training as well. This would prove an effective strategy for twentieth-century chemical companies. It was rarely enough to develop a new substance. In order to reach consumers with the right message and products, discoverers of new compounds had to train the individuals who used them to create finished goods. The reputation of the chemical brand name, in the case of both Bakelite and Sucaryl, depended on a close working relationship between chemical innovator and product manufacturer. By the 1950s, the task of building these relationships fell to a professional class of marketers and account executives within the world of chemical innovation.

The story of Abbott Laboratories' ongoing relationship with Richmond Chase, and eventually the CCG, is an example of this "middleman" approach. Skilled chemists, technologists, and marketers formed a team to promote cyclamates and ensure that purchasers like Edwin Mitchell had success with the resulting product. To understand this as a story chiefly concerning how Abbott sold cyclamates, however, is to miss its complexity. In fact, Abbott did provide the equipment and training; it literally helped Richmond Chase/CCG get Sucaryl in the cans. But it also sold expertise and assurance, "products" arguably as important as the sweetener to the canners and to the eventual success of diet goods. And it was not a one-way transaction. The canners provided an equally important service to Abbott. By believing in the safety of cyclamates and hitching their wagon to Sucaryl's success, the canners allowed their own good reputation to move cyclamates over the regulatory hurdles that stood in their way.

In September 1953, Edwin Mitchell received a diagram from A. J. Paik, Abbott's chief process engineer. Labeled "Sucaryl Liquid Feeder," it took Mitchell through the steps required to successfully place Sucaryl solution into cans moving along a conveyor belt. Not only did Abbott provide the labeled diagram, apparently free of charge; the company also gave the price (about $10,000) of the device and suggested where Mitchell could buy it.[27] Several years later, when Mitchell ran into a gelling problem with the red plum pack, Abbott again produced advice. When Mitchell's technical service representative at Abbott was unsure what was causing the problem, he went to Dr. Karl Beck, chemist and vice president of the Chemical Sales Division, who fixed the problem by raising the temperature to 175–180 degrees Farenheit. In 1961, when Mitchell faced a Sucaryl "dusting problem," again Abbott's Karl Beck had the solution: 100 pounds of free wet Sucaryl crystals for a trial run.[28]

Abbott's technical and marketing teams had ample reason to ensure that Mitchell's machines functioned properly. Since Mitchell was one of the first food technologists to adopt cyclamates, his experience—and product—would do much to make or break Abbott's reputation among peer companies. Beyond a commitment to excellence in diet peaches, however, Abbott also aimed at increasing its own profits. In 1959, after Floyd Thayer, Abbott's marketing representative to the California Canners (who had acquired Richmond Chase in 1957), returned from a visit to Mitchell's office, Karl Beck quickly followed up with Mitchell himself. Apparently Thayer informed Beck that Mitchell had "mentioned some interest" in dietetic syrup. With a formula Abbott had already developed for diet syrup, Beck included the caveat, "We do not claim that this is the best possible maple syrup." But it might, he continued, "give you an idea about where to start." He closed the letter by asking Mitchell to be sure to "let us know if we can be of further help."[29] The response suggests that Abbott was undertaking parallel research on food products in order to make well-timed observations of particular "opportunities" in product innovation. Just a year earlier Mitchell had received a suggestion from Beck out of the blue. As Beck explained it, he had recently been talking with Mitchell's sales representatives, when they "got to wondering if you have considered adding Sucaryl to your dietetic corn and peas." The inquiry, as Beck explained it, was driven by the fact that they were "always eager to see you use more Sucaryl as well as to see you improve the flavor of your products." And as early as 1954, Robert Nichols, Abbott's sales manager for the Chemical Sales Division, wrote directly to Mitchell asking if Richmond Chase would be interested in a new "ion exchange resin" that apparently would allow people to taste salt in canned vegetables but not absorb it. If the product, currently in experimental stages, succeeded, Nichols wrote, it would be "a very nice market both for you and for ourselves."[30]

Abbott's staff helped achieve this nice market for Richmond Chase by getting Sucaryl in the cans. And they helped expand the market by suggesting new products that might prove profitable. At the same time, they helped the canners navigate funding and labeling barriers by sharing insider tips on the paths of least resistance. In 1954, when Richmond Chase was struggling to finance the venture, Abbott's Karl Beck wrote to the Fischer Brokerage Company on behalf of Richmond Chase with a full description of what Sucaryl was and how it worked on the body and a summary of studies that proved its safety as a food additive.[31] This early assistance with funding was followed with regular assistance in navigating the complicated FDA rulings that affected Sucaryl content within and the labeling on individual cans. In 1958 Karl Beck replied to an inquiry from Mitchell as to Sucaryl's status under the new food additive law by explaining that sodium and calcium cyclamate were on the list of additives to receive an exception from tolerance requirement studies.

Mitchell's challenges extended beyond money and FDA approval. He also faced the byzantine details of product labeling, a process rendered particularly complex because cyclamates were neither fully food nor fully drug. Abbott recognized that the labeling issue was of great concern to prospective Sucaryl buyers. In a 1955 article in the journal *Food Processing*, Karl Beck declared, "Any manufacturer of artificially sweetened foods should keep in mind government regulations on labeling." Not only did the FDA require labels to give clear percentages of fat, protein, carbohydrates, crude fiber, and calories in a specified portion; there was also a specific sentence that had to appear on any product using Sucaryl: "This product contains X% cyclamate, . . . a non-nutritive sweetener which should be used only by persons who must restrict their intake of ordinary sweets."[32]

In private correspondence, however, Abbott urged Richmond Chase/CCG to explore the wiggle room in that labeling structure. In 1960, when Mitchell was facing regional difficulties getting label approvals for dietetic maple syrup and dietetic pineapple from the northern California branch of the FDA, Karl Beck responded with what he carefully termed "not legal advice but . . . an opinion which may be of some interest." He then quoted an expert on FDA regulation, who explained that if he were on the west coast, "I would take my labels directly to Washington. The San Francisco FDA office seems to be making drastic decisions on special dietary labeling on their own responsibility."[33] In 1962 Mitchell received a letter from Adrien Ringuette, of the Abbott general counsel office, who said he was writing after hearing from Karl Beck that Mitchell had additional labeling questions. Mitchell appears to have wanted to change the language on the label from "should be used only by persons who *must* restrict their intake of ordinary sweets" to "persons who *desire* to restrict their intake of ordinary sweets" (author's emphasis). Ringuette reported that although he had no "official clearance from the FDA on the use of the word 'desire'" and although the FDA "would not be likely if asked to provide any such clearance," he had advised their marketing division to make their own evaluation of the situation, an evaluation they would be "happy to make available to you."[34]

Mitchell, and by extension Richmond Chase and CCG, was frequently invited by Abbott personnel to imagine their relationship as one of seller/buyer *and* coconspirators. Ringuette's suggestion, given with explicit instructions to keep it confidential, effectively bypassed the advice provided to the mass readers of *Food Processing*. Here was an insider's track to success repeatedly laid out for Mitchell. When machines had to be built, when product flaws had to be overcome, when financing was uncertain, and when the FDA's restrictions threatened to prohibit the flourishing of consumer "desire," Abbott employees pointed the canners in the right direction. All of these factors, while important, hung on one small reservation that Mitchell clung to doggedly, in spite of his increasing reliance on Abbott's knowledge of regulatory agencies. Was Sucaryl actually safe?

Abbott appears to have answered this question in several ways. Most directly, Abbott told them it was. "Sucaryl is, as far as can be determined, excreted unchanged by the body [without] physiological effects other than taste . . . in human subjects," explained Edward Matson, Abbott's director of scientific relations, in a letter to Richmond Chase's president in 1953.[35] Abbott personnel relied on more than their own powers of written persuasion. Matson sent along two supporting documents: a summary of a study done at the University of Illinois involving six medical students and one "obese girl" and reprints of previous pharmacologic studies with Sucaryl completed by the FDA's chief of pharmacology. In addition to this complete data, Matson intimated that there was other evidence buttressing the conclusions. Abbott's internal researchers had reached the same conclusion as the FDA chief. And recent work with radioactive Sucaryl enabled them "to be sure" that it was excreted from experimental animals without a trace.[36]

Over the next fifteen years, Abbott kept Mitchell and the canners well supplied with such "exhaustive investigations on Sucaryl." Letters updated the company about the status of internal and external research, typically with reprints of strategic documents or summaries provided by Thayer or Beck, depending on whether an overview or a detailed account was required. The lines of communication from Abbott to Richmond Chase/CCG extended beyond research and development. Because of the steady stream of regulatory interest in cyclamates, Abbott's scientific "education" of Mitchell also involved tips on interpreting competing research studies and FDA inquiries. In January 1955, for example, in response to a request for "comments" from Mitchell on a recent report on artificial sweetener from the National Research Council (NRC), Abbott sales manager Robert Nichols replied, "As far as the report goes, we have a clean bill of health." Of course, he conceded, the report's final comment that Sucaryl's safety could not be assured when consumed in soft drinks "does not help any user of Sucaryl." The problem, as he saw it, was that "the clientele of dietetic foods can be easily swayed," especially by unfavorable data that "might be used as ammunition by packers using sweeteners other than Sucaryl." Nichols wanted Mitchell to know that Abbott was "most anxious to keep in close touch with you regarding all test data as it becomes available."

Less than a month later, Abbott was ready to communicate to all of its buyers its "astonishment" that the FDA had communicated the NRC's findings without taking into account Abbott's own contradictory data from "Sucaryl research now in progress."[37] The misgivings about cyclamates in soda had to be tempered, the memo explained, by the fact that Abbott's own investigation by a "specialist in gastroenterology" had been going on for several months and was "being tabulated" at that very moment. And for those who were persuaded more by the published than by the forthcoming, Abbott reminded its buyers that "200 million bottles of Sucaryl-sweetened beverages and billions of tablets over the past four years" had been consumed "without any reports of ill effects."[38] Only three days later, Edward Matson told Mitchell that in a study at Indiana State Prison, inmates who were given seven grams of Sucaryl a day revealed "nothing of practical significance," results that would be "promptly transmit[ted] to the FDA." A week later, yet another report arrived offering an alternative to the NRC's suggestion of uncertain Sucaryl effects. Here Floyd Thayer shared his anecdotal observations that Sucaryl safety was certainly proven by "about nine years of research and testing for safety" at Abbott and the five years of successful product marketing.[39]

By suggesting to Mitchell that it was actually the "clientele of dietetic foods" who were easily convinced to think ill of Sucaryl, Abbott skillfully required Mitchell to distinguish himself from the neophytes by disabusing himself of any similar concerns. Here the question "Is Sucaryl safe?" is answered not with evidence but with the suggestion that how one responds is a primary mark of affiliation. To think Sucaryl unsafe is to identify with the "clientele" who are easily persuaded to worry because they are not scientists. Within such a paradigm, worrying about safety is the sign of an unscientific mind. Further, as framed by Abbott's marketing team, worrying signaled that one had fallen prey to industry scare tactics driven by competitors. Even the NRC, the succession of letters seems to imply, could be motivated to ignore (or at least overlook) Sucaryl-positive research by these unnamed saccharin-using or sugar-producing competitors. Abbott called on Mitchell to do more than demonstrate his distinctiveness from those "easily swayed" from Sucaryl support by using the product. They invited him to become a "teacher" of the masses, promoting the right scientific interpretation of the product simultaneously to himself and others.

Between 1956 and 1961, Abbott provided Mitchell with ample materials to educate people within and beyond his company. In February 1956, Abbot provided a questionnaire, complete with scripted answers, of the top twenty "most commonly asked questions" by manufacturers, dealers, and customers. The sheet included a concise description of what cyclamates/Sucaryl was, what studies had proven its effectiveness as a sweetener, and how one could be assured it was safe. In April 1961, Karl Beck wanted Mitchell to have sufficient information to assure customers that Sucaryl could prevent cavities. We are "occasionally asked about the advantages of Sucaryl with cavities," he wrote; "perhaps you get questions like this also." While recognizing that it was "a controversial subject," he wanted Mitchell to know that since Sucaryl was "not metabolized," it could not "play a role in tooth decay." Apparently assuming that Mitchell would want to read more, Beck included a report prepared by the American Dental Association several years earlier on the relationship between sugar and cavities. "We thought," he told Mitchell, "you might like to have a copy of this report for your files."[40]

Mitchell appears to have paid attention to this information and communicated it to others. In 1957, after receiving data from Abbott that refuted a recent sugar industry claim that sugar "tames runaway appetite[s]," Mitchell returned the document to Abbott explaining that it was not something he could share with his buyers. Many of them, he explained, had both Diet Delight and sugar accounts and could not be trusted to determine when this information might be productively shared. "A little technical knowledge is dangerous when it is not handled by someone properly educated to absorb [it]," he explained.[41] It was Mitchell who ultimately saved his extensive collection of reports and memos provided by Abbott over the course of their relationship. He appears to have functioned as a filter between the laboratory and the factory, reading extensively to keep abreast of new developments regarding cyclamates as chemical compound and political entity. His position as chief technologist at Richmond Chase and then the California Canners enabled him to exercise wide discretion in determining how to use cyclamates and how to interpret the accompanying political risk that gradually escalated throughout the 1960s. A closer look at Mitchell's own relationship to Abbott Laboratories suggests the importance of science, faith, and masculinity in the making of diet fruit.

THE PERSONAL BONDS OF DIET DELIGHT

Edwin Mitchell's career as a food technologist reveals the extraordinary opportunities for innovation available in postwar America by altering the supply and demand for traditional American foods. Much has been written about the impact of prepackaged, heat-and-serve meals on American women and families in the 1950s. Some recent studies, particularly Laura Shapiro's treatment of Poppy Cannon in *Something from the Oven*, reveal the motivations professional women had to promote such products. Nothing, however, has yet been written about the impetus men had to create these things. In fact, as *The Abbott Tree* and popular illustrations in pamphlets by food technologists (see fig. 3.2) show, men were often celebrated in period iconography as the creators of modern innovations, including food. In *Food Additives: What They Are and How They Are Used*, a popular pamphlet distributed by the Manufacturing Chemists' Association in 1961, all "labor" has been removed from food, including the brown bodies so frequently associated with sugar production in the nineteenth century, as well as women's home labor.[42] Cornfields lie empty; a women sits in an applianceless kitchen feeding her baby from an opened can. Here white men of science have become the sole laborers converting corn to corn syrup (perhaps) and into good-tasting "nutrition" to grow the next generation of scientific men. Placing Mitchell's experiences against this backdrop helps us better understand the desires of food technologists to affiliate with chemistry and pharmaceuticals as well as their tenacity in maintaining this affiliation when, as in the case of cyclamate, the regulatory risks became apparent.

Edwin Mitchell spent his entire adult life in canning. He began as a laborer at Richmond Chase in 1937, working summers while earning a bachelor of science degree in chemical engineering at Berkeley. He returned to the company as a food technologist full time before becoming the director of research at Richmond Chase and the California Canners. Mitchell's career trajectory likely parallels that of many other food technologists who came of professional age in the postwar era of food processing and professional expansion. He appears to have been a lifelong learner who took pride in his ability to learn while doing. Years later, when attempting to describe how he had obtained the expertise required to oversee Diet Delight's production, he recalled that although he had taken a few graduate courses in statistics, food engineering, and bacteriology, most of what he learned came from "just studying on my own."[43]

Neither Richmond Chase nor the California Canners had any internal structure for interpreting animal studies or addressing regulatory agencies. As letters to and from Mitchell reveal, he quickly learned to do these jobs as well as that of chief food technologist. In his 1980 deposition, as the California Canners and Growers contemplated suing Abbott Laboratories and the federal government over the cyclamates ruling, Mitchell recalled that he had to deal with scientific literature and government processes by reading the reports himself. Without "toxicologists or pathologists on his staff," Mitchell explained, the task of determining whether cyclamates were safe and how to use them fell to him and those

Food Additives—
What They Are,
Where They Come From

*Food additives can be derived
from foods such as corn— or can be created by
food scientists in answer to special problems.*

FIG. 3.2 Illustration from Manufacturing Chemists' Association, *Food Additives:
What They Are and How They Are Used* (1961), 14.

who worked for him. Much of the time, he remembered, he looked to Abbott for this information. "I am not a toxicologist," he stated; "I am a food scientist. So I depend on the views of others for that because that is not my expertise."[44]

A close look at what "expertise" Mitchell did possess, however, combined with his own admission that much of what he learned came from studying on his own, reveals a peripatetic mind that reached beyond the bounds of food science. Mitchell recalled in a 1978 interview just a few of the processes he had used to acquire knowledge necessary to do his job of producing Diet Delight. He kept "in constant touch" with Abbott Laboratories to ensure the safety of cyclamates. He served on the Calorie Control Council (CCC), a consortium of businesses with investments in artificial sweetener, where he "attended meetings and read bulletins . . . where the safety of cyclamates was discussed." He also "received technical journals and trade publications" to follow independent research on cyclamates, including *Food Technology, Food Science, Food Processing, Food Engineering, Food Chemical News, Chemical and Engineering News,* and *Canner Packer.* And while some of these duties fell to members of his staff, the fact that nowhere in the archive is there a letter from any other technologist or chemist at Richmond Chase or the California Canners suggests that Mitchell really was the sole mind in charge of getting the science right. Although the canners' organization included 1,200 farmers and a dozen executive board members, Mitchell could count on no one else to chart a course for the substance. "None of the growers were involved in determining the safety of cyclamates," he remembered years later, since they lacked the "technical training" to do so.[45] In spite of the extraordinary effort it required of him, for decades Mitchell not only read journals and attended industry conferences to stay updated on technological innovations; he also mastered the chemistry of pharmaceutical additives, learned to interpret the results of animal and human testing on the impact of additives, grew skilled in interpreting FDA edicts, and functioned as the sole translator of all of this information back to a large organization whose profits largely rested on its accuracy. To understand why Mitchell did this, particularly as the risks of using a politically unstable chemical became increasingly apparent, one has to look closer at the rewards he received professionally and personally from his relationship with Abbott.

Media scholars have argued that technological literacy often served as a "social currency" among early professionals seeking to distinguish themselves from the ranks of nonexperts.[46] It was important for engineers to read journals and attend conferences to demonstrate that they were not merely tinkerers. Food technologists in the 1950s, unlike electrical engineers in the 1890s, had a professional association, and most practitioners had college degrees from accredited institutions. Where the similarities may be apparent, however, is in the desire to distinguish oneself from one's peers through technical information. Mitchell's generation of food scientists faced predictable career possibilities in an industry that had remained relatively stable for fifty years. Sweetening with cyclamates, however, was a new frontier.

One historian has labeled the propensity of technologists, especially those in liminal social and professional positions, to pursue, through innovation, professional and personal rewards as "technological assimilation."[47] This is a useful term for considering the relationship between Mitchell and the staff at Abbott Laboratories who blended social and scientific concerns throughout their decades of affiliation. "On the social side," began a letter from Robert Nichols to Mitchell in October 1957, "we more than enjoyed our visit with Edith and you last night. It was probably the high spot of our entire trip." Apparently reflecting on a recent business trip from Chicago to the canners' San Jose offices, Nichols speaks primarily to Mitchell as a friend rather than a business contact. "I hope that one of these days in the not too far distant future, perhaps before I bring Barbara to the West Coast, you can bring Edith back to the Chicago area with you so that the Thayers, the Becks, and the Nichols can all get together with you too," he continues.[48] The letter offers rare insight into the private social world upon which the trust and dependence essential for risky innovations is built. Nichols, by evoking his and Mitchell's wives, casts the relationship as one of business *and* pleasure. Here the bonds of sociability over dinner and drinks lubricate and consolidate the business relationship. This is not unusual in business. What is striking here is how Nichols seems to erase the class differences between pharmaceutical representatives of one of the most powerful companies in the business and a food scientist from a fruit ranchers' co-op.

One can only speculate about whether Mitchell so valued these social ties that they would have influenced his business decisions. The structure of expertise within the canning industry, however, may have motivated him to do so. In 1945, 75 percent of the cannery workers in California were female, and a substantial portion of those were Latina. Many organized, between the late 1930s and 1950, for union protection, with varying degrees of success. By the 1950s, women were increasing in numbers on the factory lines, campaigning for rights, and even running major canning factories.[49] Tillie Lewis succeeded at her Flotill canning plant in Stockton while in her thirties, prior to World War II. It was an industry in which women enjoyed a good deal of power relative to other places that a food technologist might find work. It was also an industry that was increasingly valuing Ph.D. degrees in the men who supervised technological operations. According to Clair Weast, plant supervisor for Tillie Lewis, "Everyone wanted to hire a Ph.D. for their canning operation" in the 1950s. Edwin Mitchell, with only a bachelor's degree, may have found himself somewhat marginalized by "experts" in his own field in an increasingly feminized industry.[50]

It is quite possible, of course, that the conviviality between Mitchell and his Abbott sales team was genuine. In a nearly two-decade-long relationship, it would be expected for sellers and clients to establish personal connections. A look at the field of pharmaceutical sales, however, reveals that while Abbott's representatives had been trained, as "detail men," to pursue close ties to clients, few accounts provided opportunities for easy friendship. Hired to be apostles of what one historian calls "medical modernity," men like Thayer, Nichols, and Beck were handpicked for their potential to smooth the path of a product from laboratory to consumer. They were then taught to succeed. Using texts like *Detailing the Physician*, Abbott urged trainees to project a "good appearance, a pleasing personality, physical fitness, friendliness, and a good cooperative make up." Yet their typical assignment—selling to busy physicians who often saw their own expertise as superior to that of pharmaceutical representatives—was no easy task. One guidebook urged detail men to cultivate a "fighting spirit" in order to combat "doctor fright."[51]

Their assignment to Mitchell and the canners provided Beck, Thayer, and Nichols with an easier day's work than many of their colleagues experienced. Whereas the physician's office was decorated with framed credentials and populated by "clients" wearing white coats signifying their expert knowledge, the environment of the canning factory and the men who oversaw it was similar to that of cyclamate manufacturing. "It was rather fascinating to watch the machines in operation," commented Norman Lifflin, an Abbott technical service representative for Chemical Sales, after a visit to Richmond Chase in 1957. "In some ways," he wrote to Mitchell after his visit, "it is comparable to some of the pharmaceutical operations."[52] Beyond the material similarities between the two businesses, the Abbott team may have felt a greater level of comfort in an interaction where their expertise was rarely questioned and where social bonds were easy to form.

"I sure enjoyed that evening with you folks," Jack Brennan, Abbott sales manager, wrote to Mitchell in 1964. "Fred, Barbara, and I had some pretty good laughs on the way home that night regarding . . . Fred's grandiose plans to enter the stock market and be another Ed Mitchell," he recalled. "At this stage in the game," he continued, "I don't know whether you're a good influence or a bad influence on us."[53] This tone of conviviality often blended business with pleasure. In this letter, after recalling the humor of the past night's conversation, Brennan went on to suggest that the California Canners change their marketing efforts. "Low-calorie products are for everyone . . . not just people on restricted diets," he explained. "It's just a matter of your marketing group taking the approach" before competitors like Dole "scoop the industry."[54] A year earlier, Robert Nichols had lamented that it had been three years since he had had the opportunity to "visit the West Coast and to see Edith, the girls, and you," but not before he shared his hope that Richmond Chase would be among "the early benefactors" of a new "aggressive promotional campaign" he hoped to see implemented for diet food products.[55]

Abbott's team combined friendship and business directives. And it worked. Mitchell did embark on a more aggressive marketing strategy for Diet Delight, switching from labeling language pitched to those who "must" cut calories to those who "desire" to do so, using direct-to-consumer advertising, and employing incentive programs for grocers to display the product prominently in retail outlets. Mitchell did "scoop" more prominent, national canning companies by getting to the market first with Diet Delight. And Mitchell did continue to buy Sucaryl primarily from Abbott even after Pfizer-Martens and Miles Laboratories came up with their own competitively priced cyclamates. One could argue, in fact, that the loyalty between Abbott and the California Canners was what got Sucaryl to the market in the first place. It was Mitchell who went to lunch with members of the NRC in 1958 as they were considering whether to restrict it to prescription use, ban it, or make it available to healthy consumers.[56] Shortly after, Abbott's Edward Matson wrote to thank Mitchell. "I believe that things should be much smoother with the Council now that they have seen that the canning industry has definite interest in Council acceptance and in the conservative marketing of artificially sweetened foods."[57] Twenty-two months later, the Food and Nutrition Board, a group convened by the FDA; the Department of

Health, Education, and Welfare; and the National Academy of Sciences, announced that cyclamates were safe for the special dietary purposes of individuals who "must restrict their intake of sugar."[58] There would be no prescriptions required.

By inserting an unknown chemical into a trusted product, Abbott Laboratories and the California Canners made uncertainty palatable in the form of a perfect peach. And an all-American soda. And a scoop of innocuous ice cream. A close reading of the professional relationship between Abbott and the canners reveals the intense co-branding that enabled the first generation of diet products to succeed. What Abbott did with the canners was just one example of an extensive effort to promote cyclamates to food manufacturers across the nation. There was no inevitable path that artificial sweeteners took from the laboratory to the food package. It was laid by men like Mitchell, food technologists who learned the benefits of artificial sweetener from pharmaceutical companies. By imagining the canners' experience duplicated across the country in the 1950s and 1960s, we see not only how artificial sweetener entered foods that had long relied on sugar, but also how food and soda companies came to have a vested interest in encouraging the ever-increasing consumption of their new products.

FINDING DEMAND FOR THE SUCARYL SUPPLY

Abbott, like most pharmaceutical companies, used increasingly sophisticated marketing campaigns after World War II. In what one medical historian refers to as an attempt to catch the eye of "the unsuspecting physician," Abbott sent out more than 40 million postcards in the 1950s, each masquerading as a personal greeting, complete with photos of exotic locales. Only when the recipients read the message on the back of the card did they see that the "excitement" was really about the virtues of Pentothal, an intravenous anesthetic.[59] With food companies, the approach differed in some respects: the archive leaves no trace of exotic brochures connecting Sucaryl to faraway places. Yet the attempt to grab an "unsuspecting eye" was at work there as well.

Between 1953 and 1959, Abbott personnel contributed at least seven substantive articles on the virtues of Sucaryl to major journals within the canning, bottling, and ice cream manufacturing industries. Authored primarily by Karl Beck, the articles offer information about the chemical composition of Sucaryl and the potential for its use in food products, as well as predictions of the size of a waiting consumer market. With titles like "What You Should Know about Sucaryl," "Use of Sucaryl in Frozen Desserts," and "Have You Considered Artificial Sweeteners?" the articles present a uniformly positive view of Sucaryl. And while the subjectivity of the pieces was readily apparent to readers who noted the Abbott Laboratories affiliation beneath Beck's name, their scientific content (complete, in some cases, with formulas for production) gave these a substantive air that distinguished them from advertisements. In 1955 Beck tabulated the possible consumer audience to readers of *Food Processing* as follows: in addition to the 2 to 5 million diabetics, there were "over 30 million people for whom overweight is a health problem in the U.S." By 1958, in an article titled "How to Make Dietetic Frozen Desserts," the number had increased to include "35 million people in the U.S. for whom overweight is a health problem," 3 million diabetics, and the "60 million people" who dieted each year. These vast numbers of obese, diabetic, and dieting individuals added up to one-third of the entire population, Beck reasoned, who were now "potential customers for low calorie frozen desserts." By 1962, product descriptions disappeared along with distinctions between diabetics, the medically obese, and the casual dieters. According to "Capture the Calorie-Counters' Coins," published in the *Ice Cream Review*, "Some 60 million Americans are overweight. More important, they know it and are concerned about it," explained Beck.[60]

With Sucaryl, Abbott broke from a sixty-five-year company tradition of not advertising directly to consumers. Between 1955 and 1968, Sucaryl appeared in glossy advertisements in *Life, Reader's Digest, Time, Ladies' Home Journal, Good Housekeeping, Look, Parade,* and even *National Geographic.* As Floyd Thayer recalled, the controversial decision to engage in direct-to-consumer marketing was ultimately made from necessity. "We had to go directly to the consumer for more sales," he recalled in 1959. Although Sucaryl had been selling steadily in tablet and liquid form since the early 1950s, "steady" was insufficient if Abbott was to succeed in bringing food manufacturers on board. "The campaign succeeded in bolstering the confidence of food processors who capitalized on Abbott's advertising."[61]

By 1960 it would have been difficult for food technologists and their corporate employers not to be confident about Sucaryl. Abbott's consumer advertising had made Sucaryl a household name, if not object. It is likely, in fact, that many technologists reading *Ice Cream Review, National Bottlers' Gazette,* or *Food Processing* had wives at home who "knew" very well that Sucaryl was "good," since they had seen it on store shelves, read about it in magazines, and perhaps used it themselves. Further, Abbott's consumer campaign urged users to purchase Sucaryl directly and to look for the products in which it was embedded. "Customers for our packaged Sucaryl are potential customers of food manufacturers using Sucaryl in their dietary products," Floyd Thayer remarked when explaining his products' success at gaining loyalty from food producers. By creating brand association between a well-financed consumer product and lesser-known options like Diet Delight, Abbott was able to point to ready and willing consumers to assuage any doubts technologists might have had.

Food manufacturers who worked with Abbott had ample evidence, from Abbott, that there was growing consumer demand. Abbott provided consumer surveys and statistical breakdowns of upticks in the low-calorie food markets. They produced their own pamphlets for clients like the California Canners with tips on promoting the product to supermarket buyers and encouraging the design of tasteful direct-to-consumer product displays. Two 1967 annual reports, one on low-calorie foods and one on low-calorie beverages, profiled families nationwide to determine trends in product purchasing across regions and demographics. They included consumer likes and dislikes and identified lucrative areas for future product development.[62] Letters also kept Mitchell updated with the latest market research. In December 1967, J. C. Lowey, director of chemical marketing, opened with "Did you know that 19 million American families doubled the consumption of low-calorie canned fruits in just the past year?"[63] It was information few food manufacturers could have afforded to produce on their own, and it added urgency to efforts to expand product lines and improve supermarket distribution networks.

In 1958, still early in the Sucaryl campaign, Floyd Thayer's work on Sucaryl earned him the title of "marketing man of the year." He was recognized, along with his fellow sales team members Beck and Nichols, for their multifaceted offensive that gained Abbott "a multi-million dollar sales growth." Among his achievements, the awarders noted, was "successfully pioneering new markets" by "integrating the joint efforts of sales, advertising, product development, and marketing research."[64] Just ten years earlier, Thayer admitted, the Chemical Sales Division was a "shoestring operation" at Abbott developed simply to find markets for the excess material produced in the manufacture of chemicals.[65] Thayer and his team soon realized, however, that the real market lay beyond disposal in imagining new uses for Abbott's products and cultivating the business relationships required to realize them. This was where Abbott had turned when it needed to create a nationwide Sucaryl market strong enough to withstand the competition that would surface in the 1960s when its patent eventually expired.

THE POLITICS AND PULPIT OF SUCARYL

With Thayer's success came major accounts with Pillsbury, Royal Crown, and Foremost Foods. He spent less time with the canners and more time building nationwide alliances for Sucaryl defense. Golf games and jocular letters to Mitchell and his wife were replaced with meetings of the Calorie Control Council. Beginning in the 1960s, general CCC members contributed funds to enable saccharin and cyclamate research to be conducted and for the results to be communicated to the press to increase the public acceptance of both substances. Members of its Scientific Committee agreed to be in contact with media agencies and to provide access to facilities and interviews with staff scientists and technologists to explain the truth about saccharin and cyclamates. At a typical one-day meeting of the group, the roughly twenty members reviewed unfavorable sweetener research, summarized Abbott studies in progress, and planned future research and publicity actions. Members also spent good deal of time strategizing to bring other food and beverage manufacturers into their ranks.[66] Abbott Laboratories appears to have caught up with more modern approaches to promotion, establishing committees that could cultivate favor rather than maintaining close relationships with strategic individuals within particular accounts. Abbott may also have sought to distance itself from its Sucaryl-using clients, as the future of the chemical began to look increasingly uncertain.

To explain the ultimate success of artificial sweeteners in the United States, in spite of repeated suspicions of their dangers, lawsuits about their claims, and relentless challenges by the sugar industry, one must understand the CCC. From the 1960s to the present, its members have provided a united front supporting the conclusion that artificial sweeteners are safe for human consumption and part of a healthful diet. Formed by pharmaceutical companies and supported by manufacturers of foods and beverages using artificial sweeteners, the CCC's agenda was to preserve public and government approval for saccharin and cyclamates. Their Scientific Committee, comprised primarily of industry chemists and technologists, watched for and quickly refuted negative articles on the substances. In addition to sending "corrections" to lay and industry publications that questioned the safety of artificial sweeteners, the committee members wrote articles on cyclamates for lay publications. A typical piece was "What about Artificial Sweeteners?" written by Robert Goodhart, the council's scientific director, in 1969. Few of the more than 20,000 home economics teachers who came across the piece in the journal *What's New in Home Economics* understood that it was crafted by an organization primarily formed to defend those sweeteners.[67] The CCC also published informational pamphlets sent directly to the media. In March 1969 the CCC informed its members about the effectiveness of this approach. JoAnne Shurpit, home economist for Libby-McNeil and Libby, had just appeared in a television interview and, when asked by the host about "unsafe" cyclamates, had responded with what the council called a "five minute dissertation on cyclamate safety." Members were to be thanked, the article in the CCC's newsletter commentary explained, for supporting the "almost 10,000 copies" of their latest publication, "Cyclamate Sweeteners in the Human Diet: A Scientific Evaluation." This booklet, aimed at members of the media, had proven such a success that the council was able to distribute it to universities, research foundations, food editors, and scientific journals.[68]

The CCC was a success. It increased the sales of cyclamates and saccharin; it turned health educators into advocates or, at the very least, helped neutralize their concerns; it funded research to prove cyclamate safety. Yet if Mitchell's private correspondence is any indication, at least some members felt uncomfortable in assuming the public role of Sucaryl loyalists. Prior to the CCC, uncertainty had been encouraged. Mitchell could always write to Thayer and Nichols with his doubts. In return he would receive immediate responses with friendly data. It is likely, in fact, that doubts were essential in solidifying the social and intellectual connection between the companies Mitchell so valued. The CCC afforded no such opportunity. As a political lobbying force, it had one clear goal: to homogenize the views of sweetener producers and manufacturers so that financial and intellectual resources "spoke" as a single voice in defense of the chemicals. Mitchell appears to have fully absorbed these changes in Abbott's business practices in February 1968 over lunch with Joseph

Lowey, who had replaced Thayer and Nichols. Mitchell approached the lunch as he had his previous encounters with Abbott staff: he asked for assurances that Sucaryl was safe, according to the latest research. Lowey, however, did not provide the response Mitchell had come to expect. Rather than handing over recent test data or explaining what new scientific studies Abbott was planning, Lowey asked Mitchell to stop doubting and start advocating. As Mitchell later recalled, his request for information was met with "quite a pitch" for the California Canners to join the ccc.[69]

Three days later, Mitchell was still upset by the exchange. "Frankly," he wrote to the ccg's George Bradford, "I cannot see how membership in the Calorie Control Council can be of any assistance in determining the safety of cyclamates. The cyclamates are either safe or they are not safe." The response to Mitchell's inquiry is not recorded. Seven months later, however, it appeared that Abbott was ready to bypass Mitchell altogether. Lowey's next letter was directed to the California Canners' vice president for sales, Maurice Charlat. Ironically, Lowey did provide additional data on cyclamate safety, a report on Sucaryl safety prepared by the ccc. The accompanying letter, however, frames the report as less important than the canners' financial and political backing. "I might add, incidentally," Lowey wrote, "that support of the Calorie Control Council by California Canners and Growers would be greatly appreciated and undoubtedly would help to lay the ghost of cyclamate safety to rest much sooner."[70] By January 1969, Charlat and Vice President and Corporate Secretary Henry Schacht were ready to join, though company memos suggest as much resignation as enthusiasm from Schacht. "My personal feeling is that with the stake we have in low-calorie we ought to be active in the Calorie Control Council and help to make it as effective as possible," he wrote.[71] Lowey quickly put them to work on the Scientific Committee. By July, Charlat was actively contributing the key information for a favorable article in *Reader's Digest*.[72]

For Schacht, it was a matter of business. The California Canners depended on Diet Delight's profits, and those profits depended on cyclamates. If the ccc was the best way to protect the sweetener, he reasoned, then the company should join. Schacht may have found the transition from partnering with Abbott to partnering with the ccc fairly unremarkable.[73] In some ways, the ccc was just the latest means of "protecting" the interests of the California Canners, something Abbott had long stressed was its primary endeavor. In 1965, for instance, when Mitchell considered switching to competitors' cyclamates, Nichols urged him to remember "the true service" Abbott had furnished through its years of pro-cyclamate research and public relations. "Abbott has for the past 15 years led the way in creating the atmosphere in which low calorie products have flourished," he explained. And that atmosphere was "an integral part of the price which you as a buyer pay for the product you purchase."[74] As Mitchell, Charlat, and Schacht considered whether to buy cheaper product from competitors, they were subtly reminded that going against Abbott could be very bad for business. "We assure you," closed Nichols, "that our leadership in this growing and important field will continue."[75]

Abbott's leadership increasingly demanded visible loyalty. It was no longer acceptable for the California Canners to profit from yet remain dubious about cyclamates. For fifteen years the canners had maintained, through Edwin Mitchell, the right to doubt the substance. They had become one of Abbott's biggest buyers and had consulted on the production of scientific data and navigation of regulatory protocols. Mitchell seems to have walked a fine line between the pleasures of cyclamate profit and prestige and a measure of material uncertainty. It is possible that his prestige ultimately came from being willing to be the doubter: the person among canners and chemists for whom "safe so far" and "profitable" was insufficient. His attitude likely made it difficult for him to muster the confidence demanded by his canning boss and pharmaceutical colleagues, particularly in the wake of new FDA investigations that began when sugar-sponsored research suggested cyclamates could, in some cases, be absorbed by the body with negative impact.[76]

Shortly after his lunch with Lowey, Mitchell balked. His lengthy letter to Abbott executive George Bradford is worth quoting.

> As you know George, I have always held the greatest respect for Abbott Laboratories. I still have this respect, and I am certain that Abbott Laboratories would not under any circumstances merchandise any product which was in any way detrimental to public safety. However, that recent conversation keeps gnawing at the back of my brain, and I feel it is essential that a clear statement come from you in order to purify my thoughts if for no other reason. . . . George, I have written this letter to you because I have known you longer than any of the other people now associated with the cyclamate phase of your business, and I will appreciate

your personal efforts to obtain for me the information I have requested.[77]

Mitchell's unease is palpable. His inability to get an answer out of Lowey, when confronted directly, regarding the safety of cyclamates is not merely troubling; it is "gnawing" at his brain. It is a sensation that seems heightened by an accompanying alienation. Unlike Nichols and Thayer and Beck, whose wives and golf handicaps were known to him along with the product they sold, Mitchell had no personal connection to Lowey. Nor does Lowey seem to desire one. Whereas the earlier team courted Mitchell and took his inquiries seriously, Lowey engaged Mitchell's desires only insofar as they advanced his own. Mitchell seems keenly aware that the Abbott he has just had lunch with is not *his* Abbott. His decision to write to George directly, and to evoke the long history of their business relationship, can be read as a spiritual pilgrimage of sorts, one necessary not to learn facts (and this is written by a scientist, recall) but to "purify thoughts." Mitchell takes personal and professional risks in this letter. He bypasses the chain of command by going over Lowey's head, perhaps putting the canners' relationship with Abbott and the CCC at risk. More startling is Mitchell's willingness to confront directly the question of whether he really matters at Abbott. By writing to Bradford himself and connecting this specific inquiry with an assessment of Mitchell's overall importance to the company, Mitchell is doing more than asking for one more assurance. He is asking for a validation of his faith in the product and its producers.

Mitchell appears not to have told others at the California Canners about his letter. Several weeks later, Maurice Charlat wrote Mitchell, urging him to "apply the necessary pressure to obtain a response immediately," apparently believing that Mitchell had not yet heard back. He had. Only it was not the response he had wanted. "Frankly, I expected more," he wrote Charlat in a letter accompanying the Abbott response he now forwarded. "But maybe this is all that can be said at the present time." What Mitchell received was a statement that "cyclamate is a safe substance for food use," supported by two pages of research with which he was already familiar. It was sent by Karl Beck.[78]

By 1968, "gnawing" brain apparently overruled, Mitchell agreed to serve on the CCC, and the CCG continued to be a major purchaser of Abbott cyclamates. Late that year, Mitchell went so far as to tell CCG executives that the FDA's newly convened NRC committee on cyclamate safety would soon issue a "good report."[79] In September 1969, Mitchell oversaw the canning of a year's crop of fruit. He supervised as the automatic machinery fed roughly 125,000 pounds of cyclamate sweetener into cans containing fruits grown from family farms across the state, a process similar to one that had happened year after year, as raw fruit was turned into preserved, portable product. When he was finished, he and his wife, Edith, planned their first trip to Europe. On October 17, the day before they were to board their flight, Mitchell received news that the FDA would ban all cyclamates in the United States, beginning February 1. The plane left without them.

"DISPOSAL" AND THE PARTNERSHIP OF DIET FOODS

In 1953, *Drugs and Cosmetics Industry* used the early success of products like Diet Delight as evidence that a new kind of business had been born. "Obviously," its editors argued, "the food industry and the pharmaceutical industry have become partners in the new field of therapeutic dietetics."[80] At the time, it was a premature statement. Twelve years later, with former small companies like the California Canners commanding 65 percent market shares for diet fruit, and pharmaceutical firms earning multimillion-dollar annual profits from food companies, the "therapeutic" partnership was a clear success.

Whether the story of cyclamates is ultimately one of success or failure depends on the viewer's vantage point. From the perspective of the soda manufacturers and pharmaceutical companies, cyclamates were just the beginning of a much more profitable partnership to come. With cyclamates no longer available, soda companies turned to saccharin. The consumer base they had built in the 1960s, combined with ample funds for aggressive advertising, ensured that diet soda would enjoy its largest profits yet in the 1970s and become the clear leader in the diet-food industry. Pharmaceutical manufacturers like Abbott, Monsanto, Pfizer, and Searle would continue to profit from saccharin sales. More importantly, the success of cyclamate would motivate them to further research. Sucaryl offered a powerful three-part lesson in market success: find the zero-calorie sweetener without an aftertaste, use the connections to the food industry to co-brand for access and success, and place a profound emphasis on regulatory approval. In 1982, Searle would use this approach in NutraSweet's debut.

To see the story as a failure, one has to consider the vantage point of

Edwin Mitchell and the 1,200 farmers who watched the CCG go bankrupt in 1983, a result, in part, of the significant losses sustained from the 1969 cyclamate canning.[81] "Shock, great shock," was how Edwin Mitchell recalled reacting to the ban when he first heard of it. He had been assured by Abbott, even in the face of Japanese findings on increased incidences of bladder cancer in laboratory animals, to expect—at the worst—new labeling regulations. Members of the NRC, the very body investigating cyclamates, had assured him of as much. Historians of science who have explored the ban have shared Mitchell's assessment. The research used to ban the substance under the Delaney Clause, one scholar has argued, was "inherently suspect and deviant from the proper statistical comparison with the simultaneously-run controls."[82]

In early October, after receiving preliminary data showing that rats fed a 5 percent cyclamate diet had an increased incidence of bladder cancer, Abbott personnel delivered their results directly to the FDA, the National Institutes of Health, the National Academy of Sciences, and the Department of Health, Education, and Welfare. They did not deliver those results to their clients. People like Mitchell found out from the news media.[83]

Had Abbott wanted to clear its inventory and leave the CCG holding the cans, theirs was an effective strategy. As CCG executive Jim Harwood explained of the ban, which provided food companies using cyclamates approximately four months to dispose of their entire inventory, it "couldn't have come at a worse time—when we had just finished our packing." With more than 3 million cans of Sucaryl-sweetened items in storage in several plants, just weeks after their yearly pack, the canners were caught completely by surprise and with little flexibility in reacting to the news. "Unlike the soft drink industry which bottles continuously," Harwood continued. "The canning business, in effect, packages its foods in one season for the whole year." Soda manufacturers were able to switch production practices, increasing the saccharin and eliminating cyclamates, thereby leaving only a small, pre-announcement inventory to sell to consumers after October 18. The canners, on the other hand, had millions of units of Diet Delight widely rendered "toxic" by media coverage of the ban.[84]

Much to the dismay of the CCG, consumers accepted the FDA verdict that cyclamates were dangerous. An internal company memo assessed the increasingly dire situation in late October as housewives, "frightened" by the "word cancer," sought to return "any and all articles containing cyclamate to the store where purchased." An American Dietetic Association study published in 1970 also found consumers considering safety far more than brand loyalty when deciding what to do with cyclamates before cans were actually removed from store shelves. Roughly 35 percent of both high school and college students agreed with the statement, "I will throw out any products containing this substance." Nearly 90 percent claimed to feel "grateful that the government is seeking to protect me." One *New York Times* reporter, after interviewing several cyclamate consumers in the days after the ban, noted that if people were angry at all, it was because the government had not acted earlier to protect them. Most "housewives," he concluded, "quietly accepted the situation as one of the hazards of living in the technological age."[85]

Overnight, the canners saw their best-selling product, the one on which their brand reputation was based, become a suspected carcinogen. The archival record contains no documentation of internal conversations between men like Mitchell and Charlat about the sudden reversal of fortune. The legal record, however, suggests that they did not plan to accept it quietly. A memo produced in preparation for a possible lawsuit against the government and Abbott Laboratories in November 1969 suggests that the canners were rethinking the nature of their former "partnership." Referring to a June memo they had received from Abbott, the canners' lawyer wrote, "The representations . . . could have had no other purpose than to induce Cal Can to continue to purchase cyclamate. Abbott knew that the Canners would cease to purchase cyclamates if it felt they were unsafe."[86]

In fact, Abbott had held a seminar on "non-nutritive sweetener" for its biggest Sucaryl buyers on October 8, just days before the FDA announcement. The official purpose was to provide safety assurances. Little data in the presentation, however, was new, except a message that buyers needed to begin to see cyclamates as their industry. Abbott, explained Joseph Lowey to his assembled crowd, could no longer carry "the burden of researching and answering" questions of cyclamate safety. "I would like to make clear that this meeting is called primarily for your benefit rather than ours," he announced. The burden now had to be placed on those who enjoyed most of the gains from the substance. "With well over a billion dollars a year retail hanging in the balance," he continued, "the question of cyclamate safety is, in fact, more your problem than ours." Abbott, Lowey explained, had "fathered the low-calorie food and beverage industry as it is constituted today" and therefore felt "a deep sense of obligation and responsibility to the industry we helped spawn." None-theless, Abbott had grown tired of doing "virtually the entire job of communicating the safety of cyclamate sweeteners." This would have to change, he explained, encouraging the technologists in the audience to urge their own companies to deal with what he assured would be "only minor changes in labeling" on the horizon.[87]

Nine days after hosting the seminar, an Abbott representative ex-plained, in an oft-quoted press release, that the company's decision to turn over its own research, thereby harming a profitable product, was just what a "corporation dedicated to the health and well-being of people world-wide" must do. While the canners received sympathetic media coverage for their losses, particularly the effect those losses had on co-op member farmers, Abbott emerged with a clean bill of corporate health. Diet Delight, product of the CCG, was the brand associated with the problem. And while some consumers who remembered the Sucaryl co-branding efforts of the early 1960s may have understood that Abbott Laboratories supplied the cyclamates to Diet Delight, it was peaches, not pharmaceuticals one had to avoid.

There is ample reason to suspect that pharmaceutical companies would not have received continued FDA approval across two decades to produce cyclamates without the assistance of food technologists and manufacturers. Abbott relied on Mitchell to convince the NRC that can-ners "needed" cyclamates. In person and in writing, Mitchell used con-cepts supplied directly by Abbott, even going so far as to avoid contro-versial information that might harm the approval process at Abbott's request, with the single goal of positively influencing the committee's safety assessment. Food companies like the CCG likely played a key role in gaining consumer support for Abbott food additives as well. Seen from the perspective of Abbott's executives, the Sucaryl promotion they did directly to consumers was intended to increase the business for those food companies who used it. And while this did occur, the flip side was that many consumers first bought diet food from canners, not pharma-ceutical companies. In 1959, the very time that Sucaryl sales skyrocketed, Senator Estes Kefauver of Tennessee was holding lengthy hearings into the excessive profit margins of the U.S. pharmaceutical industry. Ac-cording to journalist Herbert Burkholz, the ensuing testimony "ripped away at the altruistic façade that the companies had worked so hard to erect."[88] Frequently embedded in products like Diet Delight, Sucaryl did not elicit hard questions about its creators' profit margins and marketing

California Canners and Growers
1971-72 Annual Report

FIG. 3.3 Illustration from California Canners and Growers 1971–72 annual report.

practices. It was canners, soda companies, and ice cream makers who, by using and supporting cyclamates, ultimately helped the product bridge laboratory and pantry.

The strange story of diet fruit reminds us of the importance of the personal—even the spiritual—in transforming artificial sweetener from an experimental substitute for the few into a household staple for the many. There is no doubt that Diet Delight made a tremendous amount of money for the CCG before 1969. And Edwin Mitchell's leadership clearly won him the admiration of his peers, so much so that he became vice president of research and development and was featured on the cover of the CCG's annual report in 1971 (see fig. 3.3). The historical archive, however, leaves little doubt that profit and internal regard were not the only motivators for men like Mitchell. To understand the canners' willingness to be first to the market, to provide the solid reputation necessary for cyclamates' approval, to prime a national market for "diet foods," and to fail to accurately assess the risks at a critical moment, we must see the opportunity the chemical sweetener afforded individuals to transcend the limits of what they had come to define as possible. Twelve hundred small ranchers cooperatively canning did not expect to be industry leaders on the diet frontier. Food technologists specializing in fruit did not expect to be courted by powerful pharmaceutical companies, brought into their inner social circles, and privy to information that made them sought-after experts in a new field. Detail men did not come of professional age in the 1950s expecting to be viewed as experts by buyers and feted as marketing men of the year. Today, thanks to decades of marketing, we tend to regard artificial sweeteners as tools for making less. The history of cyclamates, however, reveals that for "diet" entrepreneurs, they have often been about making more.

PROSPERITY STOMACHS AND PROSPEROUS WOMEN

DIET ENTREPRENEURS

*Let's face it, the best diet for you is the one which you can follow
without hardship, without sacrifice . . . and without a second thought.*
—Tillie Lewis, founder of Tasti-Diet foods, 1953

In 1953, Tillie Lewis, owner of a Stockton-based fruit-canning company,
told readers of the *Chicago American* the most important fact about modern weight control: "You now know that dieting can be pleasant. You've
discovered that food research has finally produced sweet desserts and
rich dressings which make it possible to take calories out of a menu,
without removing the pleasure of eating or the texture and taste from
dietetic food."[1]

Lewis was part of a small group of businesswomen who worked with
artificial sweetener to fundamentally change the meaning of "diet" between 1953 and the late 1970s. Diets, of course, had been popular in the
United States among white women since the 1920s. Yet what diets had
in common, whether they were based on eating grapefruit or counting
calories, was an insistence that a person eat less in order to lose weight
and a recognition that this meant doing without pleasure, at least for the
limited period of time when one wanted to "lose." Grape juice diet advocates urged women to substitute it for regular meals in order to "burn

fat." Diet guides offered alternate versions of desirable meals and desserts made with less fat and less sugar. Whether it was a replacement diet or an ingredient-altering diet, taste and pleasure were not promoted as core experiences for adherents. Eating grapefruit for a meal or cooking without butter and oil was just what it seemed—a sacrifice. Eating within such a system was not a pleasurable consumer experience. The pleasure came from consumption deferred for the sake of achieving a future goal.

Tillie Lewis, along with a group of women's magazine editors and writers, and Jean Nidetch, the founder of Weight Watchers, developed a new approach to dieting wherein pleasure replaced deprivation. Diets, in fact, worked when women were able to have more rather than less of what they wanted. Instead of focusing on willpower and limited quantities, the emphasis was on plenty. This dramatic change in philosophy was enabled by artificial sweetener.

These women were not producers in a typical sense. They did not create diet foods or experiment directly with artificial sweetener—though Lewis would claim that she did. What they created was a set of meanings around the new artificially sweetened products such as canned fruits, low-calorie dressings and jellies, sodas, and desserts. They were the first to tell compelling stories about what kind of people used such products, how these products could be combined with other foods to make meals, and, perhaps most importantly, how the use of these products was a fundamentally positive—even required—practice for women attempting "healthy" living in the modern age. By simultaneously promoting eating as a proper source of female pleasure and creating lines of virtuously indulgent foods that relied upon artificially sweetened products, these women removed the taint from saccharin and cyclamates and created a profitable dynasty for themselves.

Lewis and Nidetch were among the hundreds of market researchers, food and fashion writers and editors, and diet promoters who, between 1950 and 1970, helped create a popular understanding of artificial sweetener as primarily a diet food for normal women who sought to remain thin through market choices. It is to them that we must look if we want to understand why diet soda, rather than water, and low-calorie dinners, rather than regular dinners in small portions, remain frequent choices for women (and men) who are watching their weight. Men like Fahlberg, Queeney, Mitchell, and Beck invented saccharin and cyclamates, helped stabilize their formulas, and put them in cans on supermarket shelves across the country. What they did not do was create a full set of accompanying meanings for the products, meanings that could help move them off the shelves, into the carts, and eventually into the bodies of consumers. Americans had to learn that eating less did not mean consuming less. It was a lesson that could only be taught by communicating the value of artificial sweetener, a substance that embodied the promises of the postwar era.

Women have long been valued by the advertising industry for their ability to enable product promoters (mostly men) to get into the minds of female consumers. The first women employed at the J. Walter Thompson advertising agency, for example, were hired expressly as "women's researchers" and went door-to-door talking with housewives about products as diverse as home cleaners and beauty aids.[2] It was not revolutionary, then, that women worked in the early artificial-sweetener industry. They, too, were translators, working between a new product and the possible meanings that consumers might give to it. What was revolutionary about these artificial-sweetener entrepreneurs was their message. They promoted artificially sweetened products (canned fruit, chocolate soda) alongside a philosophy about the relationship between appetite and consumption. Many of them asserted that there was simply too much food available for women to make appropriate market choices. Like cookbook writers, but on a much larger scale, they described a foodscape in which "diet" meant indulgence, not deprivation. Because artificial sweetener had changed food, women did not have to change their appetites. This message transcended the question of what to eat and addressed the very scale of appropriate consumer appetites in the postwar United States.

Diet fruit, diet dressing, and diet soda reached a national audience because they combined a set of practical benefits (fewer calories, same sweet taste) with impractical aspirations. While many individual women had experimented with saccharin during wartime rationing or had it prescribed by physicians, there was no unified image—or branding—of artificial sweetener until this era of female entrepreneurs. Moving saccharin and, for a time, cyclamates into the mainstream required savvy sellers and self-promoters; these women used personal and professional expertise to present artificial sweetener as the substance that could finally solve the problem of overeating. By presenting it as a "miracle worker" that had helped them shed pounds on their own bodies in spite of their lack of willpower, these women walked a fine line between being experts and neophytes. They crafted narratives of control and power that were built on the precarious revelation that without artificial sweetener, they were powerless. It was a message far more liberatory, ultimately, for these women than for many women who would follow their advice.

Up to this point, I have largely disputed the notion that diet foods were invented in response to American women's increasing urge to diet in the 1950s. Chemists created sweetener in the late nineteenth century quite by accident, and their customers were not weight-conscious consumers but, rather, beverage manufacturers looking for cheap sweetener. Wartime shortages encouraged experimentation among women in the 1940s; along with victory gardens and sock darning came searching the aisles of the drugstore for saccharin pills and experimenting with new dispensers and alternative canning techniques at home. And throughout the 1950s and 1960s, men in the pharmaceutical and canning industries innovated with sweetener as a means to achieve personal and professional status.

There is scant evidence to suggest that white American women woke up one morning in 1955 and determined that (1) they were overweight, (2) food products could help them lose weight, and (3) food products without sugar would help them more than anything else to lose weight. Historians have documented the increasing interest in weight-loss products in the postwar era. Others have discussed the new fascination with thinness revealed in 1960s preferences for "Twiggy" over "Marilyn" frames. Yet to see an increasing imperative for thinness is not to explain the phenomenal rise of artificial sweetener. There could have been a sudden new vogue for long walks or eating more fruit or going without dessert or eating less bread—or fasting.[3]

Today we drink diet soda without considering Jean Nidetch or Tillie Lewis, and we peruse advertisements for low-calorie desserts in magazines without considering the women in the editorial office. Though commodities of all sorts can easily be created in laboratories, market success demands meaning-makers who draw consumers to products, helping them cast off old practices for new. Because they created the messages that helped sweeteners to appeal to the masses, these promoters ought to be considered inventors as much as Fahlberg or Sveda. Men made the chemicals, but women made them relevant. Artificial sweetness required equal parts technical and cultural expertise.

PROMOTING PLEASURE IN TASTI-DIET

While Edwin Mitchell was developing Diet Delight, Elsie Orr Weast was working on what would become Tasti-Diet. Weast worked at night, in a small kitchen laboratory she and her husband, Clair, chief chemist of the Flotill Canning Company, had set up so that she could work after she put the kids to bed. The operation was modest in comparison with the Richmond Chase facilities. Photographs taken in the 1990s of the space reveal it to have held little more than a small refrigerator for storing solutions, a stove, a sink, and a countertop. Yet according to Clair, it was here that Elsie, a stay-at-home mother with a master's degree in nutrition from the University of California at Berkeley, worked to perfect saccharin solutions that could be taken into the factory and added to fruit. As Clair recalled in 2009, the canning industry "had lost all customers after the war," and he and Elsie frequently talked about how they might build the industry. "My wife and I were a bit on the heavy side and had always talked about low calories." It is easy to see how Elsie's background in nutrition and Clair's day job in the canning factory provided the tools necessary to experiment. Over a period of several years they perfected the process of mixing saccharin with pectin without the resulting bitterness that so frequently occurred when saccharin was heated in processing.[4] In 1951 the Weasts presented the first successfully packed can of artificially sweetened apricots, and Lewis agreed to market the product, Tasti-Diet fruits, locally. The product "took off like you wouldn't believe," remembers Weast. In 1952, with the Weasts' blessing, Tillie Lewis invented a story about Tasti-Diet, launching the first nationally popular brand of diet food for well people and fully eclipsing the Weasts as the product's originators.[5]

Tillie Lewis was, by all accounts, a driven and dynamic woman who had already made a name for herself prior to launching Tasti-Diet. Her business savvy and flair for self-promotion helped her capture media and public attention. But it was her story of struggle and victory as an "everywoman" who knew what it was like to lose and gain weight that made her particularly compelling. In many ways Tillie built on the desire for creativity and control that cookbook users found by counting out forty-eight tablets for their own sweetening solutions. Unlike cookbooks, however, Tillie was embodied. In her high heels and tailored outfits, strolling through the laboratories of dietary innovation, Lewis was proof that smart women could turn weakness into strength by embracing artificially sweetened diet products.

Time magazine described Tillie Lewis in 1951 as the "world's tomato queen," a woman who oversaw the processing of 75 million cans of tomatoes and tomato products each year. The feature opened with a vignette of Lewis at the elegant St. Regis Hotel in Manhattan: upon receiving two tomatoes delivered to her room on a silver tray, accompanied by a bill for $1, she commented to the waiter, "You tell Vincent Astor that these tomatoes cost him no more than $.05 a piece, that's 1,000% profit."[6] As the owner of Flotill Products, Inc., Lewis had just completed a packing season that yielded her a $1.3 million profit. She could cover the bill.

Much about Lewis suggests a classic industrial success story of postwar America. Born in 1901, she grew up Myrtle Ehrlich of Brooklyn. Her father owned a phonograph shop, and her mother had died in childbirth. In a 1979 speech, she recalled that her entrepreneurial spirit had come to her in a dream. At age sixteen, while working on inventory in a "dirty old grocery warehouse" in New York (which, she failed to mention, was owned by her first husband, a wholesale grocer whom she had married when she was fifteen), she took a can down from the shelf and read the label: "pomodori pelati, imported from Italy." She opened the tomatoes and fell in love with "their tangy flavor." Pomodori could not be grown outside Italy, she was told. Later she had the dream she felt came directly from God: "that I would grow and sell pomodori in the United States."[7]

If we look at only the first half of Lewis's career, prior to her moment at the St. Regis, she appears to have had much in common with technologists like Edwin Mitchell. Both came from food industry families and considered themselves self-taught in the skills necessary in food production. Yet differences suggest the limitations that women faced in food innovation professions. Mitchell was able to enroll at Berkeley, get a degree in chemistry, and return to his "home industry" an expert. Lewis married young, seems to have had little opportunity to attend college, and instead pursued technical information on the margins by writing letters to professors at Berkeley and teaching herself chemistry, soil science, and agriculture management through textbooks she found at the New York Public Library.[8] In 1934, when a tariff sent the price of Italian tomatoes up, thirty-three-year-old Lewis, now free from an unhappy early marriage, went to Italy, where, after working in a cannery outside Naples for twelve days, she was given four bags of pomodoro seeds, a small stash of canning equipment, and $10,000. Rumors suggested that Lewis had a romantic relationship with the owner, Florindo Del Gaizo, and that this was the motivation for his investment. The name of the company, Flotill, is, in fact, a combination of their first names. This, however, was not part of the story Lewis told.[9]

Instead, Lewis portrayed herself as a woman alone, succeeding on the power of her own ingenuity. Returning to the United States after only a few months, Lewis recalled, she traveled by train and Model T looking for a region whose climate and soil most closely matched those of Naples. After settling in the San Joaquin Valley, Lewis set about convincing local farmers to plant her tomato seeds. She eventually found several willing to overcome their skepticism that such seeds could be grown in the valley and one packer who agreed to produce (should there be a crop) the resulting canned tomatoes and paste under her supervision, in exchange for that $10,000 she had been given in Naples.[10] Lewis's prodigious energy is evident in this story, which she often told as part of her early biography.[11] After securing the growers and the canners, she found midwestern and east coast grocers who agreed to stock the still-hypothetical harvest of canned pomodoros. The story ended happily, with a growing crop, a canning process that functioned just as she had hoped, and the 200,000 cases of her first crop selling out. By 1947 she was the sole owner of Flotill Products with multiple plants in the Stockton-Modesto area, making her the largest independent food processor west of the Mississippi.[12]

Lewis took pains to present herself as a technical mind. Her story of learning chemistry without going to college, of unearthing the secrets of growing pomodoros in the Central Valley when others said it could not be done, of carrying back the knowledge from the great tomato masters in Italy by the force of her own will—all of these craft her heroically, repeatedly breaking the boundaries of what women were expected to know and do in the era. Her company's promotional materials, which we can assume were created under her watchful eye, highlight the expertise of her staff chemists and laboratories. On the page titled "Research," potential investors or buyers learn that Flotill laboratories are producing "consistently high quality canned food products" by the "latest scientific methods." Another page explains that quality "keynote[s]" every phase of the operation. Both pages feature Lewis in a hands-on role. In the first, she handles a beaker as an unidentified staff member looks on (fig. 4.1). In the second, Lewis fingers a pan of what appear to be canned fruits, standing in close proximity to her female assistant, directly in front of a microscope and other laboratory equipment. In her promotional materials, Lewis crafted the message that her products were unique because

Research

THE UNIFORM EXCELLENCE OF FLOTILL PRODUCTS
IS NO ACCIDENT—IT IS, INSTEAD, THE PLANNED
RESULT OF SCIENTIFIC CONTROL

Under the expert direction of staff technicians and
specialists, FLOTILL laboratories are completely
equipped to experiment, develop and control
in their continual search for improvement.

Starting in the field, soils, seeds and climatic conditions
are continuously checked to determine the
ideal conditions for growing the finest raw produce possible.
In the plant, careful testing and inspection
have eliminated all guesswork from
production technique and have resulted in uniform quality.

Thus, the latest scientific methods assure you
consistently high quality canned food products
represented by the name FLOTILL.

Quality in Quantity

1. Flotill Research . . . *"Flotill Products, Inc. of Stockton, Calif.
   has found a fine new food for the penicillium mold—
   old asparagus butts, which canneries discard."*
   (TIME magazine July 10, 1944.)
2. Constant examination for uniform FLOTILL quality.
3. A test field where research is put into actual practice.

FIG. 4.1 Tillie Lewis promoting her role in research, Flotill Products company brochure,
Tillie Lewis Collection, San Joaquin Historical Society.

she had a mind that was at once feminine and industrial. "The industrial symphony that today, is Flotill, was inspired and is personally directed by a woman. Because a woman fully appreciated the universal feminine demand for the highest standard canned food production possible and insisted that quality—first, last, and always—keynote every phase of the operation."[13]

Lewis, in fact, was not a technician. If Flotill was an industrial symphony, it was because of the paid and unpaid labor of people like Clair and Elsie Orr Weast, who developed the solutions used in canning and experimented with new substances like sweetener. Lewis was, in fact, prone to hyperbole when it came to remembering the role she played in technological events. According to an article titled "Woman's Idea Builds Three Canneries," from a 1953 industry publication, *PG&E Progress*, Lewis had first considered artificial sweetener in canning in 1941, and she herself had funded a "well-equipped laboratory" complete with staff for saccharin experimentation.[14] And she often told the story about how, early in Flotill's history, the water supply went out just as the canning for an entire season's worth of crops was about to take place. Had she waited for the water line to be repaired, the crops would have been ruined. Instead she "begged" the nearby railroads for a steam engine, which arrived "within an hour" to save the pack. As Clair Weast recalled, that had been his idea: Tillie was not involved in the industrial operations in her plants. "Tillie never questioned any of my technical material," he recalled. When asked about Tillie's tendency to exaggerate her own technical prowess, he commented, "That's management."[15] The Weasts wanted financial security from their diet invention. Tillie wanted fame. According to Ailea Haywood, who was hired as Lewis's secretary in 1947, had Tillie not been a businesswoman "she'd have been an actress. . . . She could make you believe black was white and visa [*sic*] versa, just by her magnetic personality."[16] It was this personal skill, rather than the technical ability to get saccharin into a can, that would make her, in 1952, *Reader's Digest*'s "first lady of diet food."[17]

The records confirm that Tasti-Diet products were indeed a huge success. According to Lewis, within days of advertising the products in newspapers, the Stockton plant office was "flooded with mail requesting where the food may be found or why it is not sold in every store." Her calculations had "more than 10,000 letters" coming into an office that had previously taken in a handful of requests, mostly from wholesalers, for products each day. Lewis brought in twelve additional clerks "just to handle requests and inquiries" about Tasti-Diet.[18] By February 1953, Tasti-Diet was advertised nationally. That same month, the Vanderbilt hotel on Manhattan's Park Avenue introduced a dietetic menu made up entirely "of Tillie Lewis Tasti-Diet foods," and within eight months the low-calorie food line was in national distribution.[19] According to the industry journal *Good Packaging*, the introduction of Tasti-Diet was "one of the biggest events in the food business in fifty years."[20]

There were practical reasons for the demand. Tasti-Diet was the first brand on the U.S. market with a full line of products. And the 1950s was an era in which white women had an intense fashion imperative for thinness. Diet plans abounded across the country, particularly in California, where Tasti-Diet originated and where programs from grapefruit-only diets to hot coffee cures were reputed in the popular press to help dieters drop pounds "instantly." Yet, the fact that Tillie Lewis and Tasti-Diet were inseparable in the vast majority of product advertising suggests that these reasons may not entirely explain the success. After all, when Tasti-Diet entered the national market in 1953, Dole and Libby also had their own line of diet fruits, along with Richmond Chase's cyclamate-sweetened Diet Delight. In spite of the competition, a small cannery from Stockton, run by a woman, did exceptionally well in the market and dominated the media. If we want to understand what once made diet fruit so compelling to American women, it makes sense to take a closer look at Tillie Lewis.

GAINED AND LOST A THOUSAND POUNDS

Unlike Edwin Mitchell, Lewis relied heavily on her own biography to promote Tasti-Diet. In newspaper advertisements, interviews, and her own recollections years later, she attested that her decision to produce a food line that was "sweet to the taste but kind to the waist" came not from her business or technological knowledge but, rather, from her experience as a woman who "failed" at diets. In spite of her doctor's strict orders, she recalled, she "rebelled at the idea of eating flat, tasteless, water pack dietetic foods." If she couldn't stay away from sweets, she liked to recall, certainly there were hundreds if not thousands of others in the same boat. Undeterred by "countless disappointments," she eventually perfected the food line and won national markets.[21]

Lewis presented herself as someone who had struggled and failed and known disappointment. But rather than giving up, she had used her money and knowledge to invent sweet products that could be consumed freely without adding unwanted calories. Evidence suggests, in fact, that Lewis was never seriously overweight. Photos taken in the years before and during Tasti-Diet feature a slim, athletic woman. This was not, however, the Lewis she presented. Instead, she promoted herself as someone who had found power in food after being rendered powerless by a doctor. One advertisement for her products, from *Good Housekeeping* in 1954, features these words at the top of the page: "Because a Doctor put Tillie Lewis on a Diet—You Now Get Low-Calorie Foods as Delicious as High-Calorie Foods" (fig. 4.2).[22] The picture below features Tillie herself, described as "America's First Woman in Dietetic Foods." Wearing pearls and with perfect hair, Lewis is shown explaining to a group of women gathered with her at a table that food pleasure is quite possible, even if your doctor has demanded that you reduce your caloric intake. Lewis's own story was often repeated in articles that advertised her diet to readers across the country. Many may simply have been interested in the instructions on how to shed pounds, but importantly, this practical advice was frequently framed within a rhetoric of "woman knows best." Lewis's story skillfully ceded scientific expertise to her doctor. It was an expert who told her to reduce, and she accepted this. The control she exercised was over continuing to pursue pleasure in spite of his admonition. By reformulating food to have sweetness without calories, so the story went, she achieved slimness *on her own terms.*

Lewis managed to turn artificially sweetened products into an experience through the twenty-one-day diet. The plan was developed by Elsie Orr Weast, but Lewis presented it as her own. Archival records suggest that Lewis contacted 350 newspapers across the country with an offer to share her plan. Papers would run it as a continuous feature, complete with recipes and information on Tasti-Diet, over a three-week period. Fifty accepted the offer, including the *New York Journal-American*, the *Cleveland Plain Dealer*, the *San Francisco Examiner*, the *Los Angeles Examiner*, and the *Chicago American*, suggesting the target audience was urban, middle-class, and predominantly white.[23] Lewis's promotional writings suggest she hoped her products would appeal to men and women, but she saw women as the primary consumers (this would have been true even if the products ultimately were consumed by men, as women became the primary shoppers in the 1950s). This is indicated not only by the text but also by the accompanying illustrations that predominantly feature women. Lewis's campaign deployed three promotional tactics:

FIG. 4.2 "Because a Doctor put Tillie Lewis on a Diet," *Good Housekeeping*, April 1954, 137.

emphasizing her own glamorous image, insisting that dieting should be pleasurable, and presenting menus loaded with diet canned foods that she produced.

Flotill canned foods had relied on a standard packaging design to capture consumer attention: attractive tomatoes, asparagus, and spinach clearly denoted what buyers would find in the can. Lewis used a very different approach with Tasti-Diet. Instead of featuring contents on the cans and showing those cans on shelves in newspaper advertisements, Lewis promoted her product through appealing visuals of a diet lifestyle. This included savory images of drinks, fruit salad, puddings, and gelatins—with eye-catching phrases such as "This Is Dieting?" Often, images were juxtaposed with quick sketches of the obese consumer—in one case, a heavy-set face apparently poses the question when confronting such appealing foods. The departure in technique is significant: here saccharin-sweetened food tempts the reader directly as something that is more appealing than fresh or regular food (spiced salad dressings, sweetened peaches, bold jellies). Rather than promoting specific foods to lose weight, the ads present "reducing" food as pleasurable and the dieting woman as pleasured.

The *Chicago American*'s fourteen-day diet plan, a modification of the twenty-one-day original launched in September 1953, was preceded by the full-page advertisement mentioned above. The viewer's eye quickly takes in the food—the cross-positioning of appealing desserts and canned/boxed saccharin-sweetened goods. Then it moves to the contrasting faces: the chuckling older woman in illustration and the soft-hued glamorous Tillie Lewis below. Her representation combines personal warmth (her scriptlike signature), her expert authority ("most famous woman in foods"), and her insistence that losing weight can be not only pleasurable but also an act of resistance. "Now you can enjoy those sweet, delicious taste treats that have been denied to you *while you lose weight*," she announces. Lewis is an expert challenging other experts in an age characterized by its "reliance on expertise."[24] The hard data highlights that Tasti-Diet had not 75 percent but "76% fewer calories." The data, combined with the humorous illustration, creates a sense of playful authority where pleasure can coexist with dietary counsel.

These diet plans urged readers to desire food. Lewis dismissed previous diet calls for restraint and deprivation, declaring instead that hers was the "eat sweets and lose weight diet." She called her products "sweet desserts and rich dressings" and declared that the "most important fact about modern weight control" was that . . . "dieting can be pleasant."[25] By drawing on nutritional knowledge that calories caused weight gain and sugar was a main source of calories, Lewis made it acceptable to desire food and to admit that one was unable to control those desires. All that was required was the good sense to fulfill that desire with the right kind of foods. Tillie communicated this message by juxtaposing non-saccharin-eating fat women and saccharin-eating thin ones. Both wanted lots of food, but only one was modern enough to make the "right" choice. In one ad accompanying the fifth day of her plan, a cartoon scale cries "Mercy" as a large woman approaches. An ad from the third day shows an overweight (and plaid-clad) woman asking, "How's your dieting?"; the formerly fat (now svelte) friend responds, "It's done wonders for me." Lewis presented a culinary landscape in which women had merely to re-orient their eating away from sugar and toward saccharin and cyclamates, and the pounds would disappear. "Let's face it," she wrote in a brief article accompanying the *Chicago American*'s first-day instructions, "the best diet for you is the one which you can follow without hardship, without sacrifice . . . and without a second thought."[26]

The Lewis scrapbook collection in Lodi, California, contains many of the illustrations that accompanied her diet plans. Among them, the twin themes of diet warriors and large-bodied women shedding pounds are the most prominent. Whether Lewis instructed newspapers to run these specific images or not, they demonstrated to readers that it was possible to battle their own bodies by developing a new strategy for eating. Tasti-Diet users appear as warriors on day one of the *Chicago American* and day eleven in the *New York American* plans. In each, a thin woman in battle fatigues aims a bayonet at a ghostly, faceless "fat" figure with the heading, "Now for the Battle of the Bulge." The military comparison between men as soldiers at war and women as soldiers against fat was likely not lost on readers in the early 1950s. Here women empowered themselves to defeat the enemy, only instead of guns they had canned peaches. The text below explains that the battle of the bulge is won when people forget about dieting, when "your food gives you pleasure without building up poundage."[27]

Vivid images combined with daily calorie plans and Lewis's own personal biography communicated to readers that they were not fighting alone. One article that appeared on day nineteen of the twenty-one-day plan, "Reducing Fits You into Fall Fashions," described Lewis as a woman who had "spent more than 10 years in intensive research in the field of sweetened low-calorie dietetic foods," before reminding the reader that "fall fashions demand good figures—this year more than in many a season." In the 1950s, popular culture, medical advice, and nutritional expertise abounded with admonitions to eat better food, eat less food, and lose weight. It was a time when the number of new food products increased exponentially; when new supermarkets emerged filled with cheap, calorie-rich foods; and when food advertisements became more sophisticated in presenting to women what one historian has characterized as the primary message of women and food of the era: "Food Is Love."[28] In this world of confusing messages, willpower was not what it used to be. And here, women could turn to Tillie, who asserted, in spite of it all, that pleasure was not to be denied. "You've discovered," she told readers who reached the end of her plan, "that food research has finally produced sweet desserts and rich dressings which make it possible to take calories out of a menu, without removing the pleasure of eating."[29]

It was liberatory language, but for Lewis the bottom line was profit. A photograph taken at a trade show in Cleveland in 1952 provides a glimpse of one side of Lewis that she did not show in advertisements aimed directly at consumers. As in her newspaper features, she wears a glamorous dress and high heels, and she is stationed in close proximity to her product. Her usual emphasis on innovation is here touted with large-font signage behind her that informs wholesalers of "Another Tillie Lewis First" and urges them to get their "share of this NEW, constantly expanding market" (fig. 4.3). Closer inspection, however, reveals a message and tone different from her public presentation. Here her pitch was finely tuned to its context, where distributors were perusing the aisles to determine which products to stock on grocery shelves. The display she chose to grab their attention bluntly illustrates how she thought about her relationship to her consumers. Her advertising campaign, it claims, was "powerful . . . two-fisted," and "no holds barred."[30]

It is difficult to know if Lewis truly took pride in strong-arming consumers to buy her products. She did understand, however, that she had power. It was Lewis who convinced hundreds of thousands of American women to diet in order to find pleasure, and her success encouraged other food and beverage producers to enter the low-calorie market and do the same. On one hand, Lewis told women that they could take control of their situation. If they weighed more than they wanted to, they could change the foods they ate rather than changing themselves or forgoing pleasure. On the other hand, Lewis's own advertisements—and

FIG. 4.3 "Another Tillie Lewis First," Tillie Lewis Scrapbook, Tillie Lewis Collection, San Joaquin Historical Society.

those that followed—actively pointed out to many women that they did, in fact, weigh too much. This message was particularly clear in her promotional materials for health professionals, like the 128,000 kits sent during a promotional blitz she titled "Operation Turnover." Each contained professional menu plans, reprints of medical promotional materials, sample ads, and postcards to order additional materials.[31] Tasti-Diet advertisements in the *New York State Journal of Medicine* and the *Journal of Pediatrics* showed unattractive, large people next to attractive, thin people and featured headlines like "Obesity Correction without Enervating Self-Denial" and text tailored to this audience: "Tasti-Diet menu plan to help your patients lose pounds . . . instead of patience."[32] Her efforts to demonstrate the problem of weight gain and present Tasti-Diet as the solution appear to have drawn attention from corporations as well. Executives from Eastman Kodak and the U.S. Navy wrote to Lewis asking for more information about the diet plan to share with employees. By sending diet pamphlets, product samples, testimonies, and photos, such

as one featuring Tillie above a U.S. map indicating that 40 million overweight people apparently possess 770 million excess pounds, she made weight an issue to emphasize in physicians' offices and company break rooms alike (see fig. 4.4). Perhaps as a result, in September 1952, not even a year into her promotions, Lewis was awarded the first annual Outstanding Woman in Food prize by the New York Institute of Dietetics' nutritionists.[33]

The effect of her advertising and her work directly with physicians contributed to what historian Jeremy A. Greene has called an era of "numerical thresholds" for health where being well consisted of looking to doctors, waiting for test results, and "knowing one's numbers."[34] It is significant that in her fictionalized account of how she herself came to "invent" Tasti-Diet, Lewis cited a physician who told her she was overweight. For all of her self-inventing power and formidable oppositional tendencies, Lewis did not, in this story, challenge the doctor's assessment. She merely accepted that excess weight was bad and sought to find pleasure in the process of dieting rather than enjoying her body as it was.

Lewis, of course, stood to make money if she could win over women who read about her products and diet plans. Kathleen LeBesco refers to such instances as "political situation[s]" that lead one to find fat "revolting" and thinness appealing.[35] Within her contemporary cultural context, however, Lewis may not have seen her campaign as a means of manipulating women into fearing a constructed fatness. Rather, since she had found for herself that looks were critically important to her own success, she may simply have sought profit by instructing other women to do as she had done: to find ways to take control by privileging beauty within a world largely stacked against women by men. "As a realist, Helen Gurley Brown understood that her contemporaries lived in a world they neither fashioned nor controlled," explains Brown's biographer Jennifer Scanlon. Brown's approach consistently advocated "working the system rather than changing it, manipulating the rules men wrote rather than attempting to rewrite the rules altogether."[36] *Sex and the Single Girl*, Brown's guidebook for women navigating singleness without the financial means to support themselves, contained advice such as how to pocket the cab fare by getting out a block away after a man sends you home after a date. If we consider Lewis and Brown contemporaries (*Sex and the Single Girl* would be published in 1962), we can see that assessing either as a manipulator of women is too simple. Instead they crafted empowering messages for women who, had they followed them, would fail to challenge the larger system responsible for their oppression. Lewis and Brown did gain control over industries and therefore were not in the same position as the women who followed them. Yet evidence suggests that both, while thin, actively controlled their caloric intake. Lewis, in fact, did not eat her company's diet foods but instead consumed only small portions of food at any meal. In 1987 Brown admitted, "I'm always feeling guilty or hungry—one or the other," and according to Scanlon, she routinely took protein tablets after "an almost non-existent lunch."[37] Neither woman appears to have been satisfied with her own body, a fact that may explain their drive to emphasize the importance of attractiveness to others.

Lewis often discussed out-of-control eaters in her own testimony and her product pitches. Yet she also stressed that the desire for sweets—the very thing that caused the out-of-control feeling—was a fundamental American right. One Tasti-Diet advertisement that ran in Iowa in 1956 reflects the election-year motif with an eye-catching, large-font declaration: "Democrats-Republicans Win! Regardless of weight, shape, or appetite! With the platform all can stand on."[38] While certainly tongue-in-cheek ("elect to try rich creamy puddings," "up with rich, zesty salads, down with unsightly bulges"), the ad contains a tone of earnestness and a clear vision of democratic food consumption in the lengthy text that is written on a scroll surrounded by Lewis's saccharin-sweetened foods. Readers are told that they have the "right" to "anticipate, experience, and enjoy a complete meal of good, wholesome, delicious, nutritious food." They have the right to the "pleasure of eating" and to "satisfy the cravings that normally lead to obesity." The ad is a powerful evocation of what historian Lizabeth Cohen has coined the postwar "citizen consumer."[39]

Americans had to learn to overpurchase, and manufacturers and marketers emerged as willing and able teachers. Through individual product promotions and organized collectives like the National Association of Manufacturers, industry leaders peppered newspapers, magazines, television, and even public school classrooms with materials designed to convince the skeptical consumer of two important imperatives: First, buying, not saving, was the means to security. Second, people needed to rethink entirely what they "needed" to buy. One issue of *Brides* magazine from the 1950s offers the following advice to newlyweds who might feel overwhelmed by the dizzying array of products facing the new suburban dwellers: "When you buy the dozens of things you never bought or even thought of before," it explained, "you are helping to build greater security for the industries of this country. . . . What you buy and how you buy it is very vital to your new life—and to our whole American way of living." Lewis's description in advertisements of the "complete meal," surrounded with images of chocolate pudding, grape jelly, maple syrup, and whipped dressing, should be examined within this cultural climate where personal indulgence furthered national security. In a society that "leads the world in abundance of delicious foods," she asks, "What advantage is that abundance to you if you can't share and enjoy it?" What is required is a way to enable those "best-cared-for" stomachs to enjoy "all the fun of normal eating" without "suffering the torment and torture of . . . deprivation . . . or starvation." The conflation of deprivation and starvation is worth considering here. Most Americans who went on voluntary diets in 1952 were not starving. They might have felt hunger pangs if they reduced their caloric intake, but they were not, in fourteen or twenty-one days, going to reach the point of near-death.[40]

What made this an effective advertisement was Lewis's ability to communicate an important cultural truth that, if spoken aloud, would have been dismissed as ridiculous. So soon after the war, most people were unlikely to toss the term "torture" about lightly. Yet something, indeed, made saying no to desserts and those abundant delicious foods intensely difficult. Delivered in this format, borrowing from the faux intensity of campaign platforms where hyperbolic language was the norm, the ad campaign could effectively communicate to readers that Tillie Lewis in fact knew the intensity of consumers' desires and took them seriously. The advertisement directly infused food choices with political import, uniting the citizen consumer and the indulgent eater in one savvy visual display. In fact, asking consumers to willingly do without a consumable when they could afford it and wanted it violated the ethos of consumer abundance many had been learning for years. Of course, refusing to eat pies and cakes did not constitute torture. But having fit two very different types of consumer ethics into the same body may have been very uncomfortable, indeed. Tasti-Diet offered to solve the paradox of American eating wherein overconsuming had become both essential and unacceptable.[41]

By skillfully turning a can of diet fruit into a pledge of allegiance, Lewis joined the ranks of artificial-sweetener inventors who had long faced the challenge of transforming an undefined material into a cohesive, attractive message. By the late 1950s, the California House of Representatives had declared a Tillie Lewis Day, and Lewis had been named Outstanding Woman in Food by the New York Institute of Dietetics. In 1966 Lewis sold Flotill and retired a wealthy woman. Her name has been largely forgotten, but her message and product, in tandem, helped establish the initial affiliation between diet and pleasure in the United States.

DIET PRODUCT PROMOTION ON THE WOMEN'S PAGE

Since the nineteenth century, readers had relied on women's pages for advice about food preparation, fashion, and etiquette. Newspapers in small and large towns alike had specialists who imagined, wrote, and delivered stories that would be of general interest to women running households. These were women who walked a fine line between professional expertise and lay interest. They were responsible for reviewing new inventions and products and suggesting how they should be used. At the same time, they had to know their readers and have their trust; achieving this depended on being local. Thus they were the ideal messengers for artificial sweetener, and many of them seem to have felt an intense attraction to Tillie Lewis, her message, and her products.[42]

"The Duchess of Diet" is how Lewis was introduced in the *Chicago*

FIG. 4.5 "Tillie Lewis' Amazing 'Diet with Sweets,'" archive copy, *Chicago American*,
September 5, 1953, 15.

American on September 5, 1953. The article was in many ways a typical
introduction to the twenty-one-day diet plan: background on Lewis; descriptions of her as "a modern day pioneer," "a woman with vision and
determination"; and details on the diet plan that would be coming, daily,
to readers. Like most, it featured a large image of a glamorous Lewis.
Alongside that photo, however, was another one: Lewis with Trudy Dyer,
Chicago American's woman's page writer and "perennial dieter." Dyer types
as Lewis chats nearby in what appears to be Dyer's office (see fig. 4.5),
and the caption below reads, "Why, wails Trudy, didn't I know about this
long ago?"[43]

Dyer was a member of the women's press corps during the 1950s. One
among tens of thousands nationwide, her job was to craft stories on fashion, beauty, and the home for "women's pages." It was these women who
helped Tillie Lewis take Tasti-Diet from a product advertisement to an
uplifting biography. Along with Katherine Harrington of the *Knickerbocker News*, Clementine Paddleford of the *World Journal Tribune*, Ann

Chester of the *Herald Statesman*, Dorothy Siez of the *Dallas Times Herald*, and Camille Jilke of the *Chicago Sun Times*, Dyer covered diet plans and new products and placed them in contexts that spoke directly to their own readers. Women's page writers offered their own opinions about artificially sweetened recipes and personal tips on how to make recipes a success. Their contribution was equal parts publicity and personalization, and their work blurred the boundaries between product advertisements and personal interest stories. By interweaving their expert opinions and their personal struggles with weight, these women provided an intermediary between the world of larger-than-life Tillie Lewis and the world that most white female consumers occupied. These women writers knew what it was like to struggle, they explained to their readers. What they did not explain was that they were being paid to promote artificially sweetened foods.

Producers of artificial sweetener had ample reason to pitch their product to women like Trudy Dyer. Newspapers were the most important medium through which consumers could learn about the properties of artificial sweetener and artificially sweetened foods in the 1950s. Lewis had found, in her own survey, that 55 percent of women who purchased her product had first heard about it from their local newspapers (compared with 10 percent from magazines and 4 percent from physicians).[44] This finding likely confirmed the wisdom of taking her story and product directly to editors and writers. After receiving word that newspapers would cover her twenty-one-day diet plan, Lewis apparently visited many of them in person. She posed for photographs with women like Dyer and commiserated about the difficulties of weight loss. This ensured that when the diet plan ran in a newspaper, it was not merely words on a page and calorie count. Celebrity-quality photographs of Lewis and women like Dyer often were the first thing that grabbed a reader's eye. When Dyer, a figure familiar to women readers, "wails" "why didn't I know about this long ago?" the Tillie Lewis canned fruits and diet plan are no longer foreign. They are situated at the heart of information production for women's dailies and presented as commodities so good that they are worth crying over.

Lewis's method of personal product delivery was not new. African American beauty entrepreneur Madame C. J. Walker had used her personal story to recruit agents from across the country for her hair-straightening products. In the 1950s, Estée Lauder refused to open a new counter in a department store anywhere in the country unless she did it personally. Lauder, like Lewis, seems to have known that only when these journalists were impressed with a particular line were they motivated to write about it.[45] And once they wrote about it, their female consumers would buy.

What is significant about the relationship between female journalists and the promoters of artificially sweetened foods is the sheer scale of the operation. Not only was Lewis crisscrossing the country engaging women writers with girl talk, but male industry leaders were courting them with press conferences and "sampling" events. The lines between the professional and the personal were blurred at events like the annual Newspaper Food Editors Conference held in Boston in September 1966. The crowd was almost entirely female, since most food writers were women and were assumed to write primarily for other women. Henry Schacht of the California Canners and Growers (CCG) delivered a keynote address titled "How to Succeed in Business without Getting Fat."

Schacht's primary purpose appears to have been to promote Diet Delight products. He had helped plan the meal that the editors ate prior to listening to the talk. According to accounts of the event, they dined on salad, entrée, and dessert, all "tastefully appealing and sumptuously prepared." Each dish contained Diet Delight or Abbott Sucaryl products. The Persian peach chicken contained artificially sweetened peaches; the string beans almandine and diet blue cheese dressing had been sweetened with Sucaryl, and the sugarless apricot mousse with fruit sauce used both Diet Delight apricots and Sucaryl.[46] The caloric total for the meal, as the menu the editors were given explained, was only 420. It is significant that the editors first learned about this new full product line of artificially sweetened goods by tasting them. Rather than merely lecturing to these women about the improved state of modern sweetened diet products, Schacht involved them directly by asking them to assess the quality for themselves.

In his address, Schacht reminded the dining writers of the significance of their professional skills and praised their unique ability to communicate directly with female consumers. "We think we have found a way for hardworking people like you . . . and like us . . . to succeed in the business without getting fat," Schacht began, quickly linking his own professional expertise as the head of a major canning and food operation to theirs as women's food writers. The evocation of "fat" likely grabbed their attention, given the frequent focus on beauty, style, and eating that occupied these women's professional (and likely personal) lives. Yet this was not a matter of vanity or profit alone. It was, in fact, a chance to address a core problem of contemporary American life. This was "prosperity stomach," a condition Schacht described as the difficulty of keeping one's "weight under control" when incomes were at "all-time highs," people had "money to buy the food we like," and machines did "so much of the work that we once did." It would be difficult to deal with the situation, given the "sophisticated audience" of American female consumers who had, by 1966, "heard everything" in the way of quick fixes and miracle products. In spite of that, Schacht urged, it was a unique moment for the diet-food industry. Consumers were turning to artificially sweetened products in substantial numbers, with $38 million worth of low-calorie fruit sold in 1965 alone. The products had improved dramatically, as the lunch demonstrated firsthand. "You know it's only the beginning" of the potential for profit by selling to what he termed "miserable harried weight watchers." It was time for these editors to embrace the promise that "fewer calories" could go hand in hand with "more champagne." "If it's good for us," he concluded, "it must be good for 79 million weight-watchers in this affluent society of ours."[47]

According to Diet Delight's sales promotion manager, Al O'Dea, who reported on the event later, Schacht's presentation "captured the fancy of these newswomen."[48] If the number of stories appearing after the event in the food sections they edited is any indication, he was right. The California Canners archive alone contains twenty articles from newspapers stretching from Albany to Phoenix to Yonkers to Columbus. With headings like "The Thin Line: How Low Calorie Foods Can Be Delicious," "Diet Foods Gain Favor," "Low Calorie Landslide," and "Our Eating Habits Are Changing," these articles, primarily in local newspapers, brought the conference and its dishes to life. The Yonkers *Herald Statesman* ran a photo of the apricot mousse along with the recipe, as did the local paper in Boise, Idaho. At least half of the articles also contained coverage of the glamorous meal consumed by the editors in Boston, and some, like the *Dallas Times Herald*, carried photographs of the meal and event. One dish, the Persian peach chicken, appears to have been particularly compelling to the editors, who returned home and decided, individually, what aspects of the event to cover. Five of the twenty articles saved by the CCG reviewed the chicken recipe and reprinted it for their readers to experiment with at home.[49]

Diet Delight's executive team thus assisted these editors and writers with the task of translating the value of artificially sweetened products from women and to women. In addition to providing them with the recipes from the luncheon, and probably also supplying high-quality photos of individual items served for subsequent reproduction, Diet Delight embarked on an advertising blitz of food editors across the country in the remaining months of 1966. In December alone, the CCG sent food editors 363 recipes for low-calorie peach cheesecake, 62 prewritten stories on a Diet Delight beauty sweepstakes contest, and 3,600 apricot soufflé recipes (with cyclamate-saccharin). The fact that the company tracked all of these publications to see if articles on diet foods would run demonstrates the premium that diet-product executives put on winning over these journalists and their editors. By January, the peach cheesecake had shown up in the *Herald Tribune* and the Pennsylvania *Pocono Record* and the Massachusetts *New Bedford Standard Times*. And in each of these stories, the writer said nothing about who had initially promoted the product. At least one story, in fact, was presented as if written entirely by the newspaper's home economist just for her readers.[50]

These were not, in fact, promotional advertisements paid for by Diet Delight. Just as the twenty-one-day diet plan from Lewis had been covered without cost to Flotill foods, editors had not charged the CCG or Abbott Laboratories an advertising fee. If we assume that newspaper editorials were similar to those for magazines in the United States, this blurring of the line between advertisement and feature made good financial sense. According to historian Vicki Howard, as early as 1930 more than 60% of revenue in women's magazines came from advertisers, and the impact stretched beyond the content of ads. Feature stories and recipe offerings also frequently highlighted the products that provided promotional revenue, leaving the stories that resulted little more than "product promotions themselves."[51] This shift had important consequences for how artificially sweetened products would be presented to U.S. consumers. Advertising dollars would circulate back into the publications, but only if consumers discovered that they had a problem for which an advertised product could provide a solution. Thus magazines and newspapers had reasons to promote problems, like being overweight, and solutions, like artificially sweetened foods.

The connection between the industry's promotional efforts and the copy that ran in these newspapers does not prove that newswomen were disingenuous in their promotions. Nor does it prove that consumers were conned into buying artificially sweetened foods against their will. The relationship between need and supply, or producer and consumer, is here more nuanced. Many of these women writers likely believed they were doing something good for consumers, as Schacht had claimed. The history of food advice and home economics in local papers, after all, can be traced back to the Progressive Era, when women frequently policed the local food supply for safety and worked to ensure that nutritious foods were available to the masses. Yet whereas women once did this in opposition to industry (consider the first antisaccharin activists), by the 1960s they did this in alliance with it. There are complex reasons for this shift, including the increasing importance of advertising revenue in magazines and newspapers that, by the 1930s, had blurred the distinction between feature and advertisement, as well as increased federal monitoring of food industries that lessened the need for journalistic oversight. For individual women who switched from their personally generated or reader-supplied recipes to those that came in the mail from Diet Delight (or other companies), however, a more immediate possibility is worth considering.

By targeting food editors, people like Lewis and Schacht found just the right audience for a pitch of guilt and absolution. Editors and writers had been, for decades, contributing to the problem. They had encouraged women to see food as their primary means of expressing love for their families and the best place for indulgence for themselves.[52] Now, confronting statistics about weight gain and the ill health that followed, some of these newswomen must have seen themselves as at least partly to blame. Schacht was offering the ideal solution. With artificially sweetened foods they could continue to generate revenue, thereby satisfying their financial obligations. At the same time, they could help their readers lose weight. With Persian chicken and apricot mousse and Sucaryl cheesecake, food editors could preach indulgence and produce (at least theoretically) restraint.

There was only one catch. These editors and writers would have to trust food companies for product and knowledge. Women had found their own best ways of using saccharin in the wartime and immediate postwar kitchen. The "two-fingered pinch" required them to experiment with ideal levels of sweetness. With few alternatives, women learned to give advice to one another in cooking guides and share information informally about canning and dessert making. By the 1960s, however, food manufacturers were supplying this information ready-made. And it pointed directly to prepackaged products in ways that benefited producers of artificial sweetener.

Even when magazine editors did not present recipes from industry as their own, they created environments increasingly friendly to diet ads. *Good Housekeeping* ran the monthly feature "You and Your Diet" throughout the 1960s with titles like "Advice for Calorie Counters," "Choosing Nonnutritive Sweeteners," "International Fare for the Calorie-Conscious," "If Your Fondness for Cooking Has the Family Gaining, Read Our Advice," "Words to Wise Weight-Watchers on Losing Pounds," and "Checking Calories." Here reader questions were paired with editorial wisdom. Sweetened products were rarely promoted directly, but the feature always emphasized the importance of calorie awareness in its presentation of healthful eating. It took little effort to get from these questions and answers to the advertisements on nearby pages featuring artificially sweetened foods. *Good Housekeeping* regularly featured ads for D-Zerta Gelatin, Like, and Tab as early as 1963. Their text frequently mirrored editorial copy, such as this headline: "Why a woman who tends to put on weight should discover D-Zerta Gelatin."[53] Thus, though officially separated, editorial advice and sweetener promotion went hand in hand.[54]

By the late 1960s, newspapers and magazines aimed at women regularly collaborated with artificial-sweetener producers and products. When *Reader's Digest*'s "Quick Complete Meals for Summer" recipe booklet appeared in 1966, readers found numerous suggestions for using artificial sweetener, such as substituting diet canned fruit for regular and using artificially sweetened dressings and jellies instead of those with sugar. They did not find any mention of the fact that Diet Delight had paid for that promotion.[55] Nor did they know that the magazine's manager, Willard Hamilton, sent an advance copy of the *Reader's Digest* article "How Safe Are No Calorie Sweeteners?" to CCG president Maurice Charlat with the note that it "should go a long way toward reducing consumer concern about the reasonable use of cyclamates."[56] By 1970 these cross-promotions were primarily handled by the Calorie Control Council, a consortium of saccharin manufacturers and corporate buyers in industry that worked full time to ensure artificial sweetener remained unregulated and appeared favorably in all forms of media. It is unlikely that the 11 million readers of *Family Circle* knew that the new weight-control section offered in January 1970 was, in fact, a planned showcase for artificially sweetened products. Advertisers had been told in advance of this "fantastic opportunity to increase sales and profits and increase acceptance of the participant's calorie controlled products at the retail and consumer levels." Consumers saw helpful tips on getting exercise and eating right, accompanied by page after page of artificially sweetened salad dressings, sodas, and desserts. All roads to health and wellness in *Family Circle* led directly to artificially sweetened food.[57] By 1970 the individual relationships and hometown recipe tips had largely disappeared from promotions for artificially sweetened products. What remained was the lack of distinction between advertising and feature. This would leave a new generation of Americans awash, without a local guide, in a media landscape where health was best achieved through the limitless consumption of diet foods.

JEAN NIDETCH: FROM ASPARAGUS TO CHOCOLATE SODA

Tillie Lewis directed women who wanted to lose weight to artificial sweetener, effectively replacing old ideas of "diet suffering" with twenty-one days of "substitute pleasure" as a means of being thin. Women writers and editors brought this message to the doorsteps of American homes and helped blur the boundaries between media advice and diet-product promotion. Jean Nidetch, founder of Weight Watchers, made artificially sweetened foods a staple of the weight-conscious woman's diet. By making sugar "illegal" and artificial sweetener "legal," Nidetch would teach millions to see saccharin (cyclamates were banned in 1969) as the only appropriate form of sweetener.

Nidetch was, in many ways, a perfect composite of her predecessors. Like Lewis, she had the compelling story of a girl from Brooklyn who made good. Like the newspaper editors, she knew how to publicize ideas as a "local girl." And, like both, she was committed to both the pleasure of food and the power of self-promotion. According to the jacket on her autobiography from 1970, *The Story of Weight Watchers*, Jean Nidetch was a "fat Brooklyn girl who grew up to be an even fatter Queens housewife" who went on to develop "the first internationally proven system of weight reduction." Nidetch's personal story, to this day, is inextricably linked to the Weight Watchers "club" method of weight reduction. It was Nidetch's well-publicized battles with her weight that drew women to her meetings, speeches, and publications. Her glamorous platinum blonde hair and svelte figure were constant features in Weight Watchers promotional materials. At the same time, Nidetch made sure that her fans never forgot she was one of them, a woman who struggled to keep cravings in check and who started it all merely to have a "club for me and my fat friends."[58]

Through the Weight Watchers program, Nidetch created a complete system of weight reduction that relied on artificial sweetener for success. She was not, however, the first. As early as 1948, TOPS (Taking Off Pounds Sensibly) was founded in Milwaukee to fight what its founder termed "food addiction."[59] Nidetch's biography introduced her own story of weight struggle and her final victory over overeating through retraining herself to want thinness more than cupcakes. Her club meetings, which began in her basement in 1963 and, by 1970, had been attended by close to 2 million people, encouraged members to go public with their weight problems and to receive support (and accountability) for their eating choices each week (the weigh-in was a key part of any meeting). Her recipes, published in numerous Weight Watchers diet cookbooks, offered ways to cook guilt-free meals at home. Her magazine, with fashion tips, life insurance ads, and food information, gave its 3 million readers a vision of the organization's lifestyle to aspire to.[60] And her prepared foods offered women a foolproof way to ensure they were eating "legally."[61]

In the pages of the magazine, readers could find the words "legal" or "maintenance" at the bottom of each ad, indicating whether the item was good for those trying to lose weight (legal) or only for those who had reached their target weights (maintenance). By rendering pleasure essential for Weight Watchers and then making "legal" pleasure rely heavily on saccharin, the organization created a system that directed dieters to indulge in artificially sweetened products.

Nidetch did not mince words with her followers. "Except for the relatively few who do have medical problems," she explained in her autobiography in 1970, "most people who say they don't know why they are fat aren't telling the truth. They do know. And you must admit it, at least to yourself, because it's such a relief to be able to say, 'I'm fat because I eat too much.'"[62] Nidetch saw no shame in loving food even to the point of obsession. The problem was allowing too much food, and the wrong kind of food, into the body. Her own seventy-two-pound weight loss came after years of binge eating kept hidden from her family. There were the candy bars for her son that she hid in the back of the refrigerator, where she could find them and he could not. There were chunks of salami and cheese eaten in single sittings. There was the entire birthday cake polished off in an afternoon. Nidetch had a deep sense of herself as an out-of-control eater whose cravings, in the face of fattening foods, could not be overcome. This formed the basis of her Weight Watchers approach. Followers were advised not to count calories or decrease the portions of desired foods. For Nidetch such approaches encouraged eaters to constantly bargain with themselves, saving calories here and there only to cash them in later on a binge. To change their weight, they had to change their food. In the early years of her program this meant that cakes, cookies, and chips went into the trash, and celery, tuna fish, vegetables, and gelatins took their place. At the heart of the Weight Watchers system were two simple words: "legal" and "illegal." Once followers learned to eat legally all the time, they would lose.

Nidetch believed that people took control not by becoming moderate eaters with casual attitudes toward food but by remaining obsessed eaters with intense attitudes toward food. The distinction was in what they allowed into their body. They could keep their eating disorder as long as what they ate was shorn of its fattening qualities. Nidetch, in fact, urged followers to love food; she even suggested that they hold their own birthday cake, smell it, even serve it to others. "It's only fattening when it gets into your stomach," she explained. "You're in control . . . so blow out the candles, serve the cake to your guests and then have half a grapefruit."[63] She also recognized that they would keep eating extraordinary amounts of food until, at some point, their desire to eat was outweighed by the pleasure they took in their own thin bodies. To prepare for these binges, Nidetch recommended that weight watchers eat before going out, refuse social cocktails, and keep a can of asparagus or mushrooms in the car (and a can opener) so they could pull over to the side of the road and gorge should food cravings overwhelm them in transit.[64]

The original Weight Watchers plan did not allow dietetic food, except sugar substitutes. "We allow the sugar substitutes simply because there is no other way—except with sugar—to sweeten food," Nidetch explained in 1970. Strawberries, an apple, or pears paired with celery and a bit of sugar substitute were recommended nighttime snacks. Diet sodas were suggested as good alternatives to alcohol at parties so that weight watchers would not feel pressured to take that glass of champagne.[65] The sweetness of saccharin was a way to make snacking on good foods or navigating stressful social situations more palatable. Nidetch was careful early on to distinguish between the habit of aggressive eating, which she believed could be switched from fattening to nonfattening foods, and the final goal when thinness would be the reward and food obsessions would dissipate with a look in the mirror. She used herself as primary evidence that it was possible, for everyone, to get to the point where food desires are supplanted by the desire to maintain thinness. "To me eating strawberry shortcake was a real emotional experience," she recalled in her autobiography. And while she admitted that "we can't diminish that desire," it was possible over time for what she called "promiscuous eaters" to foster a more utilitarian and less passionate relationship to food. "It's a fuel, that's what food is. . . . Pleasure and rewards must come from other sources." All we can do, she explained, is replace that appetite for "cupcakes with a desire to get thin."[66]

The role of sweetener and the relationship between food and pleasure, however, shifted dramatically with the mainstreaming of the organization and its arrival in print media. Just as advertising revenues played a part in food editors' "conversions" to artificially sweetened products, Nidetch herself appears to have realized she could expand her market, and her message, by promoting chocolate pleasure rather than canned asparagus to the masses.

The inaugural issue of *Weight Watchers Magazine* in February 1968 featured three separate presentations of saccharin and cyclamate products: an advertisement for Sweet'N Low with a free coupon for samples (with the Weight Watchers seal of approval), a section on "fabulous desserts for smart weight watchers" that recommended mixing sugar substitutes in gelatin and applesauce, and on the back cover, towering visions of "No Cal" soda paired with an offer for a free thirty-six-page recipe book and sample of a new sugar substitute.[67] The second issue of the magazine, in March of the same year, followed up with enticing advertisements for Sweeta, a cyclamate-based substitute that would become a mainstay of the magazine throughout the 1970s. The sexy woman on the cover was accompanied by the text "Sweeta girls have something. You can too, and just in time for summer" (again with Weight Watchers approval) and a full-page ad for Tab on the back cover. By the late 1960s, a pattern had emerged in the placement of artificial sweetener in the magazine: every few months it appeared in a new recipe, it regularly showed up in the reader question-and-answer section, it occupied three or four full-page or half-page ads, and it was featured on the back cover of most issues.

This was a conscious shift on the part of the organization. Touted as "The New Weight Watchers Program," the modified plan was presented in advertisements that told readers, "You can have foods like thick, juicy cheeseburgers" and "real cocoa milkshakes"; it positioned photos of tasty, indulgent foods next to thin women to bring the message home.[68] In addition to allowing people to eat smaller portions of higher-fat foods, the new plan relied on artificially sweetened low-calorie shakes and sodas to add pleasure. It was, in fact, not merely a new plan; it was a new view of food. Prior admonitions to change one's own pleasure objects, moving from food to the thin body, were replaced by marvels over the ability of Weight Watchers and its allied food producers to change the food itself. The new plan, however, was for old people—those out-of-control eaters prone to binges and bad choices. Therefore, it was even more important that Weight Watchers follow the organization's meal plans. Pursuing this new pleasure principle at home, after all, could mean eating an entire cake in a dark closet. By 1975 Weight Watchers was presenting itself as "The Authority" in its branding, along with the message that "losing weight never tasted so good."

The new attitude was embodied in the complete line of Weight Watchers products introduced in February 1971 with the motto "Weight Watchers, who knows more about losing weight . . . tastefully?" Here was the first of the diet-food total meal plans that organizations like Jenny Craig and NutraSystem would also provide: row after row of boxes and packets with clearly labeled calorie counts. At first the only artificial sweetener in the line was in a variation on Sweet'N Low called "Weight Watchers sweetener." By 1973 there was a full line of diet foods and sodas and a new message of "sinful indulgence."[69]

One advertisement in particular reveals the dramatic shift from the asparagus era. "Try them . . . they taste terrific!" reads the copy, clearly spoken by Jean Nidetch herself. Cans of root beer, raspberry cream, chocolate, cola, grape, lemon-lime, orange, and chocolate-twist soda frame Nidetch in this image, which appeared in the magazine repeatedly in the mid- to late 1970s. Her gleaming white teeth, blonde hair, and large diamond ring demonstrate her beauty and success to readers; the large smile suggests that she's nearly bursting with pleasure as a result of her soda consumption. Nidetch's face, framed between cans she is holding, assures the consumer that this indulgence is safe. The stark LEGAL printed in the left corner further indicates that control is exercised here.[70]

The danger was that such passions might embolden the body and weaken the head. "For those wild, passionate moments," suggests an ad from May 1976, reach for artificial sweetener. "You're dying for something to eat," reads the copy accompanying the white woman sneaking into her marshmallow-chocolate-fudge-laden cupboard late at night. "Even though your head says no, your body says yes. Now you can fight back with Weight Watchers sweetener." The accompanying offer for seven cents off on a packet allows the reader to identify with this woman in the throes of "passion," clip the coupon, and stock the sweetener on her own

FIG. 4.6 "The sure cure for Chocolate Mania!" *Weight Watchers Magazine*,
January 1973, 8.

shelf to shield her from temptation the next time she heads to the cookie
jar at 3:00 A.M.[71] Ads for chocolate sodas frequently suggested their ap-
propriateness as an antidote when desire for chocolate was nearly out of
control. "You've got that chocolate madness," read one from 1973; "we've
got that cure"—one that could satisfy "the cravings of even the wildest
chocolate maniac" (fig. 4.6). Nidetch's photo, placed near the ubiquitous LEGAL stamp in the lower right corner, sits close to the admonition
to "be prepared with these new delicious chocolate flavors."[72] Weight
Watchers artificial product line presented eaters as in need of constant
vigilance against cravings that were simply too strong to overcome. The
only defense was the decoy: give the chocolate maniac the artificially

sweetened, artificially flavored chocolate soda so she will not devour that ever-looming entire chocolate cake.

If one stayed within the Weight Watchers circuit, this hyperchanneling of passion into food could be tempered by eating the "right" things. But one could easily find the passion, so encouraged by the organization, spinning out of control. In fact, that was exactly what it was doing to the weight watcher who found herself raiding the cupboard for brownies. Nidetch herself acknowledged as much in her advice to constantly keep a photo of one's fat self close at hand—on the fridge, in the wallet—so as never to forget what could happen again (she reportedly did this herself).[73] Weight Watchers may have produced thin people. But it also produced people who knew that they needed to manage their out-of-control cravings by ingesting controlled foods. Cravings might not go away, and good choices might not be possible; but it was possible to channel impulses through prepackaged, saccharin-sweetened products and produce a thin body.

What women had once wanted with saccharin containers and self-taught techniques was an opportunity to cut calories, experience creativity, and control bodies—their own and others. This alchemy did have, at its core, an attempt to discipline the body. But it also had, at the perimeter, other desires that were empowering, that expanded women's control of the world around them. This bargain was subtly shifted by Lewis and promoters of her generation. Now the invitation was not to be the person in control of the sweetener—that was up to Lewis and Nidetch and their food scientists—but to be the person who followed the new food rules of artificial sweetener and took control of herself.

Nidetch required followers to admit their own powerlessness. Losing weight required them to acknowledge that they could not make their own choices. Choice was left up to Nidetch, who, with the help of her laboratories, scales, and equivalency charts, would find foods and safely label them "legal." By 1982, *Weight Watchers* readers were given a menu of legal choices, nearly all low-calorie, low-fat products reliant on artificial sweetener and fat substitutes. In August of that year one could find, in a single issue, advertisements for the following artificially sweetened or otherwise chemically altered low-calorie food products: Weight Watchers frozen dessert, sugar-free Sprite, diet Mazola corn oil, Kraft reduced-calorie dressing, Egg Beaters, Pepsi light, Puritan no-cholesterol vegetable oil, Alba Fit and Frosty milk substitute, Wishbone light dressing, "legal" white wine, Weight Watchers fried chicken meal, light and lean

Hormel meats, Butter Buds, Slim Set jelling mix, Sweet Taste sugar substitute, and Dia Mel no-sugar low-calorie table syrup.[74]

Artificial sweetener ultimately enabled Weight Watchers to turn the vice of excessive appetite into a virtue. Few members would have been proud of an uncontrolled urge to consume a chocolate shake with real ice cream. Yet ads frequently presented that same shake, rendered legal through skim milk and artificial sweetener, and urged members to both celebrate their desire and act on it. Through the world of her magazine, with the help of artificial sweetener, Nidetch created visual kinship between dangerous, rich, sinful foods and thin, desirable bodies. At the very least, this made for a compelling diet organization and helps explain how she was able to attract hundreds of thousands of people to the plan. Yet it may also have reframed how these dieters thought about themselves. Philosopher Lauren Berlant has argued, in her work on romance novels, that through groups that provide consolation and a sense of belonging members can acquire validation and strength.[75] One of the most powerful aspects of being part of such a group, she explains, is that it can legitimate "qualities . . . or entire lives that have otherwise been deemed puny or discarded."[76] Viewed through this lens, Weight Watchers was offering much more than a sinless chocolate shake. It was offering to redeem the very sensation of craving and the personality trait of limited self-control.

Between 1951 and 1980, an array of professional white women delivered the message that artificial sweetener was a tool for control in a world of dizzying food choices that left individuals unable to trust their own appetite as a proper barometer of healthy food consumption. These women assured audiences that food remained the proper source of intense personal pleasure and that deprivation and restraint were at the very least outmoded and perhaps even unhealthy. By promoting pleasure as personal, positive, and plentiful through artificially sweetened products, they helped build a market for diet foods. Yet by masking the primary role of the food and pharmaceutical industries in these new "miracle" products, they failed to inform consumers about the conflicts of interest embedded in this new "consumer-centered" healthy eating. By 1977, it would become clear that millions of consumers had made artificial sweetener a daily habit, and they needed it in ways that even the most forward-thinking sweetener promoters could not have imagined.

SACCHARIN REBELS

THE RIGHT TO RISKY PLEASURE IN 1977

I have never written to anybody like this before but when
your very livelihood is threatened it is time to act.
—Mrs. James Fallman, Waco, Texas, 1977

What do you want me to use to sweeten my life a little?
—J. R. Murdock, Detroit, Michigan, 1977

Life without saccharin would be dreadful.
—Lynn Hamilton (Mrs. James C. Hamilton), Bethesda, Maryland, 1977

Artificial sweeteners are chemicals. Saccharin, cyclamates, aspartame
(NutraSweet), and sucralose (Splenda) were all discovered in a laboratory, not in nature. Thus even when market and consumer forces combine to render sweeteners safe and desirable, there exists an under-
current of uncertainty and fear. This was swift and powerful in the early
twentieth century, as consumers combined unease over the chemical origins of saccharin with disdain for the industrial producers who dared to
sneak it into their drinks. Fear diminished in the postwar era, however,
as consumers engaged in their own experiments at home and redefined
saccharin and its new competitor cyclamate as compelling alternatives
to sugar. Uncertainty nearly disappeared in the 1950s and 1960s (rising
briefly in 1969) as a host of new artificially sweetened "diet" foods and
sodas entered the market promoted by dynamic entrepreneurs. But in
1977, it returned with a vengeance.

In March 1977, the Food and Drug Administration (FDA) announced to the public that beginning January 1, 1978, saccharin would be banned in the United States. Citing the Delaney Clause, a piece of legislation passed in 1958 that prohibited any carcinogenic substance, regardless of how minimal or low-risk, from entering the food supply, FDA commissioner Sherwin Gardner did precisely what the agency was charged with doing. He acted to protect Americans from danger by banning a commodity that had been shown, through experiments with laboratory animals, to increase the risk of cancer under particular conditions. The same thing had happened with cyclamates in 1969 with little public comment. But this time a very different reaction occurred.

In spite of the fact that the 1970s was the beginning of a major alternative food movement, one facilitated by books such as Frances Moore Lappé's *Diet for a Small Planet* and a new focus on eating whole foods, eating locally, and eschewing chemicals in agriculture in general, when told that there was an unhealthy chemical in their food supply that should be banned, hundreds of Americans wrote protest letters *against the agency* seeking to protect them.[1] In what should be seen as one of the largest "food revolts" in American culture since the eighteenth-century antisaccharites' campaign, concerned consumers from all corners of the country challenged government officials and their science in order to preserve what they saw as an essential commodity.[2] Without laboratories at their disposal to run their counterexperiments, these protesters instead made arguments about saccharin's value by reaching into their own life experiences. As a result, their letters provide rare glimpses into how individuals used saccharin and, more importantly, how they thought about their use of saccharin. It was, for many, far more than a tool for shedding unwanted pounds. It was a means of enhancing control and rendering ubiquitous risks pleasurable, for a change. As the FDA, members of Congress, and the president would hear loud and clear, for a surprising number of Americans saccharin had become something worth fighting for.

CONDITIONS FOR REVOLT

Over a fourteen-day period in March 1977, 30,000 Americans wrote letters to their elected representatives to tell them that the government was wrong. By December 1977, the number of letters received by members of Congress, the FDA, and President Jimmy Carter would reach 1 million.[3] Many Americans still remember this massive consumer protest, either because they participated in or witnessed the months of debate in news media and among politicians. It aroused such strong feelings from so many different citizens that veteran congresswoman Barbara Mikulski of Maryland could say, referring to the phone calls and letters that had inundated her staff, that this issue, without a doubt, "has more opposition than any other matter I have dealt with in public office."[4]

Following closely on the heels of the Vietnam conflict, the Watergate scandal, the oil crisis, and a lengthy recession, this was no minor statement.

Given the sheer scale of the protest, one would expect that a history of the saccharin rebellion would have been told already. Yet the event is largely invisible in accounts of U.S. political movements in the 1970s. Nor does it appear in histories of American foodways or consumer culture. This may be because it appears, at first glance, a "food issue," something set apart from larger concerns about the economy, pollution, politics, race, and gender that are more central to how we remember the issues of major importance in that decade. Looking more closely at the rebellion over sweetener, however, we can see that saccharin was deeply connected to these issues. For many who had disagreed with their government over wars, recessions, job losses, or environmental destruction, not until Tab and Diet Pepsi were threatened with legal action did they pick up a pen. And when they did write, they had a unique opportunity to articulate their beliefs about the relationship between consumer choice and health. The letters they wrote are powerful testaments to the ways in which artificial sweeteners, as a material and as a set of cultural messages, were deeply intertwined with the ways Americans thought about "life, liberty, and the pursuit of happiness" by the late 1970s. The letters also help us understand why average Americans supported nutritional advice that focused on ingredient substitution rather than commodity exclusion. Foods that provided pleasure were essential, many argued. And this was particularly true when pleasure was hard to find.

To understand how a simple chemical like saccharin could provide such a catalyst, it is important to piece together what it meant in 1977. It was a well-known substance that had been in mainstream (not merely diabetic) food and beverage products for a generation. It was heavily marketed in low-calorie foods such as fruits, syrups, and jellies as well as diet sodas such as Diet Pepsi and Tab. It was recommended by professional weight-loss organizations such as Weight Watchers, which, in the early 1970s, had made artificially sweetened foods a cornerstone of its new program. And saccharin was the only artificial sweetener available, thanks to the FDA's ban on cyclamates in 1969. Yet there was still plenty of uncertainty about saccharin, and it was not a perfect product. It was bitter and left a metallic aftertaste. It could not be heated. Frequent rumors that it was unsafe were fueled by studies, often funded by sugar interests, demonstrating a link between saccharin consumption and elevated cancer risk. In fact, saccharin producers were sufficiently fearful of a ban that they were already searching for a replacement (a contest that was, in fact, won by Searle with aspartame, a product already going through the FDA approval process the year the saccharin ban was announced).

This context left the FDA, members of Congress, the news media, and even the diet-food and -beverage industry unprepared for the quick and decisive anger that streamed from letter writers across the nation. Twelve days after the proposed ban was announced, the congressional committee in charge of food oversight met to discuss saccharin's fate. Several members specifically addressed the vehement response in the form of letters, telegrams, and phone calls to their offices from individual constituents, declaring them "outraged," "skeptical," "baffled" and "deeply upset." Representative Lloyd Meeds from Washington State credited the unprecedented response to the large numbers of diabetics and "Weight Watchers," a group that he described as "representing an astonishing large portion of our population."[5]

FDA commissioner Sherwin Gardner agreed. His testimony before the group reveals an office caught off guard by the public's anger and unprepared to process the letters and calls from individual consumers opposed to the ban. It was, Gardner claimed, an "essentially negative" reaction— one that his previous experiences with the agency, and specifically with the 1958 Delaney Clause that demanded this action, had left him ill prepared to understand.[6] With "almost any other food ingredient," Gardner explained, drawing on past experience, the public's reaction "would have been somewhat quieter and a different character." Not only would far fewer people have weighed in with an opinion, he believed, but those who did would have had a far different complaint. Rather than demanding that a suspected carcinogen remain in the food supply, they would have railed against an agency that did nothing to protect them earlier.[7]

There are many reasons why consumers reacted as they did. The most obvious is that people liked diet products. Nearly as apparent, from the vantage point of 1977, was that they did not like government agencies. Consumers had, in the early twentieth century, regarded the FDA as a protector of the U.S. food supply and bestowed nearly heroic status on crusaders like Harvey Wiley, who promoted the 1906 Pure Food and Drug legislation that, for the first time, regulated the American food and drug supply. But this pool of goodwill had largely dried up by the 1960s. The FDA continued to play an important role in protecting the public, with decisions such as Frances Olden Kelsey's refusal to release thalidomide on the U.S. market (thereby preventing thousands of congenital defects in newborns). Yet Americans had increasingly come to believe that the FDA was an inefficient bureaucracy controlled more by political and corporate interests than by the will of the public. Many had come to trust independent agents for consumer safety like Ralph Nader over appointed bureaucrats at federal agencies like the FDA.[8] Gardner may have expected Americans to see that the FDA's actions were designed to protect them. But even a decade earlier, one national study had found the vast majority of Americans ready to declare that federal legislation, in general, was "inadequate to protect their health and safety."[9]

A closer look at these consumer letters reveals that this protest was, for many Americans, about more than protecting a product or resisting the government.[10] Many writers shared with the FDA intimate stories of their struggles to lose weight, their experience with cancer risks in their daily lives, and their conversations with friends and relatives that "proved" saccharin's safety. Their letters are often lengthy, and their specific references to saccharin are frequently a launching point to explain in surprising depth both the kinds of risks they face daily and their attempts to control them, with infrequent success. A sample of these letters suggests that consumers were advocating for saccharin rather than protesting against its removal. Most did not merely write to say that the FDA was staffed by idiots and that saccharin was safe (although some did). They did not just say, "Put it back." More frequently they said some variation of "Reassess saccharin from my point of view and you will see that it is necessary and good." It was the vantage point that was key. To convey their message of saccharin advocacy, they had to make visible their own bodies, their own knowledge, and their own situations.

In *Inescapable Ecologies*, her chronicle of how citizens of California's Central Valley have considered the relationship between disease and environment, historian Linda Nash emphasizes the importance of viewing disease from an ecological rather than a pathogenic vantage point. The shift is one of context. A pathogenic understanding of the body sees human illness as caused by specific agents that are "revealed under the microscope." An ecological perspective, on the other hand, is characterized by what she calls "a constant exchange between inside and outside" the body and a "close dependence" between the body and its surroundings.[11]

The former definition of disease was predominant until the early twentieth century. Working with nineteenth-century advances in germ theory and biology, medical researchers had at first focused primarily on isolating factors that "caused" disease within the body itself. But in the 1960s, Rachel Carson's wildly popular *Silent Spring* refocused people's awareness on the relationship between the body and its physical surroundings.[12] Toxins from the environment could permeate the body through air, water, and food. The body/environment divide became more difficult to sustain. The disparate reactions to the possibility of carcinogens in saccharin by the FDA and consumers suggests that this divide between ecological and pathogenic viewpoints was still in place in 1977. For many at the agency, the goal was to protect physical health by preventing exposures to dangerous food chemicals. For many consumers, food chemicals could not be considered dangerous unless they were placed in the context of all of the spaces and products that bodies came in contact with, not merely those that could be easily isolated for study in a government laboratory.

The FDA, long before the 1977 ban, had been acquiring data suggesting that saccharin could have an adverse effect on human health. The agency began research on the substance in 1951 and continued with major investigations in 1953 and 1968. These were inconclusive. In 1971, a new study found correlations between laboratory animals and an increased risk of bladder cancer. While not statistically significant enough to warrant a consumer ban, these findings did induce the agency to remove saccharin from its list of additives that were "Generally Recognized as Safe" and to recommend limitations of one gram per day for adults. In March 1977, the Health Protection Branch of the Canadian government produced conclusive findings that the second generation of saccharin-consuming rats did indeed have an elevated incidence of bladder cancer. The FDA's subsequent recommendation to ban, however, was based on a pathogenic understanding of disease: saccharin was considered in isolation, given in large doses, and found to have possible negative effects on mammal health.[13]

While the FDA studied saccharin in isolation, consumers saw it in context. They argued that saccharin had to be considered in relation to other environmental risks that they faced in their homes and communities. And they demanded that their own bodies be considered evidence that saccharin was not only not unhealthy but, in fact, essential for health. From the FDA's point of view (and given the mandate of the Delaney Clause), food was one of many environmental risks posed to consumers, and it was the easiest to control. Because the environment posed many risks, food therefore should be particularly policed. Consumers disagreed. Since there were so many risks anyway, they reasoned, the policing of those posed by food should be relaxed. To make that case, many found their public voice for the first time. In order to advocate for saccharin, protesters had to also advocate for themselves.

SACCHARIN AND CONSUMER RISK

Several weeks after the FDA announced its intention to ban saccharin, Commissioner Gardner testified before a congressional subcommittee convened to consider the issue. He explained that he continued to regard saccharin as a possible carcinogen but noted that he would have liked more leeway than the Delaney Clause provided to determine if, in fact, the substance should be removed from the market. Most of the presentation was straightforward, reviewing the science used in the Canadian study and the process by which the FDA came to its conclusions. The one cultural observation Gardner made concerned risk. "The reaction to our action on saccharin," he testified, "demonstrates better than any evidence I know an important fact of life: people do respond differently to different risks based on the kind of benefits that accompany them."[14]

The people responding in this case were primarily women. The majority of administrators at the FDA, scientists in the research laboratories, and congressional representatives debating the issue were men. Official channels of information-gathering were, then, closed to the group of people who had the strongest relationship to the product. Female consumers had, over decades, developed their own relationship to saccharin and cyclamates—from experimentation and jeweled containers in the 1940s and 1950s to early "hometown" news about Tillie Lewis diet plans and new modern products to the more mainstream advertising of diet sodas with the arrival of Tab, Diet Pepsi, and Diet Coke in the late 1960s and early 1970s. This gender and experience gap created a space in which many women may have felt compelled to write to Commissioner Gardner in order to explain what saccharin actually was. Unlike the subjects of other FDA pronouncements, such as the banning of thalidomide, saccharin was not an unfamiliar chemical. It already had meaning in the lives of consumers.

The story of the saccharin "rebels" enables us to form a more complex understanding of the connection between environmental risk and women's social and political power in the 1960s and 1970s. Environmental activists like Rachel Carson and Frances Moore Lappé have been credited with connecting personal health to political activism by encouraging Americans—especially women—to look more closely at the chemical content of food, water, and air as a means to ensure the health of themselves and their families. Carson urged readers to envision a world without the sound of birds, evoking immediate geography in order to mobilize people to change policies on pesticide use. Lappé articulated a vision of eating low on the food chain and, in so doing, illuminated how personal consumption could be political action.[15] Indeed, women did mobilize to address environmental issues in the 1970s. In Love Canal, a neighborhood in Niagara Falls, New Jersey, neighborhood activists led by Lois Gibbs in 1978 uncovered 21,000 pounds of toxic waste buried under their subdivision in their quest for answers about the high rates of illnesses among neighborhood residents. In California's Central Valley, another group of women mobilized to convince legislators to link pesticides in the groundwater and soil with their own high rates of cancer. In both cases the efforts were led and staffed by women, many of whom were reacting to illnesses in their own children and those of their neighbors.

These highly publicized public mobilizations, with their place in history books and in media archives, are valuable for what they teach us about women's political activism, anticorporate sentiment, and the growing awareness about the link between environmental and human destruction. Yet they overshadow the more mundane and common mechanisms through which Americans confronted environmental risk during the decade. By shifting our view from Love Canal to diet soda, an entirely new category of environmental "activists" emerges with a very different solution to the problem of determining one's personal level of tolerable risk. Millions of Americans found that they could no longer separate drinking diet soda from considering cancer risks. The resulting letters show us, generations later, how low-level fears about the safety of artificial sweetener became part of its value. Saccharin may have been a poison, many argued, but it was a poison that one could pick.[16]

BAD SCIENCE AND LOCAL KNOWLEDGE

Several factors enabled consumers to dismiss the seriousness of the FDA's warnings on saccharin. First, and most obvious, saccharin was ubiquitous. In 1976 it was a $2 billion industry with approximately 7 million pounds produced for domestic consumption. The vast majority of those 7 million pounds went directly into dietetic foods and beverages or powdered Sweet'N Low packets that could be used as substitutes for sugar in coffee and tea and on cereal.[17] Letters from consumers leave little doubt that saccharin was primarily consumed in diet soda, tea, and coffee; the vast majority of letters that mention commodities directly cite Diet Rite, Diet Pepsi, and Diet 7-Up as important saccharin products, along with desserts, cereals, tea, and coffee that require added granular saccharin.

Second, saccharin seemed to work. While most health professionals agreed with Kenneth Melmon, who, in 1975, concluded that saccharin studies had yet to produce "a clear picture of the usefulness of the drug" in treating patients with obesity, users appear to have disagreed.[18] Many had lost weight by switching from sugar-sweetened teas and sodas and replacing teaspoons of sugar in coffee with packets of saccharin instead. Scientists wanted long-term data that illuminated a clear correlation between sweetener use and weight loss. For many consumers, the evidence that weight had come off their own bodies, even if it had returned, was sufficient. Many expressed fear that if they were to lose saccharin, they would most certainly gain (or gain back) a large amount of weight.

A final contributing factor was the well-publicized use of rats and high saccharin dosages in the Canadian study. In order to account for the metabolic differences between humans and rats, the Canadian scientists used an accepted, if contested, practice of elevating the dosages for the study animals. The result was a clear increased incidence of bladder cancer among the study's second-generation rats. The FDA unwisely sought to make an equivalent dosage for humans clear in their press announcement by explaining that rats had been given "in excess of the amount a consumer would receive from drinking 800 diet sodas daily."[19] It is difficult to discern why the FDA would use such an equivalent; perhaps the intent was to assuage fears among causal consumers about pending cancer doom. It apparently worked; consumers were certainly not afraid of saccharin.

"Now tell me, who in their right mind would drink 800 bottles of soda, much less diet soda, a day for the rest of their lives?" asked Martha

Hurd of Portland, Maine, in a letter dated March 11, 1977.[20] The figure of 800 cans of sodas appears repeatedly in individual letters as well as the newspaper articles many people clipped and sent as original sources of information. Many even did the math to demonstrate the impossibility of consuming 800 cans of soda. "It takes a person drinking a diet soda every two minutes of each day (without sleeping at all)" to reach 800 cans, explained Roberta Turel of Allentown, Pennsylvania, in a letter also dated March 11.[21] Others defended their own use of saccharin by directly comparing their typical "dosage" to the figure of 800: "I can't even drink 100 bottles a day; I don't think I've ever had more than two," explained Nancy Deardorff of Falls Church, Virginia. Sally O'Brien "promise[d]" the FDA that she would "not drink 800 cans of diet pop in one day," offering also to "cut down to one pack of diet gum per day, or even less."[22]

It would be easy to look at these letters and argue that consumers were simply stating that the emperor had no clothes. A literal chorus of "800 sodas" appears across these letters; it was obviously the primary way writers entered the dialogue with experts about "good" science. Yet to stop here is to miss the nuances of risk that lie under the surface of such ridicule. Consumers frequently offered a two-part logic to their assertions of saccharin's relative safety. On one hand, they insisted that the study was flawed and therefore needed input from people who could provide perspective. On the other hand, as long as they were providing perspective, they had a few things to tell the FDA about risk from their point of view.

People occasionally sent the FDA cartoons along with their letters protesting the proposed ban. Most of these highlight the irony of regulating saccharin, a possible carcinogen, while failing to do so for tobacco, a known carcinogen. In one letter, a creepy, skeletal figure named "Nick O. Teen" drops ash on an innocent-looking soda can labeled "sugar-free soft drinks." As the can is carted off by the law, Nick declares from behind a haze of smoke and a pile of cigarette butts that it serves the can right. Soda is a danger to public health. (See fig. 5.1.) Another illustration, aimed directly at the FDA's hypocrisy, features a murky boardroom barely discernible through a thick haze of cigarette smoke. The speaker, whose back faces the viewer, holds a cigarette and is identified with the nameplate "Food and Drug Administration." The text below lampoons an agency that would deem saccharin "dangerous to your health" while smoking, a proven threat, goes unchallenged. Both senders added their own personal notes to make sure the FDA understood they thought the FDA administrators were hypocrites. The Nick O. Teen cartoon has hand-

FIG. 5.1 Illustration sent by anonymous author to the FDA, no
date, Food and Drug Administration Records, #18899, cd5, f151.

written text at the top: "Do you suppose the tax collected on cigarettes
makes a difference?" At the bottom of the smoke-filled room illustration
is the typewritten phrase, "Need I Say More?"[23]

In moving to ban saccharin, the FDA cited consumer safety as a priority. Yet by failing to comment on the issue of cigarettes, the most obvious
carcinogen, which remained on the market, the agency was vulnerable
to critique. (The cartoonist and sender appear not to have realized, however, that the FDA was allowed to regulate only food and drugs; tobacco
fell outside its purview.) The connection between saccharin and tobacco
was, in fact, the most common point of contention. A sample of 400 protest letters reveals that roughly half of those arguing against the ban (as
nearly all did) used cigarettes to make their point.[24]

What appears on the surface to be a comparison of commodities is,
upon closer inspection, a categorization of risk by consumers. By 1977,

saccharin had become only one of myriad environmental risks that Americans were forced to confront in their daily lives. Even before the devastation of Love Canal became a national symbol of environmental degradation and danger, grassroots antipollution groups were springing up across the country in response to highly visible toxic events such as the dumping of the insecticide Kepone in the James River in Virginia. Antismoking campaigns were burgeoning, too. In May 1977 the public-interest group Smoking on Health delivered its first petition to the FDA demanding that cigarettes be regulated as dangerous drugs. President Richard Nixon's highly publicized war on cancer had done much to alert the public to the increasing incidences of the disease and its causal link to environmental toxins. Media coverage linking PCBs (polychlorinated biphenyls) to cancer similarly revealed the widespread carcinogenic risks of simply living in the midst of modern materials.[25] Among all these risks, saccharin alone afforded a contained pleasure, one whose risk and impact traveled no farther than the body of an individual consumer. It was also relatively benign when compared with perceptible toxins such as environmental pollutants and cigarette smoke. This assertion is not meant to suggest that people knowingly consumed saccharin in order to render environmental risk pleasurable. Rather, consumer response to the proposed saccharin ban provides useful insight into the constellation of factors that underlie food choices. For those who lived with continual environmental risk, the risk posed by one particular food or ingredient seemed negligible.[26]

David Kennedy, the FDA commissioner appointed in the midst of the controversy, recognized that saccharin was not the only health risk facing American consumers. His decision to support the ban even in the face of ample resistance was, in fact, predicated on his belief that existing environmental risks made saccharin more, not less, threatening. In congressional testimony on the ban, Kennedy explained that "we should not allow even weak carcinogens in the environment if we can help it. . . . Our systems may already be overloaded."[27]

Cancer risks were clearly on the minds of many saccharin consumers who wrote to protest the ban. Few, in fact, dismissed the risk entirely. Consumers simultaneously admitted the possible risk posed by saccharin and dismissed the necessity of banning it by creating a hierarchy of carcinogenic consumption. Stella Dumm of Crooksville, Ohio, picked up a pen the day after the announcement and with palpable frustration wrote, "God help us. With so many known dangers to our health—we continue to breathe polluted air, drink polluted water, foul up our lungs with cigarettes—it is just stupid to concentrate any effort or money on this avenue of remote possibility. . . . For the love of heaven, let's solve some of the really IMPORTANT problems before we attack saccharin."[28] That letter was echoed closely by one from Mrs. Lee Hoffman. For Hoffman, the really important problem was secondhand smoke. "I work with a miserable chain smoker who *stinks* with cigarette smoke and pollutes the air I breathe for 9 hours a day," she explained, lamenting that "nothing is done about that even though it can cause cancer."[29]

Letter writers frequently invoked the dangers of environmental toxins such as water, alcohol, and tobacco in order to assert their right to saccharin. Lynn Pearlman of New York City found that the risk from saccharin paled in comparison with that from the Mississippi River, which she described as a carcinogen-filled "main water supply for thousands of cities." Roberta Turel of Allentown, Pennsylvania, described her local water as "so polluted with fluoride and other chemicals" that she felt "a lot safer drinking diet sodas."[30] Phyllis Starks of Evansville, Ohio, enclosed a clipping on water pollution with her protest letter. The article appeared in her local paper the same day she penned her protest to the FDA. Its description of the Ohio River's high levels of chloro-ether, a byproduct of antifreeze manufacturing, probably motivated her to command that the agency "not take [saccharin] off the market." Given that her own city water "produces compounds suspected of causing cancer," she exclaimed, "isn't this all a little ridiculous!"[31]

Far more common than parallels to drinking water were comparisons to alcohol and tobacco consumption. For many who protested, the fact that the FDA was attempting to eliminate saccharin while allowing these substances with known health risks to stay on the market was incomprehensible. Many writers appear to have been unaware that the FDA could only control carcinogens in the food supply and that it had no jurisdiction over local water supplies, alcohol, or tobacco products. "As a nonsmoker, I'm subjected to the smoke of others, yet as a saccharin-user, I'm harming no one. Why can't I be 'warned' and allowed to proceed at my own risk?" asked Helen Duemler of Glendale, Missouri. Rose Greene of South Charleston, West Virginia, concurred, stating that unlike cigarettes, "which have been *proven* to cause cancer," and alcohol, which "a person chooses to drink . . . to excess and then gets in an automobile and drives [and] I may have to suffer the consequences," "when I ingest saccharin, my body will be the only one to suffer the consequences."[32]

Getting people to accurately assess risk was a major priority for industry leaders, policy makers, and economists in the 1970s. One 1979 study, similar to many conducted during the era, asked people to assess the risks to health and environment associated with scientific and technological advances. The researchers focused on the discrepancies between the actual risk posed (based on actuarial tables) versus the perceived risks of those polled. Whereas risk had actually declined, the study concluded, 78 percent of Americans polled agreed with the statement "People are subjected to more risk today than they were 20 years ago." The study's conclusions explained this discrepancy by considering the tremendous number of small risks confronted by individuals each day. Many were no longer able to accurately gauge such risks, the study explained, and thus they were uncertain as to which risks to dismiss and which to focus on. Within such a system, the study argued, experts needed to downplay overestimated risks by pointing out "risks that are probably underestimated so that the quality of life can be steadily improved."[33]

Not everyone, however, was clearly enjoying a more risk-free existence than that of their parents. As Ulrich Beck has argued, there is in any society a group of people denied the "private escape routes" available to those who can afford to buy safe products, reside in safe places, and breathe safe air.[34] Suggestively, many of those most angered by the FDA's action were in this category. For those who traversed daily zones of environmental risks, it was simply unacceptable to begin cleaning up the toxic by denying themselves a personal consumer pleasure.

Many writers, like Rose Greene, differentiated between risks that could harm others and saccharin, a risk that could harm only themselves. For Mary Windle of Dublin, Ohio, saccharin had to be understood through a comparison to marijuana. The latter, she explained, "with all of its known harmful and relatively harmful effects," was far more injurious than the former, which "causes no harm except to the person who uses it."[35] Many agreed with Windle that the issue was not whether or not saccharin was injurious. It might well be. But saccharin had to be distinguished from other consumer risks because it was fully ingested by its user and injured no one else. "Millions die each year because of the effects of smoking," instructed Eleanor Keller of Allentown, Pennsylvania. "And yet cigars, cigarettes, and pipes have NOT been banned."[36]

For women in working- and middle-class communities across the country, the battle was not to achieve a risk-free environment but, rather, to achieve an acceptable means of coping with and controlling risk. For some, such as Lois Gibbs of Love Canal, this required a direct confrontation with risk production and a demand to have risk removed. Her grassroots, women-led movement in 1978 to see the federal government purchase and enable the relocation of an entire community settled on a former toxic waste site is better known to history than the responses of women like Martha Hurd and Josephine Novak.[37] Yet most women had little opportunity to directly confront and alter the toxicity of modern life. "Air causes cancer, water causes cancer, the Government is a cancer," wrote Hurd, clearly frustrated by the FDA's insistence that she continue to live in a carcinogenic world without the simple pleasures of saccharin.[38] For Joyce Pike of Essexville, Michigan, the FDA's action made no sense in a world where, as she explained it, "there is danger in everything."

One of the most eloquent "catalogs" of risk was created by Josephine Novak of Buffalo; it deserves to be considered at length:

I live on the edge of Lake Erie and am, with no choice in the matter, obliged to drink water which has been heavily polluted, sometimes with known carcinogenic effluents, and rendered undrinkable by the heavy use of chemicals. I am surrounded by carbon-monoxide fumes and breathe urban, industrial air. I am peripherally affected by smokers all around me who are allowed to pursue their known carcinogenic pleasures unabated—in fact, my life is one big cancer risk, which I am powerless to control. Surely, then, if I decide to take one further, very minor, risk of developing cancer, it must be my decision.[39]

Written the day of the FDA announcement, Novak's letter makes clear that she regards saccharin as a very minor risk in a world in which unhealthy consequences are immediate, constant, and completely beyond her control. Catalogs of risks, such as Novak's, can be read in two ways. On one hand, they express the exasperation many people felt with the excessive analyses of cancer risks, what historian James Patterson has referred to as the period's "unprecedented flowering of popular doubts concerning science" and especially the "priests of the Cancer church."[40] Were this the only or even primary goal of letter writers, however, the missives could have been short: "Dear FDA: everything causes cancer, so let me have my saccharin." That most protesters said much more suggests that part of the desire to consume saccharin stemmed from the very fact that it was a risk. Protesting the ban, then, may have enabled consumers to make sense of inchoate fears: the only way to argue that saccharin was "safe enough" was to list, describe, and ultimately differentiate other risks as clearly unsafe.

In a moment when the toxic risks of modern production were clearly not easily controlled, individuals had an opportunity to choose risk in saccharin. Here was one concrete instance in which consumers proved to themselves that they were not merely paying the costs of risk but reaping the benefits as well. For Betty Anne Gibbons of Columbus, Ohio, the solution was clear: "Sell the diet drinks and saccharin," she demanded of the FDA, "and let us take our chances unless it can be proven without a doubt that saccharin is harmful. Even then though, life is too short and I am sure we need something pleasurable."[41]

Susan Bordo has argued, in the case of anorexics, that attitudes toward weight are constructed in the context of everyday experiences. Speaking of her extreme diet practices, one informant explains that what she eats "is the one sector of my life over which I and I alone wield total control."[42] There is certainly a dramatic difference between women who starve themselves and those who eliminate sugar calories in drinks and desserts. Yet at the core of many of these advocacy letters is language that suggests a writer's similar perceived lack of control over things outside the body. "Everything causes cancer," says Novak. "Let us take our chances . . . life is too short," says Gibbons. Their need for saccharin, a substance that facilitates weight reduction, also occurs within a context in which other desires are not easily fulfilled.

It is not possible, when relying on an incomplete survey of a self-selecting group of individuals, to say definitively what made saccharin an intensely important pleasure to these primarily female consumers in the late 1970s. Certainly, if asked directly, they would have said that they drank saccharin sodas instead of regular sodas to reduce dietary calories. Some may have added that saccharin-enhanced drinks simply tasted better than sugared soda. Others were clearly tired of government regulation in an era when recession left little love for regulation or bureaucrats. They wanted saccharin simply because the government said they should not. Such predictable answers, however, are formed too far from the environments in which consumers wrote those millions of letters. There one finds people living in a world of out-of-control risks, ready to hold tightly to the one they chose.

LOCAL KNOWLEDGE AND UNEQUAL RICHES

Roughly half of the protesters base their decision to dismiss saccharin's possible carcinogenic risks on their personal experiences. And roughly half of these mention sources of information that they have encountered beyond their own bodily experiences, such as quoted statistics heard on the news, discussions among friends, evidence from saccharin-using family members, or the local newspaper. The latter appears to be a particularly important source of information for saccharin consumers eager to find a context in which to understand the proposed ban. "After hearing on the news last night and reading in today's newspaper about saccharin . . . I decided it was necessary for me to write to you about your foolishness," explained Judith Robinson of Phoenix. She referred the FDA to an article she had enclosed on healthful eating (unrelated to saccharin) and asked the agency to pay particular attention to the areas she had circled. Marilyn and Edwin Ormondroyd of Woonsocket, Rhode Island, wrote to demand that the FDA repeal "this ridiculous federal law" immediately. Referring to an article titled "Saccharin Stupidity" from the *Woonsocket Call*, they wrote, "It is exactly the way we feel about the proposed action." An article titled "Big Doses Don't Hurt Monkeys" was sent by Edwina Johnston of Oklahoma City, who explained, "All the reports that has [*sic*] been printed . . . doesn't stand to reason. To drink 800 cans of diet soda a day you would have to *drink 33.33333 cans an hour*." Beverly DeVore of Laramie, Wyoming, sent with her protest letter a newspaper clipping from the Casper *Star-Tribune* with the title "Food Bans Called 'Illogical.'" And Charlotte Newport of Okmulgee, Oklahoma, enclosed "Overkill on Saccharin," an editorial from the *Tulsa Tribune*, with a brief note explaining her desire "to let you know directly that a great many people do not agree with you and are trying to get the congress to overrule your order."[43]

"I have used saccharin since World War II and have no ill effect," explained Mrs. James Fallman of Waco, Texas. "There are thousands of people right *here*," she underlined for emphasis, "that use it and have absolutely no ill effects on them either." Her adamant insistence that the FDA take seriously the bodies of people "right *here*" in Waco, Texas, closes the gap between the high science of Washington, D.C., and the working-class life of the small-town South. Fallman effectively dismisses claims of scientific authority by citing the healthy saccharin consumers of Waco. She dismisses the FDA's framing of the danger as one of future risk, instead arguing that if people do not have cancer in Waco at this moment, then there is no cancer risk.[44]

Arjun Appadurai has argued that the "negotiation of the tension between knowledge and ignorance" itself is critical in determining how commodities flow from one point to another in a society with vast distances between the origin and the consumption of goods. Describing the "interplay" of knowledge and ignorance as a "turnstile," he imagines a process in which knowledge is not merely something absorbed by individuals through the goods they consume but, rather, a negotiation process whereby goods are allowed in when they are "known" in a way that meets local needs.[45] American studies scholar Julie Sze adds to this in her work on environmental justice activists in New York, arguing that an important part of knowing, especially for marginalized citizens, is the ability to understand the meanings provided by experts and challenge them. Particularly important to the success of asthma activists, for example, in protesting transit stations was what Sze calls their ability to understand government "technocratic language" without "letting this perspective dominate their worldview."[46] It was a process that in fact had two goals: changing city planning policy and prioritizing the voices of marginalized community members.

Individuals who protested the saccharin ban were not involved in a formal political protest. Nor did they come together as communities and articulate shared values in opposition to social systems. Yet in individual letters they clearly share their dissatisfaction with their environments, and their sense that their experiences are largely ignored by those in positions of power who might address the problem. Arguably, it was the opportunity to make visible their local spaces and validate their individual perspectives that motivated many to write down their thoughts and mail the letter to Washington. Some were women who lived in working-class areas, who faced the toxic risks associated with low-income/low-power geographies, and who had little political power. Others were dieters who classified themselves as either overweight or at risk, without saccharin, of becoming so. According to Arnold Brooks, the president of the Eastern Pennsylvania Weight Watchers in Allentown, the ban would never have been proposed in the first place if what he termed the "overweight . . . users of sugar substitutes" had not become "the forgotten people." His words, printed in the local paper, appear to have resonated with many readers; more letters originated from Allentown than any other city in the sample.[47]

There is ample evidence that many of those who relied on saccharin to control weight gain were, in fact, forgotten in 1977. The repeated evocations of risk in these letters offer compelling evidence that these writers were politically disempowered. As Ulrich Beck argued, risk does not disperse in a society equally; instead, a society creates "social risk positions" in which poverty (here either poverty of income, power, or education) attracts "an unfortunate abundance of risk."[48] Work emerging at the time on what was being termed the "obesity epidemic" also suggested that weight control was more difficult for "subjects moving downward in social status than it was among those who remained in the social class of their parents."[49] One study bluntly stated that research had found what it termed an "inverse relationship" between "the level of fatness in the adult female and the levels of education, income, and occupation."[50]

Historians have found that the late 1970s were an era during which the whites of Brooks's Allentown had become politically and socially invisible. Working-class Americans, Beth Bailey argues, failed to enjoy "full membership" in American society after prolonged periods of domestic unrest and economic decline. The loss of visibility occurred not only in the places many of these letters originated from—Allentown, Detroit, Indianapolis, and Kansas City—where the well-documented off-shoring of manufacturing decimated blue-collar jobs; it also occurred in popular culture. Analyzing the coterminous defeat of labor strikes and the replacement of Archie Bunker with more middle-class media heroes, historian Jefferson Cowie argues, "It was not simply that specific groups of workers were defeated at specific places, but that the very idea of workers in civic and popular discourse were defeated."[51]

"It's bad enough we can't afford to even buy a cup of coffee, but [now] we can't even have sweetener to go with it," complained J. Murdock of Detroit. "What do you want me to use to sweeten my life a little?" "I don't know if my letter will have much effect, but I can try," wrote Deborah Kessler of Roseville, Minnesota. "I'm only one person and it's so hard to be heard," wrote a protester who did not even include her name on her letter. A number of letter writers expressed a similar doubt that their words would have an impact on a government agency in Washington, D.C. "Do you even know we're out here?" asked Lois Havenker in her letter from March 11.[52]

While many letters were typed, some even on company letterhead, revealing the professional knowledge of their writers, far more common was the handwritten note. A fair number of these were penned on decorative stationery. Havenker's letter is written on small-sized paper with a basket-weave border. Other letters appear with edging featuring hearts, animals, and whimsical scenes. On a small notecard featuring embroidered borders and a portly man selling vegetables from a pushcart (see fig. 5.2), Rosanne Shuster of Waban, Massachusetts, declared it "humanly impossible to consume that much saccharin." Nancy Townsend of Evansville, Indiana, described herself as "a fat person who craves sweets," on personal stationery with NANCY in a large block letters in the upper right corner.[53] Both Shuster and Havenker gesture in their notes to their own vulnerability, Havenker by doubting that the FDA knows she exists and Schuster by ending her note "Please help—." Townsend went further, declaring, "I must be allowed saccharin or I shall die." Writers like these may have taken pride in addressing the FDA (and the president) on their own informal paper. Others may have considered such stationery best suited for this purpose. But some, one imagines, were made very aware of the distance between themselves and Washington, D.C., through the act of expressing themselves without a typewriter or professional stationery.

Regardless of the paper they used, writers were adamant that their experiences mattered. Many felt they had to educate the FDA to understand that they were not rats. "We don't put ourselves in the class of experimental rats, but as human beings we can testify that saccharin is not harmful," wrote Marilaw Smith of South Bend, Indiana. "As a long time saccharin user I would like to add my information as a human to yours with the mice etc., for all its worth," wrote Marilyn Martin of Plainfield, New Jersey.[54] Donna Jeanne Morean of Newport Beach, California, explained, "We're tired of being compared to rats continually."[55] Mrs. Gynie Baker of Danville, California, who described herself as a seventy-seven-year-old who had used Sucaryl sweetener for "as long as I can remember," declared, "I'm not a rat and should not be treated like one."[56] Certainly none of these women believed that the FDA had lost the ability to discern a human from a rodent. But they did see the FDA as an agency that knew far more about rats than about people like them. While the majority of letter writers seemed satisfied with expressing their disgust at the FDA's ignorance, others took the opportunity to educate the agency. "As you know Americans have more of a weight problem than any other population," explained one woman from Silver Spring, Maryland. Others sent both local articles clipped from their newspapers and national coverage

FIG. 5.2 Letter of protest, Rosanne Shuster to FDA, no date, Food and Drug Administration Records, #903, cd1, v15.

of the futility of the ban; they seemed to believe that if the FDA knew the issue better (as they did), it would reverse the decision.[57]

VISIBLE BODIES AND RELEVANT DATA

One scientist, writing about the saccharin controversy after witnessing the public hearings held on the issue in March 1977, recalled the unorthodox methods used by saccharin advocates to make their point. The majority of witnesses who explained to elected representatives why, in spite of the FDA recommendation, saccharin should remain on supermarket shelves used their own bodies as evidence. The scientist recalled that they brought with them only "anecdotal evidence" about how saccharin had helped them lose weight and improve their health. Rather than presenting blood tests or physicians' testimony, these speakers pointed to their own struggles to lose weight, the amount of weight they lost, and their conviction that without saccharin they would be fat again. One woman had gone so far as to insist to Congress that she should be considered "living proof that diet foods help people lose weight."[58]

A high percentage of people who wrote letters to the FDA offered their bodies and their experiences as a counter to the FDA's scientific knowledge of the dangers of saccharin. What for the scientist was strange and anecdotal was, for many of these women, the most important argument to be made for saccharin's positive effect on health. Because they had come to see health as synonymous with weight loss, these women felt confident in declaring that whatever cancer risk might be found in a laboratory was simply not as important as the fat risk they knew from their own "body laboratories" located in towns far from the purview of Washington, D.C., lawmakers.

This line of argument is significant for several reasons. First, it illuminates a satisfied saccharin user different from the type presented in advertisements during the era. One popular campaign just prior to the FDA announcement, for instance, included the Tab "mind sticker" commercial. It shows women—universally thin, well dressed, and young—who capture and keep the attention of men because they drink Tab and are thin. "Stick in his mind," says the male voiceover as soft music plays; "be a mind sticker."[59] Along with magazine and newspaper advertisements, the commercial campaign strongly asserts that the primary purpose of saccharin-sweetened soda is to produce a perfect, thin body that is worth remembering.

Letter writers' assertions of their saccharin-aided weight loss, however, focus on their bodies for their own sake. There is an intense emphasis here on the process of weight loss and the virtues of a struggling, if still-imperfect body. For these women, saccharin is not producing thin perfection; it is producing a means of working toward it. Second, these letters reveal an intense pride in the materiality of the writers' bodies *as they are* and *where they are*. Some stood up before Congress with before-and-after pictures, and many more sent records to the FDA of pounds lost and measurements gained. "I feel wonderful and have never had *any* ill effects whatsoever," wrote Mary Rogers of New Berlin, Wisconsin, to Commissioner Gardner on March 23, 1977. Her insistence that the decision to ban saccharin should be "left up to the American people" was based solely on her own 160-pound weight loss, facilitated, she believed, by daily saccharin use.[60] Women like Mary claimed their right to be seen and their right to have their perspectives taken into account by the nation's lawmakers. To do this, they used vivid arguments of falling short of perfection, laboring to attain it, and living lives attached to others who were doing the same. These were not just "dieters"; they were women whose experiences made them worthy of being seen and heard.

A large percentage of the letter writers opposing the ban noted their affiliation with Weight Watchers. Mary La Pointe of Allentown, Pennsylvania, enclosed, along with her protest letter, her Weight Watchers attendance book for the previous sixteen weeks. "I feel that I can be justifiably proud of my 44¾ pound weight loss," she explained, attributing it "to some extent" to "the use of artificial sweeteners and artificially sweetened beverages." The document overwhelms the letter; its sixteen small coupons, each dated and inscribed with a weight, chart La Pointe's minimization. She closed her letter with the descriptor "proud weight watcher and user of saccharine [*sic*]."[61] Others, like Linda Sanders of Montgomery, Alabama, sent specific physical measurements at the beginning of their letters, effectively framing their argument for saccharin around an imagined body. In large print Sanders details her height (5′ 3¾″) and weight (279½). Her letter suggests that she understands that her body is out of the bounds of normal consideration: she explains parenthetically next to her weight that the measurement is in "pounds not ounces!"[62]

Many of these women were emboldened by Weight Watchers to make their own weight-loss struggles public. Founded in a New Jersey living room in 1964, by 1977 the organization had 9 million registered members and $30 million in revenues.[63] Letters arrived from all over the country from women who identified themselves as Weight Watchers members. Several of these letters suggest that members discussed the pending saccharin ban in their group meetings. One member, Sandra Kew of St. Clair Shores, Michigan, explained to the FDA that she had "discussed this subject" at her last weekly Weight Watchers meeting. Reporting to the FDA the results of a spirited conversation among attendees, Kew concluded that it was "unanimous that saccharin not be taken off the market."[64]

It is difficult to discern what was said in conversations among these 9 million registered members of Weight Watchers in the weeks after the announced ban. Few letters discuss specific conversations between group leaders and members. Yet the sheer number of letters that refer to Weight Watchers membership as a self-identifying feature suggests that that organization was on the minds of many consumers as they composed protest letters. Two explanations arise for the connection. On one hand, Weight Watchers had created a system of weight loss heavily reliant on saccharin-sweetened foods. According to Jean Newcombe, a member from Farmington, Michigan, Weight Watchers' own recipes were a "big asset" in the organization's efforts to help the obese. "Most all of these recipes," she explained, "call for a sugar substitute and diet drinks." Nancy D'Amico of Louisville, Kentucky, lost eighteen pounds by substituting saccharin for sugar in the "so many nice and tasty recipes" she made. For Patricia Amador of Brooklyn Center, Minnesota, the ban on saccharin would "put a damper" on what she called "this new enjoyable diet." It would also make it more difficult for individuals recently attracted to the organization to stay on their weight-loss programs. Only by enabling members to consume things like saccharin-sweetened Jell-O and pancake syrup, which she described as "the fat foods," would the diet plan remain a "feasible one."[65]

By 1977, the success of Weight Watchers as a mass-marketed, relatively pain-free program depended on saccharin. Had saccharin been removed from the market and another substitute been unavailable (aspartame would not be approved by the FDA until 1982), Weight Watchers would have lost a good deal of money on memberships and prepared foods. Certainly this was a motivating factor for group leaders who facilitated conversations about the proposed ban. Yet for consumers who followed such advice and actually wrote, a second purpose emerged. Many articulated a clear resistance to the ban by identifying with the organization. Theirs was more than a diet defense; it was an articulation of power and a demand to be heard.

"I'm a Weight Watcher, and we are legion," wrote Norma Lee Mc-Mullen of Louisville, Kentucky. "Back off and leave us alone."[66] McMullen is not merely asking the FDA to reconsider its proposal. She is demanding it. By embedding her own body within the strength of the organization, McMullen presents herself as a force to be reckoned with. It is significant that next to Allentown, another Weight Watchers stronghold, the largest percentage of letters from a single city were sent from Louisville, the site where McMullen felt herself part of a "legion." Writers frequently couched their personal logics of protest within the framework of organizational membership. As "members" or "life members" or simply "Weight Watchers," these women were emboldened to become the front line of defense against the FDA's action. The protest necessitated that their private struggles against weight be taken public in defense of the greater good.

In his history of dieting in America, *Never Satisfied*, historian Hillel Schwartz traces the obsession with weighing and measuring bodies in order to assess health back to the 1920s. The rise of universal life insurance produced actuarial charts of desirable ratios of height to weight that were used to determine insurance eligibility across the country. Conscription during World War I had also contributed to a new fixation on weight. The aggregate numbers of individual soldier's "weigh-ins" revealed that an alarming number of American men were being medically judged too heavy to fight effectively. By the 1920s, Americans had become familiar with calorie counting, thanks to nutrition research that had identified the ideal amount of calories each individual should consume and revealed the caloric value of common foods. Yet, in spite of a new educational emphasis on calorie-conscious eating and a dramatic uptick in the purchase of private scales for home weigh-ins, most Americans continued to regard their weight as a private matter, something to be tracked with the door closed (if one could afford a scale) or to keep between oneself and one's physician during a physical examination.[67]

Within this climate, Weight Watchers was unique. It required members to declare their weight publicly—repeatedly—and to promise never to forget what life was like at one's highest weight, even years after the pounds were shed. Meeting leaders, always successful members on "maintenance" for reaching their goal weights, would often stand up in front of a group with a large "before" photo next to them in full view, to remind everyone that they were not always thin. Schwartz refers to this technique of motivation as "anamnesis," or a "calling to mind," and demonstrates that it was practiced famously by Nidetch herself. For years after she reached her size 12 goal weight (and became famous), Nidetch told people how she woke up every morning and tried on her size 44 dresses, just to make sure she would "never get to the point where I think I've always been thin." This intense emphasis on visual girth created an organization, at least in the 1970s, in which many women agreed with the assessment of one member who had reached her goal weight: "We know we're not cured. We're merely arrested."[68]

Not every woman who wrote to the FDA was a Weight Watcher. But many shared this dual emphasis on power and powerlessness that emerges in the term "arrested." They had control over their cravings because they could satisfy those cravings, at least in part, with a sweet, pleasurable substance that did not make matters worse. And when they wrote to the FDA to tell them this in ways that made their own experiences visible, they converted the private practices of dieting (measuring, calculating risk, fearing backsliding) into their own political power. Yet the panic in these letters suggests a building dependency at the root of this description of success and empowerment: individuals simultaneously tout their achievements and hang their continued success on a lifetime supply of saccharin.

SACCHARIN AS A CONSUMER LIFE LINE

"Please do not take away my life line," wrote Wanda Wright. "Life is not worth living without diet foods," explained Virginia Tamarin. "Please help, people are at the end of their rope without saccharin," explained Mrs. Victor Kundert. Linda Sanders required three exclamation points to make herself clear: "please, please, please reconsider. . . . In this overweight nation we desperately need saccharin!!!"[69] According to one official at the FDA who had the unenviable job of answering the phones and recording consumer sentiments, most who called were exceedingly upset, and "some of them [were] in tears." With some exceptions, most letters demanded that the FDA keep saccharin on the market and did so with intended emphasis: underlines, bold print, and multiple exclamation points were frequently used to add intensity to the requests.

Wanda Wright and Virginia Tamarin, like thousands of other letter writers, understood clearly the risk of not having saccharin. "Saccharin and sugarless gum and drinks are my allies," explained Tamarin, who described herself as one who "[tries] hard to control my weight and count my calories." Wanda Wright described herself as "thin" after having lost 105 pounds eight years ago after being "overweight for 40 years of my life." The very thought of losing saccharin, however, left her "prepared to March on Washington DC"; she ended her letter with a cry of "Help!!" Virginia Allee closed her letter with "Please help us!" after scolding the FDA for failing to understand that "we are dealing with life and death issues" when we "tamper with the . . . needs of persons fighting to keep their weight within bounds. The battle is hard enough without this low blow!"[70]

Not far below the surface of consumers' fight for saccharin is their fight against a culture that makes it nearly impossible to eat right if "right" means thin. Particularly difficult, for many, was resisting the urge to eat sweets. "I am shocked and personally frightened by the decision to ban saccharin," explained Josephine Novak. She described herself and her husband, both in their late thirties, as having "suffered from a life-long struggle with obesity." Theirs was a world rife with control and resistance in which the nearly constant temptation to indulge in sweets could only be combated by saccharin. "In all other ways we are extremely aware of proper diet and nutritional balance and feel that we are capable of making these choices and judgments," she explained. But when it came to sweets, she explained, "we both strive at diet control." Only with saccharin-sweetened diet sodas and dietetic chocolate puddings had she and her husband achieved what she termed "an equilibrium whereby we receive sufficient palate gratification to resist any more."[71]

What frightened Josephine Novak was her own appetite. Her statement suggests a well-educated woman with ample nutritional knowledge. The food desires of her and her husband, however, are impervious to both intellect and willpower. Saccharin provided the "equilibrium" required to balance their cravings for sweet foods with the maintenance of a weight she characterized as "healthy." She does not suggest that altering her appetite or changing her physical routines to expend more calories are options. Hers was a world in which "palate gratification" was required; thus the only way to pursue health was to ensure that the sweet products she and her husband frequently required could be rendered calorie free.

Novak was one among thousands of women who wanted the FDA to understand that saccharin was the only thing that stood between them and significant weight gain. "In order to continue my weight control program, I feel the availability of these products is essential," explained Mrs.

David Corbin of Bridgeport, Washington, who had lost seventy pounds in the past year. Mrs. Ernst Bold of Schnecksville, Pennsylvania, who described herself as "inclined to overweight in the extreme," reported that she had lost sixty-five pounds twenty-five years ago "with the help of artificial sweeteners." Norma Emory of Louisville, Kentucky, urged the FDA to consider the "plight" of the obese in the United States, offering her own 105-pound weight loss "with the help of products that contain saccharin" as evidence of what would transpire in the wake of a saccharin ban.[72]

For many, a future without saccharin was a future with lots of sugar and, consequently, fat. "You are giving me and *many* others no alternative but to turn to sugar," explained Susan Richardson of Indianapolis, Indiana. "There are many millions of Americans who are fat," chided Darlene Roy of Lyndon, Kentucky. "What are we going to do? Are we going to have to go back to sugar and be fat the rest of our lives?" Pamela Magee of Kennard, Indiana described the proposed ban as "very disturbing" and herself as "very concerned." Facing a medically demanded weight loss, with 100 pounds already shed, she wondered what she "and millions of other people" were supposed to do for sweetness without saccharin.[73]

Saccharin defenders frequently presented as a truism that if saccharin were discontinued, they would consume sugar, and if they consumed sugar, they would be fat. It is tempting to see their analysis as extreme. Certainly one option, were saccharin to be banned, was simply to drink water and avoid dessert. Two conditions may have made such an option extraordinarily difficult. The first, and most obvious, was the rise of diet products that had enmeshed sweet pleasure with weight loss and maintenance for twenty-five years. The second was surely the rise of soda consumption, in general, in the United States. According to the 1977 dietary report of the Senate Select Committee on Nutrition and Human Needs, there had been a "sevenfold" increase in the amount of refined sugar consumed by Americans since the early twentieth century, mostly due to an astounding increase in the amount of soda and sweetened teas being consumed. "Beverages now comprise the largest single industry use of refined sugar, accounting for over one-fifth of the total refined sugar in the U.S. diet."[74] In American culture in 1977 there likely appeared two options for pleasurable nonalcoholic drinking: diet soda and regular soda. The disappearance of one would have necessitated the adoption of the other unless one was willing to take extreme measures and drink water. Among letter writers there was no virtue in doing that.

As early as 1958, historian John Kenneth Galbraith argued that the continual stoking of postwar consumer desire would lead to a situation where consumers would no longer be able to trust their own instincts to know when they had been satiated. In an essay titled "How Much Should a Country Consume?" he saw appetite itself as a problem that had to be confronted. In a society where citizens were constantly encouraged to buy more, what would happen when we reached a point where desire could not be satisfied? "What of the appetite itself?" he inquired. "If it continues on its geometric course, will it not one day have to be restrained?"[75]

Over the next twenty years, between Galbraith's question and saccharin rebels' answers, manufacturers of artificially sweetened products like Diet Delight and marketers like Tillie Lewis and makers of sodas like Tab had to directly confront this problem, so aptly described by one diet-industry executive as "prosperity stomach."[76] By promoting artificial sweetener as a way to continue to indulge in pleasurable eating in spite of the clear caloric limits of actuarial tables' definitions of health, popular cultural messages enabled appetites for sweets to stretch beyond the bounds of what consumers could control without a technological intervention. Read in this context, the saccharin rebellion was a moment in which consumers were forced to fully confront the dangers of their own intensified appetites. It is impossible to say, without examining extensive demographic and nutritional factors, what caused their weight problems or even if letter writers were honest in claiming their own weight-loss success. And it is beyond the scope of this book to do so. What is possible to discern from this evidence is that the letter writers believed their appetites were dangerous without saccharin, and that saccharin had become the one substance that enabled them to find equilibrium between sufficient pleasure and appropriate weight.

"We need help in this affluent society," wrote Elizabeth Shaw Plummer of Silver Spring, Maryland, in her letter to protest the ban. "Reverse your decision on saccharin," she demanded, noting that her access to saccharin-sweetened products was necessary to ensure "that we can continue to have an edge on the battle of the bulge." Returning to Beck's analysis of risk societies, insatiable consumer desire should be read along with the other perils of modernity he discusses. The increased requirements for energy produce nuclear meltdowns; the desire to lower costs and increase production leads to groundwater and air contamination; the search for cheap labor leaves people unemployed and invisible. And the need for a market for what is produced demands insatiable consumers. The pleas of Weight Watchers and women like Plummer, then, reflect more than individual struggles or group cohesion. They are also signs of the larger risks of consumption that had to be "prevented, minimized, dramatized, or channeled" in order to ensure the smooth flow of goods.[77]

THE CALORIE CONTROL COUNCIL AND PRO-SACCHARIN MOMENTUM

It is possible that consumers would have defeated the FDA on their own. Within the first week after the proposed ban was announced, 6,000 letters had been sent from across the country, and the vast majority were opposed to it. In the end, however, individual consumers had a powerful ally in the artificial-sweetener industry. The week after the FDA's announcement, the Calorie Control Council (CCC), an organization of Japanese and American makers of saccharin, soft drink companies, and pharmaceutical firms, took out two-page advertisements in major newspapers across the country. In bold-faced text they spoke directly to consumers: "If you find this action ridiculous, you're not alone," they told readers of the *Los Angeles Times* who might have been contemplating their own verdicts. According to these advertisements, it was not 800 cans of soda humans would have to drink but 1,250. Declaring the FDA's research faulty science, the CCC invited readers to imagine themselves as part of a large community of outraged consumers. It was time, the ad announced, to conduct your "own experiment . . . in democracy" by calling congressmen and the FDA. Another version of the ad that ran in the *Wall Street Journal* made certain that consumers were sufficiently emboldened to put pen to paper: "Remember . . . it's up to you to make this experiment in democracy really work." The ad concluded with "Let yourself be heard!" and a list of influential people to contact, including President Carter.[78]

The CCC made resisting the saccharin ban as easy as cutting out an advertisement and putting it in an envelope. And many consumers did just that. A number of items in the FDA archives are envelopes with only the CCC-produced and -financed words enclosed. Newspapers across the country printed variations on an advertisement clipped and sent in May by one anonymous consumer. Bold text at the top reads "You've got two weeks to be heard!" (see fig. 5.3). Below are names of "government leaders" who are reported to have an unclear but ominous-sounding "special

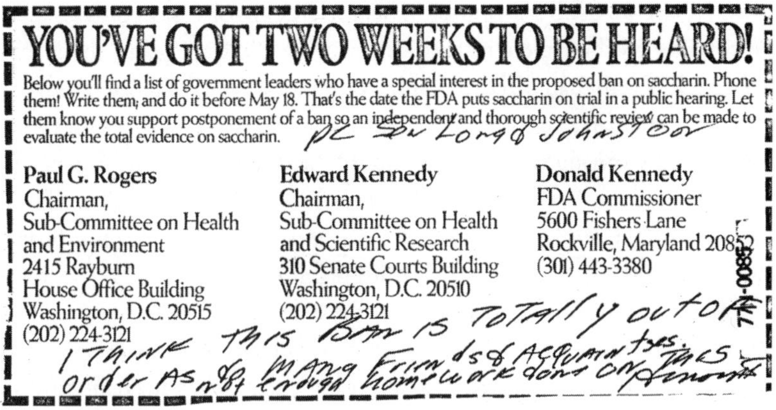

YOU'VE GOT TWO WEEKS TO BE HEARD!

Below you'll find a list of government leaders who have a special interest in the proposed ban on saccharin. Phone them! Write them, and do it before May 18. That's the date the FDA puts saccharin on trial in a public hearing. Let them know you support postponement of a ban so an independent and thorough scientific review can be made to evaluate the total evidence on saccharin. *[handwritten]*

Paul G. Rogers
Chairman,
Sub-Committee on Health
and Environment
2415 Rayburn
House Office Building
Washington, D.C. 20515
(202) 224-3121

Edward Kennedy
Chairman,
Sub-Committee on Health
and Scientific Research
310 Senate Courts Building
Washington, D.C. 20510
(202) 224-3121

Donald Kennedy
FDA Commissioner
5600 Fishers Lane
Rockville, Maryland 20852
(301) 443-3380

[handwritten] This ban is totally out of order as do many friends & acquaintances. Think I think this ban is totally out of order as do many friends & acquaintances. Not enough homework done on this.

FIG. 5.3 "You've got two weeks to be heard!" advertisement, received by FDA May 11, 1977, Food and Drug Administration Records, #28994, cd15, v519.

interest in the proposed ban on saccharin." Consumers are told to "let them know you support postponement of a ban" until more scientific studies are completed. The accompanying names and addresses easily allowed consumers to send copies of the ad directly to two senators and the FDA commissioner. The archival copy suggests that many people used this ad as a backdrop on which they could write a few sentences of their own: "I think this ban is totally out of order as do many friends and acquaintses [*sic*]; not enough homework done on this."[79]

Between March and July, the CCC spent roughly $890,000 for "lobbying, advertising, and public relations" in an effort to block the FDA's proposal.[80] It was apparent to people at the time that CCC had an enormously influential role in calling consumers to arms through local media and presenting the industry's point of view in national media.[81] When the letters are closely examined in context, the appeal of the CCC's consumer campaign is clear. Many of the individuals writing to the FDA and Congress were engaging in politics for the first time. Many were from small towns and communicated their experience of being unable to regulate their behaviors. The clip-and-send-your-opinion campaign connected these individuals to a national, organized effort and made their voices essential for success. It let many consumers literally pen themselves onto the national agenda. "I am writing to you at the suggestion of the Calorie Control Board as presented in the *Wall Street Journal*," wrote June Mansfield of Simi Valley, California. "I have just finished reading the two-page insert in the March 14th *Wall Street Journal*," explained Martha Hertz, who declared, "I fully support the Calorie Control Council's views."[82] "According to the article in the 'Kansas City Times,'" began the letter from Phyllis Callahan of Spring Hill, Kansas, before explaining the facts that made the ban a bad idea. Callahan asserted that she and her husband were "hard working people" who could "still determine for ourselves, to some degree, what we can and can not eat or drink." At the end of the typewritten letter, she included a P.S. explaining that she "just heard on the ABC News" that the ban "would result in loss of jobs and billions of dollars."[83] Consumers repeatedly cite the media as a trusted source of information over government agencies and science. In these letters, individual citizens explained the sources of their own education in this matter, the validity they believed these sources to have, and their conviction that it was now their duty to use this new knowledge to educate the ignorant in Washington, D.C.

It is not surprising that consumers who had spent twenty years following stories in local papers and national media about the virtues of artificial sweeteners were ready, in 1977, to argue that saccharin should stay on the market because "the media says so." Yet the media-driven defense of saccharin seems to have largely bypassed minority consumers. Newspaper and television coverage of consumers in grocery stores hoarding saccharin products features only whites, and typically women. The congressional debate took place between white elected officials representing, one assumes, primarily their white constituents. And while letters cannot definitively be related to race without further research, no letters directly mention race or nonwhite communities. Certainly, African Americans had little reason to join a media-generated protest for a product that had been aimed primarily at white people for twenty-five years. Diet Delight and Tasti-Diet seem not to have advertised in African American newspapers or magazines, and no black journalists appear to have been invited to the diet luncheons or visited by Tillie Lewis on her tours. And while Jean Nidetch featured African Americans in her biography, suggesting that they participated in her Weight Watchers program, the magazine she founded (and promoted artificially sweetened products in) overwhelmingly featured white women in advertisements and content well into the 1980s.[84] As advertisements for Tab, Diet Pepsi, and artificially sweetened desserts became regular features in publications like McCall's and the Ladies' Home Journal in the 1970s, they were notably absent from Ebony, the beauty magazine aimed at black women. Such advertisements appear, in fact, to have favored blondes.[85] Not until

1984, when Pepsi, Coke, and Diet Coke shifted to diverse product promoters to expand market share, did black women appear in diet soda ads in mainstream publications with any regularity. *Ebony* featured its first diet soda advertisements in 1983 with Diet Coke's "just for the taste of it" campaign that ran through 1987.[86] This disjuncture between the white and nonwhite experience of saccharin is significant. On one hand, nonwhite women may have been less inclined to use diet foods and so were not directly affected by the ban. On the other hand, because they were not major saccharin consumers, many were excluded from a political protest that elevated the importance of many middle- and working-class women over male experts.

Though it did not speak to everyone, the CCC's media campaign was phenomenally effective at mobilizing consumers of artificial sweetener for political action. It may also have been effective at misleading them. "The industry confused the public, perhaps permanently, on the value of animal tests," commented FDA spokesman Wayne Pines in 1980.[87] According to a public opinion poll commissioned by the CCC, 80 percent of people polled in the months after the proposed ban thought the FDA acted prematurely without sufficient evidence.[88] Yet what scientists saw as confusion, consumers may have seen as clarity. The issue, as presented by the CCC, was that the government was interfering with consumers' right to a commodity. By reminding consumers that this was no mere matter of convenience but, rather, an essential "experiment in democracy," the CCC effectively connected saccharin consumption to the Vietnam conflict. The fact that this group of manufacturers stood to lose millions were saccharin to be banned was beside the point. What the CCC wanted consumers to consider was that their own dietary desires were healthy, and that a government that would seek to interfere would have to be challenged.

The CCC's rhetoric may have helped consumers link their own struggles, and potential failures, to those of the nation. "While I am perturbed about the effects of the saccharin ban on my lifestyle, I am more concerned about its effects on the nation's economy," explained Joan McDermott of Baltimore. Banning saccharin would, she believed, "hurt the saccharin industry and put people out of work. You will also severely damage those industries, both large and small, who use saccharin to manufacture dietetic foods." It was a common refrain in letters that appeared in the days after the ban was announced, and it drew directly from the responses provided by the CCC in the local and national press. "What of all the millions of jobs you will take away from men and women?" asked Roberta Cox of Omaha, Nebraska. Deborah Kessler of Roseville, Minnesota, agreed. She chided the FDA for failing to consider the impact on saccharin workers. "In a country where unemployment is already very high, this ignorant act will force thousands of more people out of work," she scolded.[89] Another way consumers drew on arguments made in CCC anti-ban materials to connect their health to national health was by evoking the right to choose. "Your ban takes away my right to choose the kinds of food that I consider essential to my health," wrote a "disgusted" Barbara Didrichsen of Cincinnati on March 11, shortly after the ban was announced. "I use sweeteners constantly . . . and I am angry. I'm sick and tired of you and all your cohorts in Washington restricting more and more the rights of the American people."[90] By the next week, just after the CCC ad campaign appeared, Barbara Wackly of Kansas City would argue, "I for one have used saccharin for more than twenty years, and it IS my privilege to use it in any form I so desire, in any amounts at any time. I once said I'd rather be dead than red, but is this not a form of communism?????"[91] Wackly's insistence that the FDA's ban on saccharin amounted to communism was extreme. Many letters, however, echo the sentiment that there was a right to saccharin. And it was a right that involved much more than one's diet plan or personal pleasures. Saccharin, with the help of the CCC, became an essential guarantor of democratic freedoms.

In the end, consumers did not get clean air and water, nor did they get their colleagues to stop smoking or driving drunk, as a result of the saccharin protest. But they did get their saccharin. The Senate hearings in 1977 concluded with the decision to push back the ban's implementation date for several years to enable more tests to be completed. The date was quietly rescheduled again, repeatedly, until in the early 1990s the ban was dismissed entirely. It is fair to say this was a major victory for consumers seeking the right to determine their own market risks. It is also fair to say that it was an even bigger victory for a diet industry that had grown heavily reliant upon saccharin in the absence of all other viable low-calorie sweetening options.

Saccharin would largely disappear from the American marketplace on its own in the early 1980s, eclipsed by aspartame, a new noncaloric sweetener widely regarded as superior in taste. The quest for what Susan Kloberdanz of Cedar Rapids, Iowa, called "preventative medicine," or a sweetener that gave more of the good and less of the bad, would be carried over into the first globally advertised artificially sweetener, Nutra-Sweet.[92] For Kloberdanz, this meant quite literally a sweetener that she could ingest in large quantities without the undesirable effects of obesity and diabetes. The phrase, however, is an apt description for a new era of artificial sweetener that was articulated in 1977 and continues today. Had the FDA not sought to ban the substance, it is quite possible that saccharin would have merely been a diet product so ubiquitous as to attract little attention. But by inspiring a million users—regular and casual—to defend saccharin in writing, with arguments buttressing their point of view, the FDA's threatened ban demanded that consumers portray saccharin as a positive good to combat the agency's rendering of it as a certain bad. And consumers did so with the materials at hand. The fight for saccharin enabled participants to connect diet products to pleasure, power, and authority in an era when those things were scarce for many Americans. That, in doing so, they ultimately protected the artificial-sweetener industry was a fact not lost on Searle, the pharmaceutical company that was, in 1977, already trying to bring NutraSweet to market.

NUTRASWEET NATION

PROFIT, PERIL, AND THE PROMISE OF A FREE LUNCH

> One of the cardinal rules in Western cultures is that pleasures have prices.
> ... What we are saying to people is "you can have the pleasure without
> paying the price." That's like saying there is such a thing as a free lunch.
> —Bob Shapiro, president of NutraSweet Company, 1987

Between 1975 and 1984, Americans increased their consumption of artificial sweetener by 150 percent. Some of this dramatic growth can be attributed to the general rise in dieting in the United States and the proliferation of saccharin-sweetened products in the mid-1970s. Some of it is owed to the controversy over saccharin that forced many Americans to become advocates for the chemical in their own defense. Most of it, however, is because of NutraSweet, the third artificial sweetener sold in the United States.

NutraSweet, the brand name of the new artificial sweetener aspartame, became phenomenally popular in the 1980s. As a product, it made good on many of the promises of its predecessors. Like cyclamates (and unlike saccharin), it had no bitter aftertaste. It dissolved easily in cold drinks and hot, so iced tea and coffee became easy to sweeten with just a pinch of powder. It could not be heated because its components break down at high temperatures, so it was not a substitute for sugar in home baking and canning. In the era of processed convenience foods, however, this did not detract from its appeal. Puddings, yogurts, and gum sweetened with NutraSweet rapidly arrived on supermarket shelves, creating new categories of low-calorie treats for consumers to indulge in. Most significantly, it could be added to soft drinks, producing for the first time a product with no bitter aftertaste and no calories (cyclamates had to be combined with sugar, so products that contained it were not calorie free). This combination of malleable material and potent marketing, anchored by its ubiquitous red swirl, made NutraSweet a household name in the 1980s.

This was either a good thing or a bad thing, depending on one's opinion of the product. NutraSweet was a lightning rod for praise and controversy in the 1980s, and it remains so today, as an Internet search will quickly reveal. It was in many ways ideally positioned for success. Just as national attention was being drawn to obesity rates, a new superior artificial sweetener could remove sugar calories without sacrificing taste. Just as an early wave of environmental disasters had drawn attention to health problems caused by chemicals, the red swirl campaign effectively freed NutraSweet from the laboratory and presented it as nature, with the bad stuff stripped out. And just as a new day of neoliberal legislation moved health care increasingly out of the public sector and into the market, NutraSweet's model of "purchasable" health enabled consumers to make the "good choices" now essential for its achievement.

At the same time, a new rumbling of anti-artificial-sweetener sentiment began. It was a drama in which the cast (now consumer health activists rather than bureaucrats) changed more than the plot from the early twentieth-century antisaccharin campaigns. According to anti-NutraSweet crusaders, the product represented the failure of government regulation to put citizens first and the triumph of greedy corporations who cared more about profits than human health. Through films, websites, and local organizations, NutraSweet's critics urged consumers to pay attention to what was really in their diet sodas and desserts. *Sweet and Deadly*, the name of one such documentary, aptly described their perspective. Pharmaceutical corporations had duped the American public into ingesting massive amounts of their products by presenting them as healthful. It was time for American consumers to wake up and realize that their headaches, dizziness, fatigue, and in some cases paralysis were in fact caused by aspartame. Similar to saccharin advocates who had demanded that their knowledge mattered, anti-NutraSweet activists undertook their own investigations into a food-pharmaceutical establishment they deemed fundamentally unhealthful.

The distance between these two assessments suggests that the debate was about more than the merits of a new form of artificial sweetener. At stake was the viability of NutraSweet's assurance that consumer indulgence was compatible with health.

A NEW ALCHEMY: FROM ASPARTAME TO NUTRASWEET

In 1965, James Schlatter, a bench chemist at G. D. Searle pharmaceutical company, inadvertently discovered aspartame while developing a new ulcer medication. The event was in many ways similar to others in the history of artificial sweetener: a chemist licks his finger while researching a nonfood product, only to discover a "shocking" sweetness that shapes the course of history.[1] (If the history of artificial sweetener is any indication, the finger lick is an unsung investigative technique in American chemical innovation.) In this case, the compound was roughly 200 times sweeter than sugar, calorie free, and formed from the methyl ester of two natural amino acids, aspartic acid and phenylalanine.[2] What was different about this particular discovery at Searle, relative to previous sweetener stories, was how carefully and powerfully it would be positioned for success. In 1965, there was a budding industry of artificially sweetened products, thanks to entrepreneurs like Tillie Lewis, Edwin Mitchell, and Jean Nidetch. Supermarkets were carrying diet lines, and the profit potential had attracted most major soda manufacturers to develop their own offerings. At the same time, it was clear to many in the industry that saccharin and cyclamates continued to be controversial substances subject to government regulation. It remained an uphill battle for makers and marketers to assure the Food and Drug Administration (FDA) and consumers that these chemicals were safe. What was needed was a new substance, something that could finally put the chemical past of saccharin to rest and build on consumer receptivity to maximize the potential profit of artificial sweetener. What Schlatter found in his accidental combination was a taste nearly indistinguishable from sugar.

Searle immediately invested resources in this new substance and worked to isolate it for mass production and to create a formula that would enable it to be integrated into food and beverage products and, most significantly, meet FDA standards. A decade passed, during which Searle perfected the product, conducted hundreds of studies on its safety, and pursued agency approval. At the same time, aspartame's primary competitors—cyclamates and saccharin—were increasingly embattled by negative press, safety concerns, and threats from the government to ban them entirely. In 1977, the same year that the FDA announced its intention to ban saccharin, and only eight years after banning cyclamates, Searle took dramatic steps to ensure that aspartame would be ready to take its place. For the first time in the nearly 100-year history of the company, Searle hired outsiders. Former three-term congressman, U.S. ambassador, presidential aide, and secretary of defense (a role he would reprise under George W. Bush) Donald Rumsfeld was brought in as CEO; former Firestone executive James Denny became the new CFO; and formidable lawyer Bob Shapiro was chosen as president. The three-member management team possessed political experience and executive power that was a far cry from that of the nostrum-manufacturing company begun by Gideon Searle in Omaha, Nebraska. It was a dramatic change in company culture and a massive investment in a product that had neither cleared government regulatory hurdles nor been chosen by a single food or beverage manufacturer for use. Searle, like all pharmaceuticals involved in the development of sweeteners, was well aware of the FDA's research into saccharin and the possibility that the substance would ultimately be banned. The potential for profit was clear.

NutraSweet did succeed, making millions for Searle and ultimately for Monsanto, which purchased Searle's NutraSweet division in 1985, nearly a century after beginning to manufacture saccharin. So, too, was NutraSweet profitable for the soda and food manufacturing companies that entered co-branding agreements to use it. They would dominate the market until the arrival of Splenda in the late 1990s. The story of Nutra-Sweet is, first and foremost, a story of business savvy. Searle learned from the problems of previous manufacturers and marketers, in terms of both how artificial sweetener was pitched and how the government was handled. The company perfected the marketing message of its product, working to ensure that NutraSweet was seen as both safe and natural. Searle capitalized on the success of earlier products like Diet Delight that had used trusted, "local" food products to appeal to new consumers. Most significantly, they developed a cohesive brand message wedding aspartame to choice, pleasure, and health.

Aspartame was a significant improvement over previous sweeteners. Like cyclamates and saccharin, it contained roughly as many calories per part as sugar (about four), but because it was far sweeter, less of it was needed to sweeten a food or beverage. The result was a nearly or totally calorie-free sweet. And it tasted, to many, like sugar. In fact, one 1991 chemists' guide to artificial sweeteners remarked that in taste aspartame was "essentially indistinguishable from sucrose."[3] Unlike cyclamates and saccharin, aspartame also enhanced other flavors in products—something food and soda manufacturers found particularly appealing during the 1980s push to prepackage a new array of low-calorie products, including microwave dinners, puddings, and liquid meal replacements.[4]

By 1985, after NutraSweet had been on the market in dry form for only four years and as an ingredient in drinks and foods for two years, Americans were consuming roughly 800 million pounds of it each year. Five years later, there were more than 1,200 products containing NutraSweet on the shelves of U.S. grocery stores.[5] Diet Coke was selling nearly as well as regular Coke, a staple of American imbibing, and one nearly a century old. Puddings, gelatins, cereals, gum, and yogurts with the NutraSweet label often outsold their sugar- and corn-syrup-sweetened counterparts. NutraSweet did not merely convert those who were already using saccharin; it also converted a significant number of consumers who had never used artificial sweeteners. NutraSweet fundamentally changed the way many consumers defined healthy eating.

WHAT WAS NEW IN NUTRASWEET

Searle Pharmaceuticals did not originate the marketing of artificial sweeteners, but it did revolutionize it. Searle's research, development, and marketing teams benefited in two specific ways from the company's unique vantage point as a latecomer to the artificial-sweetener market, entering when full lines of artificially sweetened products had developed loyal consumer bases. First, diet products had become relatively mainstreamed. Low-calorie desserts, snacks, and sodas were commonly advertised in newspapers and magazines and on television. Thanks to the highly publicized and unsuccessful battle of the FDA to ban saccharin, many consumers saw artificial sweeteners as a necessity and a right. Second, and just as important, artificially sweetened products were set to benefit from a general shift in food marketing toward fun and away from functionality. Historian Warren Belasco has argued that the selling of food as fun began in earnest in the 1960s and was a direct response to the "apparent biological limit" of 1,400 to 1,500 calories a day that the average person could consume.[6] At the same time that Henry Schacht was instructing editors of women's magazines on the problems of what he termed a "prosperity stomach" specific to the diet-food industry, food executives across the country were working on ways to sell products to people who were not hungry.

Within this context, NutraSweet encountered consumers who were already facing a conundrum. Because food was now marketed most often as a way to experience happiness and satisfaction, consumers who were receptive to advertised messages were hard pressed to make good food choices that would leave them ingesting an appropriate number of calories.[7] If food was supposed to be fun, saccharin was not a great substitute ingredient. It was not, in fact, very fun. There were and still are legions of fans devoted to saccharin (and they have websites) who insist that the bitter, metallic taste of this sweetener is, in fact, pleasurable. But the majority of people found that the taste of saccharin made it an inferior substitute for sugar. Thus, much saccharin advertising emphasized how much fun it would be to be thin, rather than how much fun it would be to eat saccharin. "One crazy calorie," read the copy that accompanied a seductive close-up of the newly redesigned Tab bottle from 1969. "Unsticky, unstuffy, uninhibited. . . . Not so sweet. With 1 crazy calorie . . . it's what's helping so many people to keep slim and trim. . . . What's happening to the nicest shapes around."[8] Close-ups of bottles and cans, along with thin spokespeople or "average consumers" using the product (as in the Tab "what a beautiful drink for beautiful people" campaign), were common tools in the promotion of saccharin-sweetened products. By the early 1980s, prior to NutraSweet's debut, similar marketing techniques proliferated among a wide array of products, including sugar-free Wrigley's gum, reduced-calorie Ovaltine, Light n' Lively Kraft cheese, sugar-free Fresca, and Weight Watchers reduced-calorie meals.[9] Saccharin could help you lose weight, and it could make that weight loss more pleasurable; but it was, ultimately, a functional product.

As the food industry was promoting "food fun," government experts were redefining the terms of healthy eating in favor of "good ingredients" rather than "good eating practices." Michael Pollan, in his recent *In Defense of Food*, illuminates the importance of 1977 for those who seek to understand how sugar (and later fat) substitutes could suddenly emerge as healthful choices in American culture. That was the year that the FDA decided to overturn a rule in place since 1938 that had required the clear marking of all packages containing substitute ingredients with the word "imitation." It was also the year that the Senate Select Committee on Nutrition and Human Need released its report, five years in the making, *Dietary Goals for the United States*. Its findings backed down from the committee's original goal of changing Americans' eating habits to lower the risk of heart disease and diabetes and combat the climbing rates of obesity. Instead of urging people to eat fewer meat and dairy products, the printed version was altered, after lobbyists' objections, to focus on the part rather than the whole—and to make consumer choice the ultimate arbiter. While these changes did not address sugar specifically, they would create a market climate conducive to NutraSweet sales. "Choose meats, poultry, and fish that will reduce saturated fat intake," the report read. Taken together, the change in ruling and the guide to nutrition left the door wide open for a new era in artificial promotion. What was once a "sarcastic sham" would no longer even be an imitation. Artificial sweetener would emerge as a healthful replacement for what was really bad: sugar calories. All that was required was marketing genius to render NutraSweet the ideal form of eating pleasure.

THE ANNOUNCEMENT OF NUTRASWEET

In 1984 my house was one of the 5 million reached by Searle Pharmaceuticals in its direct gumball mailing campaign designed to introduce NutraSweet, or aspartame, to American consumers. Searle found us in Riverside, California. It also found Bonnie Garde in Freehold, New Jersey; Janet Saksa, in Mountain Home, Arkansas; and Pam Ernst in Leader, Texas.[10] I remember receiving the small package of brightly colored balls. They popped out of a see-through candy wrapper printed with the single word "NutraSweet" (see fig. 6.1). It was our first taste of Nutra-Sweet, a product we had never heard of but that would, within a couple of years, effectively replace sugar in our house. And it was telling that it came in the form of a gumball, a material symbol of fun and playfulness, more closely associated with childhood indulgence than adult dietary restraint.

NutraSweet rode into American lives on a new wave of artificial-sweetener marketing enabled by superior taste and lax nutritional regulations. No longer were diet products something you had to seek, something you had to settle for once you found them. They were now delivered directly to your door; like samples of new dishwashing detergent, they were presented as something everyone could use. By fusing artificial with "nutra" and making its ingestion fun, the gumball campaign announced a revolution in sweeteners. For Karen McLean, who found

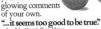

What's better than reading what people say about NutraSweet is tasting why they said it.

Send us your name and we'll send you some free gumballs.

"NutraSweet is great." —Virginia Claflin, Chicago, Illinois

And not just any gumballs, mind you. But ones sweetened with NutraSweet™ brand sweetener, perhaps the most amazing food ingredient you'll ever taste.

One taste and you'll completely agree with what people have been saying about NutraSweet. In fact, the gumballs may even inspire you to write some glowing comments of your own.

"...it seems too good to be true." —Janet Sokol, Mountain Home, Arkansas

NutraSweet tastes just like sugar but with far fewer calories. As a result, food products sweetened with NutraSweet let you watch calories without watching and weighing every morsel you eat.

"I can't believe I'm chewing a gum that is so sweet and yet not made with sugar." —Bon Garde, Freehold, New Jersey

A cup of hot cocoa sweetened with NutraSweet instead of sugar has only 50 calories, not 110. A rich, creamy milkshake, only 70 calories. Not the 250 that it has with sugar. A gelatin dessert, only 8 calories. Instead of 81.

"It will save me many calories and probably a lot of dental work on the children." —Joice Ann Ominsez, Hayward, California

"I never would have thought they are sugar-free." —Teri Read, Houston, Texas

NutraSweet isn't like anything else called "sugar-free." NutraSweet and saccharin, for example, are two completely different sweeteners. NutraSweet has no bitter aftertaste, for one thing.

"I am extremely impressed with the taste." —Pam Ernst, Leander, Texas

And unlike saccharin, NutraSweet is made of two of the building blocks of protein—two amino acids, actually—so your body treats NutraSweet exactly like it treats any natural food you eat.

"I normally won't eat anything that's 'sugar-free' because of the horrible aftertaste. Yours is terrific!" —Sandy Gescheidt, Plainfield, New Jersey

"...I now can give my children sugar-free products..." —Mrs. J. Kohl, Cary, Illinois

The fact that NutraSweet tastes as good as it does means there's every likelihood that it could become an important way to satisfy your family's "sweet tooth." That's important in trips to the dentist alone.

And even more important when you consider that the average American family of four people eats 400 pounds of sugar a year. (Where does it all come from? Well, much of it is "hidden" as an ingredient in such foods as peanut butter, breakfast cereals, catsup and fruit-flavored drinks).

"...so pleased to have a good tasting sweetener that isn't harmful or full of calories." —Pat Miller, Tomball, Texas

"Please advise how I can purchase NutraSweet." —Doris N. Rooney, Boca Raton, Florida

You can't buy the gumballs but we'll send you some free. Actually, you can't buy NutraSweet, either. At least not the way you're used to buying things. NutraSweet is only an ingredient. There's only one way to buy it, and that's in foods and beverages that have been sweetened with it.

"I am definitely looking forward to seeing more use of NutraSweet in the future." —Susan Lewy, Portsmouth, Ohio

Just look for the word "NutraSweet" on labels when you shop. More and more products with NutraSweet are showing up on supermarket shelves every month. And still more are on their way.

"...the best thing since the invention of food." —Karen McLean, Baytown, Texas

But enough reading. It's time you got to the free gumballs and some serious tasting.

"I love NutraSweet." —B. Elleby, Aurora, Illinois

A free taste of gum and discounts on other products sweetened with NutraSweet.

Yes, I'm very interested in NutraSweet. Please send a sample of five gumballs along with discount coupons for other products sweetened with NutraSweet to:

Name
Street Address
City_____ State_____ Zip_____

Send to Searle Food Resources, Inc., P.O. Box 1174, Glenview, IL 60025. (Allow six weeks for delivery.) Gumballs available while supplies last. Void where prohibited. N-4

NUTRASWEET™

FIG. 6.1 Package featured in "What's better than reading . . . ," *Newsweek*, January 9, 1984, 60–61. Also printed in *McCall's*, July 1984, 2–3.

NutraSweet in her mailbox in Baytown, Texas, it was simply "the best thing since the invention of *food*."[11]

The NutraSweet gumball approach was so successful that it would become a case study used in advertising and marketing manuals. It was the brainchild of a highly skilled executive, political, and marketing team.[12] "We think that the intersection of marketing and technology holds very few companies that are good at both. That's where NutraSweet is positioned," explained Bob Shapiro in the late 1980s.[13] With Rumsfeld at the helm, Searle tightened its research and development expenditures, cutting business by 20 percent in order to focus on profitable ventures. Once leaner, Searle was able to invest significant resources in aspartame, patented as NutraSweet. The primary concern was convincing the FDA that it was safe for human consumption.

Between the late 1960s and the late 1970s, Searle conducted, wrote up, and delivered to the FDA dozens of studies into the effects of ingesting NutraSweet's component chemicals, particularly phenylalanine, which can be dangerous in some forms, and methanol. All of the studies found aspartame safe for human consumption when ingested in amounts typical for even heavy users. It was Rumsfeld who navigated the tricky terrain of FDA counterstudies, independent review panels, and political opinion. As the FDA worked on its own with independent experts to explore fifteen of the dozens of Searle-submitted studies, Rumsfeld worked the political machines. In 1981, after more than a dozen FDA studies had found aspartame safe in such amounts, the organization's public board of inquiry continued to have questions about the long-term effects of ingestion and the conditions of Searle's original experiments. President Ronald Reagan's appointment of Arthur Hayes in 1981 to the post of FDA commissioner effectively ended the inquiry. In 1983, one of his first major acts was to declare aspartame "one of the most thoroughly tested" food additives and to announce that it would be released in the form of tabletop mixtures and ingredients in foods.[14] In 1984, the gumballs heralded its arrival in packaged foods and drinks; in 1985, Equal powder brought Nutra-Sweet to the table in ubiquitous blue packets. It was Rumsfeld who, in his capacity as advisor to the newly elected Ronald Reagan on the appointment of the FDA commissioner, had helped put Hayes at the helm.

The introduction of NutraSweet marks a fundamental turning point in the history of artificial sweetener. From peach canners to pharmaceutical representatives and women's page writers, diverse individuals over generations have used creativity and narrative talent to expand demand for these accidentally discovered chemicals infused into manufactured products no one needed in 1900. At the same time, consumers have experimented with them at home, fashioned for them containers and travel cases, and purchased new foods containing them to be eaten at new times and in new contexts. Much of this history is about exchange. Producers push for consumption, but consumers alter meanings, do things in unanticipated ways, resist what they ought to desire, and desire what they ought to resist. But this story shifts with NutraSweet. The team that manufactured and marketed NutraSweet created such an intensely effective message around the product, ensured that it would appear so ubiquitously in the U.S. food supply in a matter of years, and pushed through the regulatory apparatus in such a way that the balance between producer and consumer was altered in its favor.

According to business writer Joseph McCann, from the vantage point of the late 1980s, the NutraSweet team had been comprised of "some of the most unusually creative and aggressive managers for any firm I have witnessed." Searle's alliance of tenacious innovators and skilled political networkers extended through the division. They were young, male, and unorthodox. What was particularly unusual about these NutraSweet producers was that they occupied a sort of third space between the pharmaceutical and the food industries. They were lawyers, admen, and salesmen. They did not have backgrounds in chemistry that would enable them to understand what aspartame was or what it did, on its own or when added to food. Nor did they come from agricultural roots or possess direct experiences with food manufacturing and sales. According to McCann, this was precisely the training Searle wanted in its NutraSweet staff. Searle looked for aggressive, creative, driven employees who would see opportunities where others saw limits. This meant looking outside the food and drug industries for talent.

Searle's NutraSweet staff bonded quickly and closely with the young account executives at Olgivy and Mather. They were given the invitation to think big, to imagine that their ideas could make millions, and to work nonstop on a push to get a unified NutraSweet message directly into the hands of consumers after the FDA's sudden approval in 1981. Everyone was aware that the clock was ticking on their ten-year exclusive patent in the United States. The internal research and development staff at Searle worked so closely with the Olgivy advertising staff that the latter could frequently be found "camped out in the NutraSweet offices."[15]

The result of hiring an unorthodox staff and creating a climate in which a risk-oriented culture could thrive was the NutraSweet marketing campaign. It demanded no less than a transformation of artificial sweetener's reputation. NutraSweet's team knew they had the right product at the right moment. Joseph McCann tells the story of Donald Rumsfeld presenting President Bob Shapiro with a stuffed toy monkey shortly after the early profits from NutraSweet began coming in. The gift, as he explained it, was to symbolize the fact that "even a monkey could sell this stuff."[16] The story suggests the hubris at the heart of the effort but belies the team's intense efforts not only to overcome regulatory hurdles and mass market a superior product but, more importantly, to turn consumers into fierce product advocates.

"Where can you buy it? You can't. Not by itself anyway. NutraSweet is only an ingredient. The only way to buy NutraSweet is in the dozens of foods and beverages sweetened with it," read an ad in *Newsweek* in June 1984.[17] The text may hardly seem revolutionary from our twenty-first-century vantage point. We live in a culture of direct-to-consumer advertising where television commercials diagnose our ailments, show us pharmaceutical cures, and tell us to "ask our doctors about" them. But in 1984 and 1985, directing consumers to search for an ingredient—a chemical ingredient no less—was a dramatic change from previous food marketing strategies and accepted logics within the artificial-sweetener industries. In the swirl of NutraSweet, Searle found a way to signal its value and convince consumers to push for its inclusion in foods and beverages. But to do that, the swirl first had to come to mean something very different from "saccharin sweet."

The first NutraSweet product most consumers tasted was not for sale. The five gumballs that came in the mail were free. Advertisements in newspapers and magazines followed, all with small forms one could cut out, fill out, and send in. Doing so would bring more free gumballs in the mail. According to media critic Philip Lawler, NutraSweet's marketing gurus consciously unleashed an early "blitzkrieg of advertisements" to create customer brand loyalty.[18] The technique, known as "supplier initiated ingredient branding," relied on consumer education as a means to increase product consumption.[19] It was part of a two-pronged approach by Searle: Get a handful of food and beverage companies to use the ingredient so that it is on the shelves, but insist that they clearly label the food as containing "100% NutraSweet." Simultaneously push the ingredient directly to consumers, who would then look for that label and increase the profits of those first early users who had adopted NutraSweet, while applying indirect pressure on other food and beverage manufacturers to give up saccharin, which was cheaper. By enlisting consumers as the ground troops in its battle to win over large food corporations, Searle created a group of potential buyers ready to demand their right to aspartame-sweetened foods. Searle, through its Olgivy marketing strategy, went beyond campaigns for saccharin and cyclamates that had settled for convincing consumers that these products were safe, effective, and appealing. By combining an active education campaign with a symbol that enabled people to connect what they knew to products on the shelves, Searle created knowledgeable consumers who could build its market.

"Just look for this red and white symbol," read the bold text underneath the headline "Why some things taste better than others," in a two-page NutraSweet advertisement from *Good Housekeeping* in October 1984.[20] A quick glance at the ad revealed not a product or a person but a swirl. The red-and-white NutraSweet symbol was ubiquitous in all of the company's early marketing campaigns and branding efforts. Nutra-

FIG. 6.2 NutraSweet brand sweetener label, *Newsweek*, October 1984, 60.

Sweet positioned its logo to do three things, and each of them built upon the previous history of consumers' use of artificial sweeteners (see fig. 6.2). First, it enabled consumers to identify the product on the shelves quickly, as had the Sucaryl/Diet Delight campaigns of the 1950s and 1960s. Second, it visually communicated a wedding of opposites into one whole, enabling science and nature to commingle. Third, it was combined in advertising copy with women's fingers choosing the product by grabbing the symbol—effectively rebranding the appealing notion of two-finger consumer control that cyclamates had originally used.

According to company president Bob Shapiro, the primary goal of the NutraSweet swirl campaign and the text that accompanied it was "simplifying the informational task for consumers."[21] Advertisements took great pains to explain exactly what NutraSweet was through its "Good Stuff" campaign that placed a special emphasis on its "naturalness." They also made sure consumers knew how to convert this information into choice by searching for that red-and-white symbol. Print and television advertisements spent a great deal of space and time breaking down the facts of NutraSweet into digestible parts. For example, the "twelve interesting tidbits" campaign that appeared in *Newsweek* in November 1985 explained that NutraSweet was discovered in 1965 (tidbit #1); it's in everything you eat because it's a protein, just like a "peach or tomato" (also tidbit #1); no food ingredient "has ever had to withstand such scrutiny," and so therefore it's safe (#4); it's in over 40 countries (#7); it's metabolized, and so therefore it's nutritive and blessed by the American Medical Association (#6).[22] The campaign aimed to undo unappealing ideas about saccharin, replacing them with an origin story in which cartoon-rendered tomatoes lend their protein and banana cream pie releases its calories, after white-coated (and white-skinned) scientists produce the idea of Nutra-Sweet. It is a vision of pleasurable foods stripped of their bad calories, as nature always intended. As Shapiro explained in the *Wall Street Journal* in 1987, "We're inherently saying you can have pleasure without paying the price."[23]

NATURE AND CHOICE IN THE NUTRASWEET CAMPAIGN

The NutraSweet Company's main innovation was not the invention of aspartame or the co-branding with major food companies like Coke and Jell-O pudding, as important as those things were. Instead, it was the re-casting of artificial sweetener as not a man-made invention designed to simulate the taste of a natural commodity but, rather, a natural commodity with one offending attribute removed.

"Banana plants don't make NutraSweet; neither do cows, but they might as well. If you've had bananas and milk, you've eaten what's in NutraSweet." Television viewers in 1985 and 1987 received thirty-second NutraSweet primers in the form of a new campaign tying NutraSweet to nature. A direct response to swirling concerns among consumer groups and medical professionals about the product's safety, the campaign was the result of the company's shift away from "good taste" and to the core message that NutraSweet was just like nature, only better. Rather than explain that roughly 1 in 10,000 people did have phenylalanine reactions and therefore could not safely consume aspartame, the company situated phenylalanine within an array of safe, natural foods. "Bananas, milk and NutraSweet all contain phenylalanine, one of twenty-one amino acids that form the 'building blocks' of protein," the commercial continued. "Nature doesn't make NutraSweet. But NutraSweet could not be made without it."[24] Similar descriptions of NutraSweet as formed from pro-teins and "just like fruit" also ran in print media at the same time.

Because aspartame was descended from a line of chemical sweeten-ers that were understood by the majority of Americans to be substitutes of questionable safety, the NutraSweet Company could not increase its market share substantially without considering these concerns. Saccha-rin had many defenders in 1977, but the majority of them, as letters reveal, understood saccharin to be a chemical that, in certain conditions, might not be safe. They argued not that saccharin was risk free but that the risk, all things considered, was worth taking. This was not an adequate message for the ambitions of NutraSweet's product team. They wanted this market share, but they also wanted an additional group: the consumers who were not yet consuming diet products or who would consume more of particular food and beverage products if they could do so without increasing calories. This was a direct competition for consumers of sugar and corn syrup, and that audience could not be reached unless the sweetener were closely tied to nature. Several years into NutraSweet promotions, this theme remained commonplace. One commercial from 1986, for example, for a children's vitamin sweetened with NutraSweet, featured a child asking his mother, "Why don't they put NutraSweet in broccoli?"[25]

Most consumers were not moved to consider NutraSweet just like cow's milk and bananas or better than broccoli, in spite of the innovative marketing. More likely, this approach tempered lingering unease with artificial sweetener, generally, and aspartame's component parts of methyl ester and phenylalanine, specifically. It also capitalized on an increasingly complicated food landscape within which consumers typically found twenty to thirty ingredients listed on a box of crackers. It was a moment in which popular nutritional information had emphasized the importance of individual ingredients for eating healthy (more fiber, less fat, lower cholesterol, more omega-3) at the same time that industrial food production was requiring an increasing number of flavor enhancers, preservatives, and binding agents to keep packaged products edible across vast distances of time and space. The messages produced a challenging imperative: one needed to know one's food by knowing ingredients that were largely unknown. Within this climate, NutraSweet's assurance that its chemical composition was "just like milk," if not entirely satisfying, may have been more than people knew about most food ingredients. And given the obvious benefits of its inclusion (as opposed to, say, hydrolyzed yeast extract), consumers had reason to settle for less than perfect clarity.

If television campaigns brought NutraSweet close to nature, simultaneous antisaccharin print campaigns undertaken by the NutraSweet team helped make sure consumers would associate saccharin with all that was negative about artificial sweetener. In 1984, Pepsi and Coke embarked on their "soda war" to convince consumers which diet product was superior. Comfortable with its market share, Diet Coke had resisted shifting from saccharin to the more expensive NutraSweet until August 1984, when it

FIG. 6.3 "Check the Facts," *Ladies' Home Journal*, February 1985, 173.

introduced a blend with part NutraSweet and part saccharin. Diet Pepsi's marketing team saw an opportunity to distinguish its product by making the switch to 100 percent NutraSweet first, in November, and publicizing its competitor's continued reliance on the old-model sweetener. The result was a multi-month battle that came to a head in December 1984 in the popular press. "This product contains saccharin," said Diet Pepsi of Diet Coke in Pepsi's "Check the Facts" campaign that ran in major dailies (see fig. 6.3). Readers could squint and see the familiar warning on the Diet Coke can: "This product contains saccharin which has been determined to cause cancer in laboratory animals." By Christmas, Diet Coke had shifted to NutraSweet and offered a new response, delivered in "An Open Letter to Santa Claus," a full-page ad that ran on Christmas Eve. "Dear Santa, please be sure that the people at Pepsi-Cola headquarters each get a bottle of diet Coke with 100% NutraSweet so they can see how great it tastes and why it is the fastest growing soft drink in the world."[26]

As the battle between Coke and Pepsi continued, NutraSweet's success was enhanced by its emphasizing of saccharin's questionable reputation. These advertisements ultimately helped instruct consumers to distinguish between saccharin and NutraSweet: the former was unsafe and closely associated with the word "cancer"; the latter was a product so pleasant one would want to write to Santa about it. The approach enabled consumers so inclined to continue to hold on to their unease about artificial sweetener. This was, after all, a commodity that only a few years earlier had faced a ban at the request of the federal government. Yet by amplifying that risk and associating it with saccharin, NutraSweet was able to make the old technology the dangerous technology. Simply by not being saccharin, NutraSweet was good. For consumers tired of two decades of chemical controversy, a pleasant story about proteins may have been a welcome respite.

At the same time that NutraSweet made artificial sweetener seem natural, it also made Americans' voracious appetites for sweets seem healthy. Advertisements frequently portrayed NutraSweet-sweetened products as items that felt good and were good for you. This was particularly true in marketing aimed at women. "I believe in Crystal Light 'cause I believe in me!" was the most famous of the many NutraSweet product promotions that spoke directly to American women. One campaign from *Good Housekeeping* in 1985 that echoed throughout the decade featured a leotard-clad white woman (in this case Linda Evans from the TV show *Dallas*) featured in a close-up against a backdrop of Crystal Light (fig. 6.4). The copy described the Caribbean Cooler, Luscious Grape, and Citrus Blend drink mixes, all with "only 4 calories a glass," thanks to NutraSweet. It was, as Evans explained, how "I enjoy looking and feeling my best."[27] Crystal Light was one of the first fully NutraSweet-created products; unlike Diet Coke and Diet Pepsi or low-calorie puddings and coffee mixes, it was originally formulated with aspartame. And it was made to be consumed in bulk. With only four calories per serving, the powder came in packets that made no less than a gallon at a time. By wedding its lemonade, iced teas, and fruitlike drinks to svelte women in leotards (some ads offered coupons for the leotard as well as the drink

FIG. 6.4 "'Now!
I've got 3 *new* ways to
enjoy Crystal Light,'"
Good Housekeeping,
May 1985, 64.

mix), Crystal Light visually linked consumption of sweet beverages to
thin bodies. The same approach was used in products that were chocolate substitutes, such as Famous Amos–NutraSweet chocolate soda and
the more popular Suisse Mocha instant coffee beverages, pitched in the
1985 "Lucky Me" campaign as "rich, creamy, delicious," filled with "choc-
olaty goodness," and perfectly suited to "celebrate the moments of your
life."[28]

By late 1985, this message of "indulgent thinness" was ubiquitous in
the "Just for the Taste of It!" Diet Coke campaign. Brightly colored cans
were emblazoned with the "less than 1 calorie" and "100% NutraSweet"

signs and were commonly held by thin women in pleasurable surroundings. Advertisements increasingly featured children, especially young girls, consuming NutraSweet in scenes sanctioned by nearby adults. "It's rich, it's creamy, it's here," read the text under a photo of Bill Cosby holding a bowl of sugar-free Jell-O. In 1985 he was well known as America's most famous dad from *The Cosby Show*. Below, a white mother and daughter smile as they take synchronized bites of Jell-O chocolate pudding. NutraSweet promotions sought to appeal to American women and their daughters simultaneously with scenes of guiltless food pleasure.[29]

By 1985, the production, distribution, and sale of NutraSweet had become a "billion-dollar business."[30] In 1988, NutraSweet sales reached $736 million worldwide. By 1989, that number climbed to $869 million. Diet Coke Super Bowl commercials were topics of media commentary. In 1988 and 1989, 200 million Americans opened their mailboxes to find coupons for free cans.[31] By 1990, three-quarters of the U.S. population had tried NutraSweet in one form or another. In that same year, NutraSweet was approved for distribution in seventy-nine countries and was used in more than 2,000 products. General Foods, Coca-Cola, and PepsiCo had created massive new markets in low-calorie foods and beverages. Kool-Aid alone saw its sales increase by 40 percent within three years of switching to NutraSweet. According to Joseph McCann, NutraSweet generated "over 300 million dollars a year in new sales" for users in the late 1980s and replaced "about a billion pounds of sugar" in American diets.[32]

THE APPEAL OF INDULGENT RESTRAINT IN THE 1980S

NutraSweet's message resonated with consumers because the product was perfectly positioned to deliver on the seemingly impossible paradox that one could consume more and somehow end up weighing less. According to Warren Belasco, "light" food as a category has always had two distinct meanings to consumers and producers. While consumers understood "light" to mean fewer calories and therefore less weight gained or retained as a result of eating, the industry has seen "light" primarily as a means to an end. Light foods enabled the industry to multiply existing food products by two without the added research and development costs for new products and the imperative to create new marketing materials for unknown goods. Regular and light products could be sold to the same family, effectively doubling the market share for companies whose caloric goods might appeal to children, for example, but not to their mothers. One could, in fact, argue that aspartame/NutraSweet was just another growth commodity in a fifty-year-old light market. This is how the artificial-sweetener industry's public relations professionals saw things. "The availability of aspartame to food manufacturers worldwide has been one of the major factors responsible for the growth of the 'light' and 'low-calorie' segments of the food industry," explained Lyn O'Brien Nabors and Robert Gelardi, writing on behalf of the public-relations-focused Calorie Control Council (CCC) in 1986. The emphasis was on continuity. Using this logic, NutraSweet was important because it sold more, not because it sold differently.[33]

Two perspectives challenge this interpretation. In fact, 1983 was very different from the 1950s, when low-calorie products such as diet sodas and diet fruits were first produced. Understanding NutraSweet in the context of the Reagan era's New Day consumer optimism and its predecessor, the regulate-ourselves-or-else spirit of the Carter administration, helps us see why NutraSweet was not simply an expansion of an old thing. It was a dramatically new way of ordering the relationship that mainstream Americans had with excess through the chemical alteration of their food.

The FDA's approval of aspartame for mass consumption under the brand name NutraSweet came exactly ten years after President Nixon had first introduced "project independence." This plan to achieve energy self-sufficiency by 1980 encouraged Americans to reduce their driving speed to fifty miles per hour, reduce the oil used in their homes and businesses by 15 percent, and lower their thermostats by six degrees, all with an eye toward lowering the consumption of petroleum products to strengthen the economy and address the depletion of oil reserves and an increasing reliance on foreign oil.[34] It was a suggestion that Carter tried to turn into a mandate in April 1977 in an address to the nation on "the energy problem." "Ours is the most wasteful nation on Earth," he admonished, warning that if Americans continued to ignore calls for voluntary reductions in consumption, "we will face an economic, social, and political crisis that will threaten our free institutions."[35] Finding that his suggestions were largely going unheeded, Carter was ready two years later to diagnose Americans as suffering from a syndrome of empty consumption and indulgence. In a speech that is largely credited with turning the tide of public opinion against him (especially in the face of the protracted Iran hostage ordeal), he preached a state of the union wherein "too many of us now tend to worship self-indulgence and consumption" rather than industriousness and restraint. From our current vantage point, it is a bittersweet moment: an opportunity to check the very practices that would lead to national deficit, the credit crises and subprime mortgage bailout, and ceaseless military action in the Middle East. For Carter it was a misstep. With the decisive Reagan victory in 1980 on a New Day platform, Americans would instead embrace neoliberal government reforms, aggressive international relations, and admonitions to secure continued economic growth through consumer spending and tax breaks for businesses.

NutraSweet was not Reagan's New Day in a can, but it was close. Anthropologist Arjun Appadurai suggests that the most important information produced by any group of people who run a financial market is not specifically about the commodities for sale in that market. Rather, information is "directed at producing the conditions of consciousness in which buying can occur."[36] Sociologist S. Bryan Austin has taken this idea further, applying it specifically to the diet industry by looking at how that industry has created "semiotic transformations" that should "not be viewed facilely as a natural evolution of lay parlance." Austin refers to the words on cans and boxes: "light" is good, "low-calorie" is desirable, and "zero grams of fat" will create a healthy body.[37] People do not merely decide that they want to buy lower-calorie items over higher-calorie items. Marketers actively commodify a palate of meanings that consumers can choose from in matching their desires to purchasable products. Except for a brief period in the early 1950s, this has been true in the diet industry, where foods have literally come from nowhere and had to build loyal consumer bases.

What Appadurai and Austin help us imagine, if we stretch these concerns to the most macro of levels, is the ways in which the cultural and political climates outside the diet industry also contribute to the conditions in which purchases take place. It is inconceivable that the majority of consumers who reached for Crystal Light because they "believe[d] in me" were unfamiliar with the competing messages of restraint and indulgence created by back-to-back administrations. One might very well support Reagan's new message of unfettered markets and spending resuscitation. But that belief was built on a well-established insecurity about shortages and admonitions to restrain oneself for the good of the nation. Bridging these messages was a complicated task: people do not simply wipe away the past; they build a present that helps explain that past in light of new current priorities. Here NutraSweet could resonate far beyond its specific message of calorie reduction for weight loss. With this chemical, one could experience a reality that otherwise was an impossible contradiction: Carter's restraint paired with Reagan's indulgence, producing the healthy citizen.

The claim might seem far-fetched, but given that one of the key tenets of overcoming "stagflation" was an appeal to individual action and "rational" markets, it makes sense to look to individual commodity purchases as being particularly rife with cultural meaning. In fact, evidence from 1984 suggests that people often saw the pursuit of health through particular food choices as a means of achieving health. According to anthropologist Robert Crawford, who interviewed a number of men and women about their definitions of good health, being healthy in the NutraSweet era was "almost equivalent to pursuing health through adopting the appropriate disciplined activities or controls."[38] People did not make healthful decisions lightly, he found. Instead, for many, the labors over thinking about health were so significant that "the means to health acquire the quality of an end in themselves." Crawford was particularly interested in what he saw as two competing motifs in how individuals thought health could be achieved. In the first, "health as control," people limited caloric intake, got up off the couch and walked rather than watch TV, and avoided drinking too much. In the second, "health as release," people satisfied their urges to indulge in desirable activities because desire in itself was good. He found growing obesity rates and poor food choices created by the way people sought to reconcile these messages. Many believed that health was their responsibility to secure, thanks to a "virtual media and professional blitz for a particular model of health promotion" that emphasized lifestyle change and individual responsibility, where health is a verb, "essentially a do it yourself proposition."[39] At the same time, they could not help but overindulge in calories, given the media messages and packaged food produced within an economy that "normally requires ever greater levels of consumption." In the end, Crawford lamented, "no wonder bulimia emerges as one of our most common eating disorders."[40]

NutraSweet advertisements often promoted the product as a way for consumers to appear more virtuous than they were. Nearly ten years after NutraSweet's introduction, television advertisements continued to capitalize on the product's reported ability to create thin bodies without work. "I pretend that I work out all the time and eat the right things, but I really don't," claimed actress Lauren Hutton in an ad with Raquel

Welch at her side. Together the sex symbols revealed their secret to viewers: "One thing I really do is use Equal."[41] These examples presented even the sexiest American women as in on the new secret of NutraSweet. In spite of well-publicized nutritional knowledge and intense emphasis on exercise in the midst of the aerobics craze, these women were admitting that even though their very livelihoods relied on their thinness, they could not be bothered to eat right and exercise. By "really using Equal" they were able to get away with pretending to work for their bodies. The beauty of thinness, then, was not a physical manifestation of healthy living. It was a sign of being in-the-know, just as was reaching for the blue packet instead of the white.

Hutton and Welch probably did exercise to maintain their weight. And most women who saw these advertisements probably did not fully believe that if they, too, used Equal, they would be thin and glamorous. Yet the advertisements represent the culmination of decades of packing virtue into sweetener campaigns. From early cyclamate cookbooks to Tillie Lewis's twenty-one-day diet through the No-Cal advertisements promising mountains of chocolate soda, the promise of artificial sweetener was that women, usually white women, could eat for pleasure in excess of the number of calories that would normally mean weight gain. With the NutraSweet campaigns, they were now encouraged to keep this secret to themselves. In these ads, aspartame emerges as a shortcut for women in-the-know, one that might even enable them to promote exercise as the best way to achieve thinness without actually participating in it themselves.

While Welch and Hutton were letting their readers in on their little secret, Americans were learning about the nation's obesity problem. Beginning in the mid-1990s, studies would emerge that demonstrated a "steady and dramatic" rise in national weight averages since the 1970s. By the next decade, this would be referred to as an "obesity epidemic." As Eric Oliver has suggested, these increases were never convincingly tied to any documented elevation in health risk for individuals with a higher than average body mass index (BMI).[42] In fact, one can attribute the epidemic more to the way BMI has been calculated than to an actual national weight gain, given that BMI has been adjusted downward several times in recent decades (with corresponding rises in obesity percentages). In spite of questionable data, the popular media seized on prognoses of a "fattening" America, particularly among those who were not white or middle class. In news specials, talk shows, and documentaries, while corporations shouldered some of the blame, individuals who lack self-control were most frequently presented as the real source of the problem.

Were the obesity epidemic merely a problem of weight alone, the unexamined role of artificial sweetener in its production would be less troubling. Yet with the absence of clear medical data explaining the root of the problem with excess weight, moral judgments about fat people frequently fill the void. "Right or wrong," write the authors of *Slim Down Sister*, the 2001 diet guidebook aimed at African American women, "thin and average weight people, men and women alike, view overweight people as having no self-control, no willpower."[43] It is curious that ads for artificial sweetener have always urged their target audience—usually white women—to admit that they have no control and no willpower. One would assume, in such a climate, that the Nutra-Sweet generation would have had a great degree of empathy for those who struggled with weight. Arguably, however, because NutraSweet heightened that out-of-control potential in eaters' bodies only to channel it into the "thinning" consumption of sweetener, it gave users the ability to judge others who had so clearly failed at the task. Moreover, the NutraSweet message may have made the figure of the large body all the more alarming, given the fact that sweetener advertisements had heightened the risk of just such a "problem" for decades in order to sell more product as the solution (recall Jean Nidetch urging weight watchers to put their fattest photo up on the fridge as a deterrent). By constantly pushing eaters to embrace their desire for more food, within a culture that had for thirty years urged consumers to consume more of everything, artificial sweeteners may have helped create the climate of fat fear that transforms someone else's large body into a threat. By creating and disparaging the specter of the out-of-control heavy eater, "diet" Americans may in fact confirm the virtues of their own, hidden appetites.

PUTTING THE "NUTRA" IN NUTRASWEET

In 1906, saccharin was nearly banned because of the work of food reformers—educators, home economists, politicians, and early nutritionists—who joined together to fight what they saw as a dangerous infiltration of the nation's food supply by profiteers. In the 1960s and 1970s, similar coalitions questioned the safety of cyclamates and saccharin. In the 1980s, however, there was no professional counterbalance to NutraSweet's claims. A survey of contemporary nutrition textbooks suggests that even for consumers who questioned NutraSweet's definition of aspartame as natural and healthy, going to "experts" would, in fact, reinforce the notion that aspartame was a better choice than sugar.

Hutton and Welch's strategies for good health were not very different from the official nutritional advice provided the nation in 1991. *Improving America's Diet and Health: From Recommendations to Action*, a report authored by the government-commissioned Committee on Dietary Guidelines and Implementation, suggested to medical professionals, nutritional experts, and food producers across the nation that there were three "general tactics" for "increasing the prevalence of healthful eating patterns." Tellingly, the first two were "altering food supply by subtraction," such as reducing the fat in meat and cheese, and "altering food by addition," such as fortifying breads. It was possible, the report revealed, that people might eat less processed food or less food altogether. But these were not deemed as desirable as technological mechanisms for changing the food itself in response to what were apparently natural consumer appetites for excess. The final section of the report, "Suggestions for Promising Future Research," included as the third of six recommendations a call to "continue research to develop new food products and modify both the production and processing of existing products to help consumers more easily meet dietary recommendations."[44]

The few nutritionists who did address aspartame directly suggested to readers that there was little reason for concern. Looking across the 1970s and 1980s, there is only a small spike in attention to artificial sweeteners with Searle's market entry. *Understanding Nutrition*, for example, had a section in its 1981 edition titled "Sugar: Is It Bad for You?" that explored the varying perspectives on sucrose's effect on health. By 1984, an updated edition of the same textbook had changed this section to "Sugar Stands Accused." Both editions had the same sentence informing people that "there is no reason to believe that the moderate consumption of sugar is in any way dangerous to the normal, healthy human being." In the 1984 edition, however, two new paragraphs were added to address artificial sweetener directly. NutraSweet/aspartame, unlike saccharin and cyclamates, the authors explained, "seems remarkably free of attendant risk . . . so far." The editorial change is a good indication of the overall approach among nutritionists who did discuss it: cautious acceptance of what seemed to be a better artificial sweetener, but a continued assertion that for most people consuming reasonable amounts of sugar was just fine.[45]

Most nutritionists in the years of NutraSweet's tremendous U.S. market expansion paid little attention to artificial sweeteners. They focused instead on new recommendations for exercise and more high-profile concerns like cholesterol and the intake of saturated fat. The result was a vacuum of reliable information for consumers who might seek to evaluate NutraSweet's claims. In spite of the rapid increase in the number of consumers using diet products and the lengthy history of the use of artificial sweetener in the United States, most nutritionists gave little space to sweeteners in their guidebooks for the lay reader. Those that did rarely went beyond suggesting that sweeteners be used "in moderation." Very few seem to have arrived at the conclusion of one group of food chemists who, in 1983, argued that the "growing demand by consumers" for low-calorie foods was fueled primarily by a frequent misperception that "the simplest way to reduce caloric intake is . . . a drive against the consumption of carbohydrate, in particular sugar." This made little sense from a nutritional standpoint, they concluded. It would be "more reasonable to urge consumers to reduce their level of intake of normal foods, rather than to require food manufacturers to create the illusion of normality."[46]

Nutrition professionals were in some ways marginalized in the mid-1980s. The ingredient-focused, neoliberal approach to public health had produced a generation of educated consumers who relied on their own understandings of good health rather than looking to professionals as they had generations before. Aerobics instructors and coed gyms were creating a following around celebrities such as Richard Simmons and Jane Fonda, who had their own diet plans, exercise videos, and clothing lines. Diets like the Beverly Hills Plan, which began with ten days of fruit only, had tens of thousands of adherents. Food corporations were developing an array of fortified products and substitutes, typically with their own on-staff advisors. Within this climate, nutritionists appear to have been hesitant to encourage or dissuade prospective aspartame users.

Nutritionists' silence on the possible problems with pursuing health through the ample consumption of aspartame likely made it easier for Searle to freely make its claims for the "Good Stuff." At the same time, the field did little to combat the increasingly strident screeds against sugar. According to a 1979 New York Times article, "Candy consumption in this country has been dwindling for years. As a health hazard, nutritionists rank sugar-laden candy somewhere between unfiltered cigarettes and cobra venom."[47] The antisugar campaign has a complex history that stretches back well into the nineteenth century. There have long been nutrition experts and morality monitors worried that the widespread availability of sweets encourages unhealthful eating. Others have been concerned about how sugar consumption supports oppressive political regimes in the countries where it is produced. The sugar industry was one of the major forces that built the African slave trade and sustained it well into the nineteenth century. At the same time, as historian Wendy Woloson and anthropologist Sidney Mintz have argued, sugar has been considered a source of easy, inexpensive calories and therefore useful to both working-class families and a capitalist economy. In the 1970s, nutritionists began to pull away from this middle ground, suggesting that sugar consumption had reached an unhealthy level in the United States and the United Kingdom. A push also came from popular writing that rendered sugar a deadly substance.

In 1988, a nutrition textbook designed to be a sourcebook for quick reference for laypeople and physicians alike listed sugar as contributing to what it termed a "global outbreak of the 'diseases of civilization.'" Along with animal fat, salt, and cholesterol, sugar was contributing to high rates of heart disease, obesity, and diabetes.[48] It is unclear just what contributed to these fears about sugar. The professionalization of the artificial-sweetener industry and its attendant claims, the rise in packaged products and "hidden sugars," and the campaign on the part of the American Dental Association to encourage children to chew sugarless gum coalesced in the 1970s. The focus on ingredients rather than eating practices also encouraged pointing to sugar as a societal problem. It is also likely that Americans themselves began to distrust sugar and that consumers brought this concern to physicians and food manufacturers. If that indeed was the case, John Yudkin was partly responsible.

Yudkin's *Sweet and Dangerous*, published in 1972 in the United States and Britain, probed the steamy underbelly of the sugar industry for a popular audience. The cover, a combination of a stoplight flashing red and a sugar container with its spilled contents threatening to bury the stoplight (and looking quite a bit like cocaine), announced sugar as a "Quiet Killer" that can cause "heart disease, diabetes, ulcers, and other often-fatal diseases." In bold text, the book declared that "if only a fraction of what is already known about the effects of sugar were to be revealed in relation to any other material used as a food additive, that material would promptly be banned."[49]

Yudkin's research was roundly dismissed as flawed by medical experts.

Nevertheless, his book was a best seller, and his claim that sugar was an addictive product falsely promoted as safe by a vast network of corrupt scientists and producers reached tens of thousands of readers. According to Yudkin, Americans were consuming 102 pounds of pure health risk a year; the British, 18 more. His conclusions for consumers were made quite clear in a chapter titled "Why Sugar Should Be Banned." Here, after outlining the risks to health, he concluded, "There is no doubt whatever that sugar can do a very great deal of harm."[50]

Sweet and Dangerous is a good example of how artificial-sweetener promotion and sugar disparagement were intertwined in the 1970s. Whereas Yudkin points to the sugar industry as responsible for false health promotions, his own promotions are clearly linked to the food and pharmaceutical industries. It is to these companies that he owes the very support that made his university research program possible. His acknowledgments thank food and pharmaceutical companies for "over twenty-five years" of "constant and generous support in the building up and maintenance of the department of nutrition" at London University. In the book, this section is separate from his assessment of the healthfulness of various sweeteners, where he reveals his preference for the "low-calorie soft drinks" over those that contain sugar, a decision driven by the fact that he did "not at all accept that you run any risk from taking the saccharine that they contain."[51] Given that his laboratory equipment and research program were supported by the very industries that produced saccharin, this conclusion may not have been entirely objective.

By the mid- to late 1980s, many nutritionists were ready to weigh in on what they perceived as misinformation about "dangerous" sugar. In 1985, two years into the NutraSweet campaign, the *Atlantic Monthly* ran a story by Ellen Ruppel Shell titled "Fear of Sugar: Has It Gotten out of Hand?" Interest in the subject is suggested by the *San Francisco Chronicle*'s decision to reprint the article in its entirety. Based on a survey of leading nutrition experts and public health professionals, the author found "no clear evidence in the available information on sucrose that demonstrates a hazard to the public when used at levels that are now current and in the manner now practiced." This was particularly true, she noted, regarding reports about sugar consumption creating hyperactive children. In spite of the public's concerns, the study found, there was in fact "no conclusive evidence to support a cause and effect relationship between sugar intake and behavioral disturbances."[52]

Between 1988 and 1994, a number of studies emerged from nutrition and medical experts dismissing the most common health ailments attributed to sugar by the American public. In 1987, the American Council on Science and Health included a special section in their *Diet and Behavior* guide directly addressing what they termed a recent "great deal of public attention [that] has focused on the possibility that sugar might cause hyperactivity." Their own studies found that "very few" children had responded in this way to sugar. Far more common was the opposite reaction whereby children actually became less active after eating sugar.[53] The *New England Journal of Medicine* concurred in 1994 with a study involving fifty children given both sucrose and aspartame. Neither substance, they concluded, "affects children's behavior or cognitive function."[54]

Neither did sugar really cause cavities, the experts proclaimed. The addition of fluoride into the U.S. drinking water supply in the 1970s, combined with the rise in fluoride-enriched toothpaste, had actually led to a decrease in cavities in spite of the rise in per-capita sugar consumption during the decade. In spite of the heavy promotion of aspartame-sweetened gum as "sugar-free" and "recommended by dentists," many experts continued to see the real culprits in tooth decay as chewy "natural" foods, including granola bars and raisins.[55]

It was probably too little too late. Sugar had been vilified in countless articles on the benefits of low-calorie diets for women and low-sugar intake for children. Popular weight-loss gurus touted the benefits of a low-sugar diet. Writers such as Yudkin found audiences in two countries eager to hear that by cutting sugar they could feel better and live longer. Such ideas combined with advertisements from NutraSweet made a compelling national case that health was best achieved by switching to a chemical sweetener. Evidence suggests that by the 1980s, most American women, who were the primary food purchasers for households, made decisions about health and food based on what was presented in women's magazines. In 1988, the authors of *Essentials of Clinical Nutrition* lamented the fact that so often this reliance was ill advised. "Much of what is published is unreliable," they concluded, citing a study of the coverage of health and nutrition in most popular women's magazines. The survey of nineteen popular publications found most were inconsistent, at best, and unreliable, at worst. Nutrition experts who sought to combat a misinformed public or present a more complex account of "healthy eating" than what appeared in *Cosmo*, *Vogue*, and the *Ladies' Home Journal* had an uphill battle. "It is legal to publish material that has been proved false," they reminded their audience of nutrition educators. When it came to dealing with the American female public, it was good to keep in mind what they were reading. "A great deal of published nutrition information is simply wrong."[56] And this did not include the ads. By 1989, *Weight Watchers Magazine* provided a statistic that reveals how valued a source of nutritional advice popular magazines had become. In what we may grant is a slightly inflated statistic (owing to the fact that it appeared in an ad designed to attract advertisers to the monthly), the magazine claimed that more than 60 percent of its readers were not only being informed about healthy food products by reading but regularly "taking action on material appearing in the magazine."[57]

By the late 1980s, some nutritionists were ready to raise a red flag. Joan Gussow, professor of nutrition at Teachers' College in New York, worried that the food industry, through "synthetics," was encouraging consumers to sever "our contact with nature and that's dangerous." Michael Jacobson, director of the Washington, D.C., watchdog group Center for Science in the Public Interest, raised specific concerns about the ultimate impact of the preference for highly sweet, calorie-empty NutraSweet. "The tongue can be fooled but the body still wants its calories," he commented. As experts quietly debated the real dangers of sugar and the possible risks of NutraSweet, hundreds of thousands of Americans were consuming gallons of it each week.[58]

NUTRASWEET SYNDROME AND CONSUMER REVOLT

For the vast majority of users, aspartame was and is an occasional product: a packet or two in a cup of coffee or a Diet Coke instead of a soda sweetened with sugar or high-fructose corn syrup once or twice a day. A minority, however, have consumed much more. For many of them, the NutraSweet story has a darker side: "NutraSweet syndrome." Thousands of American consumers believe they have acquired an illness resulting from consuming too much aspartame. Instead of finding choice and pleasure, these consumers find addiction and injury. Their stories reveal that we have not, in fact, jettisoned the first fears that motivated antisweetener advocates in the early twentieth century. Claims of dangerous chemicals and manipulative businesses abound on websites, pamphlets, and published books generated and consumed by members of this self-educated and self-identified tribe. They describe an underbelly of the

NutraSweet success story and point to fissures in the promises that we can, in fact, have that free lunch.

In early 2000, filmmaker Cori Brackett took to the road. A self-described former heavy user of aspartame, Brackett had started experiencing headaches, dizziness, and blurred vision first in the 1990s. After numerous visits to physicians and specialists, she began to isolate items in her diet. Only after eliminating foods and drinks sweetened with Nutra-Sweet/aspartame did the symptoms subside. As a result, Brackett was driven to ask, Why? Was aspartame toxic for people? Why had no one told her that this "safe" ingredient could be the cause of her suffering? What did people know about the real effects of the substance? If it was dangerous, how had it gotten on the market in the first place and stayed there so successfully for more than twenty years?

Sweet Misery documents Brackett's travels across the country, providing the backdrop for interviews with former aspartame consumers, internists, FDA employees, citizen advocates, and lawyers. Spliced together into the film, they make a compelling case for the dangers of aspartame and the corruption that enabled it to appear in the American food supply. Brackett highlights stories of permanent vision loss, grand mal seizures, blinding headaches, and chronic fatigue, all of which, according to consumers and physicians, stemmed from aspartame ingestion. In *Sweet Misery*'s story, NutraSweet succeeded because of FDA corruption, encouraged by the Reagan administration, that enabled Searle to bring the product to market with insufficient testing and protected the product in spite of hundreds of complaints directly from consumers citing dramatic, unpleasant reactions to the substance. Perfectly normal people—lawyers, salesmen, and emergency medical technicians (who all happen to be white)—are presented as innocent victims. They did nothing more risky than shop at the supermarket and consume puddings, iced teas, sweetened coffee, and soft drinks. They made what they thought were healthy choices by using products with fewer calories and no sugar. Many, in fact, were attempting to lose weight by drinking and eating aspartame.

Brackett's movie is the most in-depth account of these cases, which can also be found on websites, in newsletters, and in a number of books published between the mid-1980s and the early 2000s. These include H. J. Roberts's *Aspartame (NutraSweet): Is It Safe?* (1990); Russell Blaylock's *Excitotoxins: The Taste That Kills* (1994); Janet Starr Hull's *Sweet Poison: How the World's Most Popular Artificial Sweetener Is Killing Us* (1999); and Joseph Mercola and Kendra Degen Pearsall's *Sweet Deception: Why Splenda, Nutra-*

Sweet, and the FDA *May Be Hazardous to Your Health* (2006). Taken together, the books illuminate themes similar to those in Brackett's film: the FDA did not adequately test aspartame before approving it for Searle—a decision motivated by the friendliness between the commissioner and Donald Rumsfeld more than by a judgment about good science; there have been hundreds of documented cases of headaches, blindness, and vertigo as a result of aspartame use, and these have been covered up by the FDA and largely ignored by the medical establishment; crusaders for truth and justice are out there trying to make this information known and prevent others from suffering because of a "deceptive" industry and its "poisonous" product.

The antiaspartame crusaders fall into two camps: the physicians who see suffering and diagnose it against the grain of their profession and the consumers who struggle to ameliorate their own suffering. They all share a self-proclaimed expertise, one that frequently emerges only after either directly experiencing the physical effects of aspartame or witnessing those effects in a number of individuals. And both consumers and physicians find authority in their diagnoses. Physicians such as Joseph Mercola (author of *Sweet Deception*), H. J. Roberts (*Aspartame*), and Russell Blaylock (*Excitotoxins*) do not write merely to describe what they see happening with patient sensitivity to aspartame. They also write to explain their own understanding of the connection between aspartame and the physical symptoms. Roberts describes himself as having a busy internist practice, content and not looking for controversy. Only after sixteen-year-old Tammy has a seizure in his office does he realize that aspartame is dangerous and that he must speak out. And only after the medical establishment refuses to believe what they call anecdotal evidence but what Roberts considers firsthand patient observation does he decide to take his message directly to the public with his book.[59] Russell Blaylock was a neurosurgeon whose "excitotoxin" theory—that MSG and Nutra-Sweet contained chemicals that cause neurodegenerative brain diseases such as Parkinson's, Huntington's, and Alzheimer's—made him suspect among medical professionals. Mercola's training as an osteopathic physician also sets him outside the realm of regular medicine.

Looking closely at consumer advocates in "aspartame illness" narratives, power, enfranchisement, and knowledge emerge as key drivers of their passions. Roberts saw ill patients become well after they stopped drinking and eating aspartame-sweetened products. Blaylock saw cases of early-onset Parkinson's disease improve after MSG and aspartame were removed from diets. Mercola confirmed that "Peter's" vision turned up-side down as a result of consuming two aspartame-sweetened sodas a day for two weeks, and that it returned to normal after he stopped.[60] Yet were these the only stories being told, these would be short books. In fact, each one is well over 200 pages. What each of these authors is try-ing to do is present an alternative vision of health: to cite a new theory of neurodisease, to return to respect for the "eyes on" diagnosis, and to encourage people to adopt a more holistic approach. It is a vision that prioritizes the authors' unique knowledge. Thus the evidence on which Brackett, the filmmaker, looked to make sense of her suffering is not neu-tral. It provides a platform for experts who are disenfranchised from the "party line," as Roberts put it, to have an audience.[61]

Mary Nash Stoddard is one of the most active antiaspartame cru-saders. Founded in 1987, her Aspartame Consumer Safety Network ex-ists primarily as a website and a toll-free hotline number. Thousands of people have come to her site, directed there by films like Brackett's (in which Stoddard has a prominent role) and books like Roberts's. Stod-dard's description of the disease etiology for aspartame illness is much the same as Baylock's and echoes the explanation provided in Brackett's film. She calls aspartame an "excitotoxin," one that "artificially stimulate[s] the taste buds and neurotransmitters in the brain, causing cellular dam-age and destruction."[62] Stoddard's website places her very much at the foreground of the battle against aspartame. Her photo is featured promi-nently on the site's home page, and the description beneath it presents her own experience and efforts as central to the movement to expose the risks of aspartame.

> Responsible for taking the anti-aspartame campaign international in 1987, following the brain tumor death in 1985 of her forty two year old husband. Stoddard went on to expose the massive hidden epidemic of aspartame related disease and government cover-up, using her skills as a former broadcast journalist and member of the Texas Radio Hall of Fame. Thousands of serious adverse reactions fill her organizations [sic] database files. She gave testimony at the Senate Hearing on Aspartame Safety, November 1987. Stoddard initiated a worldwide Pilot's Hotline for reporting adverse reac-tions to aspartame, after being asked by an F-16 pilot to address the issue of flying safety and aspartame ingestion. Hundreds of calls have now been registered on behalf of the international

flying community. Stoddard edits the underground best seller: *Deadly Deception — Story of Aspartame*. Stoddard receives standing ovations on her multi-national lecture tours.[63]

Stoddard presents herself as a skilled layperson whose expert medical knowledge has been acquired through dogged determination to uncover the truth after the loss of a loved one. It is easy to conflate the power of her impact with the sheer power of her personal narrative. This may be, in part, what is so compelling about her advocacy. She did not set out to question the efficacy of NutraSweet. She was a regular person who professed no expert medical knowledge or research skills. Yet, in the face of information about the cause of her husband's illness that she believed to be untrue, she began to do her own research. Via the Internet and her self-published exposé and her speaking tours, Stoddard was able to achieve the improbable in becoming a housewife who has taken on the pharmaceutical/food industry and "won" (at least in the court of her audience's public opinion).

There is a religious zeal to her quest, and that of other antiaspartame advocates, and an opportunity for communal healing through participating in these knowledge-building communities. By her own account, her interviews on television have generated more than 50,000 inquiry calls. Calls to Stoddard and visits to her website enable individuals to connect to multiple networks of antiaspartame crusaders and to read numerous stories of individuals who have come to understand their own illnesses as caused by the sweetener. While her own story is very much central to the narrative, it is presented in a way that strengthens the entire community of believers. It requires a conversion experience in that individuals must come to see that what they have been told by experts about the health-giving properties of aspartame are fundamentally wrong and must be overturned. Instead of trusting doctors and nutritionists and food producers and advertisers, converts must learn to trust their own bodies and the interpretation of their physical symptoms by the communal network of antiaspartame advocates. These believers, once empowered, can take on the force of evil in big business and restore their right to healthy bodies. It is perhaps not a coincidence that Stoddard was featured prominently on the Christian evangelical show *The 700 Club*. Viewed from this angle, Stoddard's exposés connect the antiaspartame advocates to a much longer tradition of religious food reformers, from Sylvester Graham to Gwen Shamblin. By declaring the body a pure environment and seeking one's own true path to health, followers are able to achieve a physical state of grace.[64]

IN *SWEET POISON*, Janet Starr Hull documents her own path from aspartame illness to antiaspartame advocacy. In the early 1990s she found herself plagued by intense headaches and weight gain, and she was losing her patience with her husband and children. The transformation was particularly troubling since Hull herself had a Ph.D. in nutrition, exercised frequently, and generally pursued a healthy diet in line with nutritional guidelines. Not until she gave up her daily diet soda consumption did the symptoms subside. According to *Sweet Poison*, it was Hull's frustration with doctors who failed to diagnose her and scientific research that produced no information on what she was sure was a widespread problem that motivated her to write and speak on behalf of aspartame victims. Her website is part information (What is aspartame? What does it do to the body? Why is avoiding artificial sweeteners the best option?) and part self-promotion. Like Stoddard's site, the most prominent thing on the home page is Hull: a face shot, close up, is done in soft golds that give her an angelic air, while her firm expression suggests that she is watching out for you. The biography describes her as a "former university professor, firefighter, hazardous waste specialist and emergency responder," as well as a certified nutritionist, fitness professional, author, and aspartame victim. Her services include hair and skin analysis, whereby a sample can reveal to her the level of "aspartame toxicity," which she can reverse through her patented Aspartame Detoxification Program. She "exhibits excellent verbal and written communication skills" and can be contacted, via an address in Melissa, Texas, for speaking engagements or individual consultation.[65]

Hull and Stoddard, both based in Texas, along with Sharon Roth of Ocala, Florida, who founded Aspartame Victims and their Friends in 1990, and Betty Martini, who founded a similar organization in 1993, have circulated valuable information to consumers that would not otherwise be easily found within what historian of science Anne Harrington calls "physicalist" medicine.[66] They provide an avenue for action to those suffering from vague symptoms that might, in the nineteenth century, have been termed neurasthenia or, in the twentieth century, chronic fatigue syndrome. At the same time, their vigorous self-promotion enables them to combine this message with a compelling American Horatio Alger story where the improbable protagonist rises to power by pulling tight on her bootstraps. Here were victims who through their intellect and community ties were able to turn the tables on experts and build followings of their own.

It is significant that all of these antiaspartame crusaders are white. It is possible that people of color did self-diagnose as aspartame sufferers in the 1980s yet were not featured in the websites and films. Yet ample evidence suggests that nonwhite consumers, particularly African American women, rarely became the kind of heavy users who would have seen themselves as susceptible to these ailments. Certainly African Americans were less likely to equate science with progress and trust industry in the first place. Beckett and Stoddard's shock, in the 1980s, that some government and medical professionals could not be trusted, whether true or not, would likely not have been news to many nonwhite consumers.[67] It was not only a mistrust of science, however, that distanced African Americans from the six to eight doses of sweetener many of these antiaspartame activists had consumed each day. Culture also played a large role. The Seventh-day Adventist church, which has more African American than white members relative to the total population, has long urged followers to avoid processed foods as part of their religious practice. The church has, in fact, disparaged artificial sweeteners specifically, even featuring Beckett and Baylock in small-group discussions to publicize the dangers, physical and spiritual, of aspartame.[68] African American cookbooks rarely feature artificial sweetener as a weight-loss tool, even when sweet recipes are altered to produce light versions. A collection of essays written in 1994, *Body and Soul: The Black Women's Guide to Physical Health and Emotional Well-Being*, suggests that African American women may not have had the same encouragement to see artificial sweetener as a weight-loss aid in the 1980s and 1990s that white women had. One author acknowledges the desire of African American women to be thin, citing an *Essence* readers' poll that found 71 percent of respondents "terrified of being overweight." Yet she specifically recommends against using artificial sweeteners in order to shed pounds because they "are made of chemicals that may be dangerous."[69] Another guidebook for black women written in 1990 and republished in 1994 suggests that the key to weight loss for African Americans is to "get back to our more natural ways" by substituting homemade chicken stock for ham hocks in seasoning cabbage and replacing salt with a "squeeze of lemon."[70] Patti Labelle, in her cookbook, *Lite Cuisine: Over 100 Dishes With To-Die-For Taste Made with To-Live-For Recipes*, published in 2003, also advocates healthful food—

specifically recipes from African American culinary heritage—over low-calorie substitutions. "Usually, when people are feeling stressed out they want a pill," she explains, "but honey, give me a pot."[71] And while she is likely discussing mood-elevating pills rather than sweeteners, her admission suggests that she had little in common with the early cyclamate kitchen chemists. More research is needed to make a definitive claim, but African American cooking and health guides from the NutraSweet era suggest that black women, unlike white women, may have had a cultural and culinary line of defense against aspartame's more compelling claims.

Antiaspartame advocates have more in common than their whiteness. They are also predominantly working-class people who are employed in fields that expose them to risk and uncertainty. Unexpected crises often factor into their stories, becoming part of the narrative of illness that is told around aspartame. Of the three individuals prominently featured in Brackett's documentary, one is an emergency medical technician, another is a traveling salesman, and the third is a struggling stay-at-home mom. These individuals had limited power as bodies, either as productive bodies in the workforce or as physical bodies that were visible within the medical system. Tammy first went to the emergency room when she had symptoms, since she had no regular physician. Mary found herself plagued by medical bills as her illness lingered. Bill was out of work with no savings to rely on when his headaches made driving impossible.

Within these narratives, sufferers are often cured as soon as they name aspartame as the cause of their symptoms and give it up entirely. Many on antiaspartame websites share their stories of the epiphany—the moment they identified the source of their problems and eliminated the sweetener. The recovery can be nearly instantaneous, with victims finding their blurred vision gone, vertigo subsided, and headaches cleared in a matter of hours after consuming their last aspartame-sweetened product. Such dramatic physical improvement over quite serious symptoms raises the question of whether these ailments are primarily psychosomatic. Is it possible that so many sufferers only imagine that NutraSweet is the cause of their undiagnosed malaise?

According to media critic Philip Lawler, sensational media coverage has certainly provided Americans with an opportunity to believe artificial sweetener is the cause of many ailments. His review of NutraSweet coverage in the popular press revealed an imbalance between accusations about impropriety and possible side effects and investigations into the evidence on which such accusations are based. The "bewildering phenomenon" of people who claimed to have been plagued by vision problems, sluggishness, seizures, and even menstrual irregularities after using aspartame simply does not, he concludes, bear out under actual research.[72] The studies submitted by Searle to the FDA were, through multiple replications, found to be accurate. Very few people experienced adverse reactions to the substance, a number Lawler characterized as one-hundredth of 1 percent.[73] In spite of this data, by 1986, 600 letters containing complaints about symptoms related to aspartame consumption had been sent to the Centers for Disease Control.

Lawler concludes that these unfounded complaints must be driven by the media. It is possible, however, to pose another explanation. Legal scholars argue that trials have civil and cultural functions. On the civil side, they determine the line between producer culpability and consumer responsibility. On the cultural side, they "structure narratives about injuries and differences; they are a key site where a common sense about object use, design, and consumer expectations is both constituted and articulated." As such, "they are central to the valuation and reproduction of consumer culture."[74] Aspartame syndrome is not an issue in a legal trial, but the rhetoric produced on advocacy websites strongly implicates producers as at fault for promoting a dangerous product founded on unsafe scientific protocols. At the same time, the websites' stories extend well beyond factual information about physical symptoms, creating instead "structural narratives" about the innocence of consumers (promoting them as wives and mothers, pursuers of health, persons who were fit prior to aspartame use) and the strength they acquired to break away from producer abuse (self-taught expertise about the illness, courses of study pursued to understand the issues fully). Their authors disassemble the reputation of NutraSweet in order to assemble their own. Consumer culture is, in fact, protected in this process. The problem here is defined as one bad commodity and a dishonest pharmaceutical-industrial-medical complex. The problem is not one of consumer action. What has to be exorcised is the chemical itself, thereby empowering consumers to be more than they were because of their consumption, while at the same time shifting their desire from one thing to another (back to sugar, to detoxification programs, to fitness studios).

When individuals name a set of symptoms as constituting the effects of a particular disease, they are profoundly affected by the environment in which they live and work. According to historian Linda Nash, "In a world where outright resistance to the processes of unrestrained capitalism has become incredibly difficult to sustain, concerns about illness and its relationship to an industrialized landscape provide an important means for galvanizing different kinds of people to question the trajectory of their own modernization."[75] This is, perhaps, easier to imagine in the case of farmworkers mobilizing to fight industry by researching high rates of cancer. Yet it may also apply to antiaspartame crusaders whose landscapes of job and personal stress caused by low wages, lack of health care, and insufficient education provide ample reason for them to question their own trajectory. By declaring that NutraSweet had made them ill, these individuals may, on some level, have been asserting that the unfettered consumption it promoted had not brought them the "Good Stuff." Such a conclusion, possibly accompanied by corresponding changes to diet and health, may in some cases have produced actual physical improvement.

Individuals in Beckett's film discuss in great detail their physical ailments, their quest to find medical answers, and their disapproval of the food corporations and federal agencies that have harmed rather than fed them. Only after looking at several of these stories does one begin to notice the massive amounts of aspartame many have ingested. Roberts's *Aspartame* provides several case studies: a twenty-nine-year-old man who had seizures drank eighteen twelve-ounce aspartame-sweetened colas a day; a thirty-five-year-old woman had ten to fifteen cups of soda and about fifteen presweetened teas each day; a thirty-five-year-old pilot had convulsions and slurred speech that ended when he gave up his two to four sixteen-ounce cans and two one-liter bottles of diet soda, two to four cups of hot chocolate, puddings, gelatins, and gum—all sweetened with aspartame—that he previously consumed each day.[76] A 1987 United Press International story featured several aspartame users who had recovered from seizures after giving up diet beverages and desserts. One was drinking a liter and a half to two liters of diet soda a day; another was drinking sixty-four ounces of Diet Coke and a few glasses of diet lemonade every day.[77] Among the crusading women (Roth, Hull, and Brackett), such consumption was not uncommon. Roth believed her partial blindness was due to her daily consumption of four to eight aspartame-sweetened coffees and iced teas. Hull drank diet sodas throughout the day. Brackett revealed a habit of six to eight Diet Cokes a day that lasted over a decade.

These amounts may seem excessive. Yet they fell squarely within the guidelines established by the American Diabetes Association: by its calculations, a 100-pound individual could safely consume twelve cans of diet soda per day.[78] In the late 1990s, in fact, Coke had a term for those consumers who regularly drank six to eight diet sodas a day: loyalists. And there were enough of them to fill focus groups across the country to test new products and product messaging. This was in many ways a logical outcome of the artificial-sweetener marketing that had begun in the 1950s. Because artificial sweetener removed what was "bad" from sweets (i.e., calories), consumers were finally free to indulge in pleasure without worrying about restraint. As marketing grew more sophisticated, soda drinking became normalized, and soda prices dropped to the levels where consuming more than a six-pack a day could be accommodated in an average American budget. "Without restraint" could shift from meaning a couple of sodas to a couple of gallons of soda a day.

Whether aspartame syndrome is indeed a medical problem caused by this artificial sweetener remains a point of controversy. Most medical studies suggest that it is not, and unless individuals have extreme sensitivity to phenylalanine, they are not at risk from consumption, even at higher levels. If we assume that such findings are correct, the question arises as to whether these illnesses are more cultural than physical. At some point the level of soda consumption may simply be unsustainable. Articulating aspartame—and the diet drinks that contain it—as the cause of these discomforting illnesses may be a way for consumers to express their own addiction and unease, and feel better.

ASSESSING THE FREE LUNCH

By 1994 the market for what were termed nonnutritive sweeteners in the United States was almost $1 billion, and the majority of those sales were of aspartame. Figures from 1993 reveal close to 19 million pounds of the substance consumed within the United States and more than 2,000 aspartame-sweetened products in circulation worldwide.[79] The NutraSweet Company continued to dominate the market, even after its exclusive patent on aspartame expired in 1992; its market share continued to hover between 90 and 95 percent. A decade later, there is little doubt that NutraSweet has been a phenomenal success.[80] Its makers and promoters took a product no one had heard of, in a category plagued by consumer doubt and safety questions, and earned hundreds of millions of dollars for themselves and their corporate customers by selling it to consumers as a health food.[81] At the same time, research was beginning to emerge suggesting that in spite of all of this low-calorie-sweet consumption, Americans were finding themselves increasingly unable to satisfy their cravings. One 1988 study found that sugar eaten before a meal made people significantly less hungry than did artificial sweeteners—especially aspartame. "Aspartame," it found, "produced large and statistically significant increases in hunger and desire to eat."[82] What the study found that was particularly intriguing was that this was not merely a matter of calories ingested. While one expected sugar to satiate, given its caloric content, aspartame produced notably more hunger in its consumers than did water.

We know very little, even today, about what aspartame does to us physically. What we do know is that it did not reduce the amount of sweet calories consumed by the average American. In 1975, the per capita sugar average was 118.1 pounds; in 1984, just as NutraSweet consumption was skyrocketing, that average climbed to 126.8.[83] Add to this the extraordinary rise in high-fructose corn syrup that entered packaged goods during the decades of NutraSweet's rise, and it is clear that while many of us are reaching for Diet Coke to cut sweet calories, those calories are sneaking back in, often undetected, in our cereals, crackers, and breads. Hunting for aspartame rather than syrup may have left many of us consuming more sweet calories rather than less. Furthermore, the highly exaggerated sweetness that we have become accustomed to, thanks to NutraSweet, is skewing other foods toward sweet so that we will find them palatable, as a quick check of the ingredients in Wheat Thins reveals.

This history reveals that NutraSweet has meant multiple things to multiple people. Massively marketing a chemical as a health food has been a way for businesses to control profit and to expand the market for foods in spite of caloric limits. Ingesting NutraSweet has been a way for consumers to control pleasure by jettisoning old fears of substitutes and replacing them with a vision of guiltless consumption and calorie-less food as nature intended. At the same time, consumers may have found choosing other products or developing other practices difficult, since the "healthful" vision of NutraSweet was delivered largely in a vacuum lacking alternative points of view.

NutraSweet effectively promoted a new means of healthful eating and a line of products that enabled consumers to achieve it. It also gave rise to an era in which foods could be engineered free of unhealthy consequences so that consumers would not have to restrain their appetites.

This became clear in an industry conference held in October 1989 financed and organized by the NutraSweet Company. "The task for the twenty-first century is to improve our understanding of nutrition in order to produce the right foods from which to select a healthful diet," explained the conveners of the event, titled "Ceres." And the only way to do that, they explained, was for scientists and food executives to help close "the ever-widening gap between burgeoning scientific and technological know-how and the public's ability *to understand and accept it*."[84]

NutraSweet has enabled hundreds of thousands of people to lose weight, to enjoy sweets otherwise denied by dietary restrictions, and to exert a palpable control over caloric intake. It has also dramatically increased the total amount of food and beverage consumed by American bodies and sold by American corporations, enabled a new definition of pharmaceutical chemicals as "healthy" food choices, and proven impotent in stemming the tide of national weight gain. These are not compatible narratives. While we do not know yet what the cultural and physical impact of normalizing sweetener consumption in the 1980s will be, we may not want to wait to do some reassessing of our own. History strongly suggests, in spite of claims to the contrary, that that the free lunch promised by NutraSweet did not arrive.

CONCLUSION

SPLENDA, SUGAR, AND WHAT MOTHER NATURE INTENDED

In November 2004, Merisant, manufacturer of the table-top, aspartame-based sweetener Equal, sued McNeil Nutritionals, a division of Johnson and Johnson and the manufacturer of Splenda, for false and misleading advertising in Splenda's "made from sugar, so it tastes like sugar" campaign. Merisant evoked the Lanham Act, which prohibits false or misleading advertisements to American consumers, to stop McNeil from making several claims in television and print advertisements that suggested that Splenda was like sugar, only with the calories removed. After three years of fighting in the courts, Johnson and Johnson settled, just before the jury was to return what appeared to be a ruling awarding damages in favor of the plaintiff. According to the *New Jersey Law Review*, the Lanham Act clearly provided justification for accusing Splenda's "made from sugar" campaign of being misleading. Sucralose, the chemical in the brand-named product Splenda, does, in fact, originate with the sucrose (sugar) molecule. It then undergoes a process of molecule replacement, however, that renders it qualitatively different. Along with this change in molecular structure comes the addition of chlorine, leaving it not only "not" sugar but also distinctly man-made in final form.[1]

The controversy in the case was not whether Johnson and Johnson had made a misleading claim. It was fairly clear that the language in advertisements claiming that Splenda is "made from sugar" had implied to many consumers that Splenda in some way actually was sugar, but with the calories stripped out. What is curious is why so much time had passed between the debut of this campaign, in 1999, and the lawsuit from Merisant. In fact, only after five years and $235 million in Johnson and Johnson advertising expenditures did Merisant file its accusation.[2] The delay suggests that Merisant's quest to expose the truth was motivated by legal and market concerns. Only after Splenda became the number one sweetener in the nation, eclipsing the primacy of NutraSweet and Equal, did Merisant take action on the claim.

The exchange reveals much about where we are as a society today in our understanding of artificial sweetener. It was not the government that stepped in to point out that Splenda was falsely suggesting it was "made from sugar" and therefore "like sugar," though many Americans believed this when they began using it as a beverage sweetener, baking with it, and buying products with the Splenda brand name. There was no major consumer revolt when Johnson and Johnson aimed their advertising campaign directly at the parents of children, highlighting the healthfulness of Splenda-sweetened cakes and cookies, baked at home. Nor did major corporations with loyal "health" and "organic/sustainable" consumers balk at inventing new Splenda-made products like "Enlightened Smoothies" at Jamba Juice and "Sugar Free" lattes at Peet's Coffee. The first public claim of false advertising came, instead, from another artificial-sweetener manufacturer, one that ironically had made its own claims of "made from nature" to gain market share just twenty years earlier.

When the case was settled in 2007, with damages awarded to the plaintiff but no ruling demanding that the Splenda advertising campaign be changed (in spite of the fact that the jury was going to find Johnson and Johnson in violation of the Lanham Act), the true goal of the process became clear.[3] Merisant got money, thereby recouping some of the revenue it had lost since Splenda's debut, and Johnson and Johnson got to continue the same campaign without any mandate that it adopt a more truthful presentation of its product.

In the summer of 2008, Splenda's website featured a claim quite similar to that of 2004: "Just What's Good—it's made from sugar. It tastes like sugar. But it's not sugar."[4]

In January 2008, McNeil Nutritionals was sued by the Sugar Association under the Lanham Act. According to the association's lead attorney five months before the court date, his clients "look[ed] forward to presenting the truth about Splenda to the jury and focusing on the very real effect of misleading advertising. We are confident that the outcome will be a victory for consumers everywhere."[5] Three months later, McNeil had settled with the Sugar Association for an undisclosed amount.[6] History, however, might have told us that there was little reason to hope that squabbles between the Sugar Association and manufacturers of artificial sweeteners would be resolved to the benefit of consumers. It was sugar money that produced the research data that led to the banning of cyclamates in the 1960s and the attempted ban on saccharin in the 1970s. The association has shown their primary goal to be selling sugar, and selling sugar is easier when artificial sweeteners are strictly regulated. Yet the research the association conducted to achieve that goal has struck consumers as excessive, extreme, and impractical. We continue to live with the reverberations of the attempt to ban saccharin, when consumers repeatedly rejected the "science" of the Food and Drug Administration, claiming that they would have to drink "gallons" of soda a day and be "rats" in order to truly be at risk.

Over the past half-century, artificial-sweetener manufacturers *and* sugar manufacturers have produced scientific data and consumer marketing that have been designed to increase company profits and have, as a result, ultimately confused more than educated consumers. Between 1964 and 1969 alone, for example, sugar interests contributed $500,000 to research into the health problems associated with cyclamate.[7] And they have done this in a virtual regulatory vacuum. Citizens who, in groups or as individuals, once worked with the federal government to question the claims of food and chemical companies are difficult to find today. Certainly there are websites manned by fierce opponents of artificial sweeteners. Rare, however, are forums with balanced views that offer a true assessment of what artificial sweeteners do that is good and what they do that is bad. The battle between sweetening industries for market share, driven by individuals in search of power and prestige, has not yet produced information that helps consumers make healthy choices when they reach for sweets.

Consumers, for their part, appear much less trusting of the food industry's claims than they were in the 1980s. While Splenda and NutraSweet fight over who can claim the closest relationship to sugar, many Americans are well aware that none of these options, in fact, is healthy. While some industry executives continue to promote diet products as "health and wellness brands," others declare such claims to be increasingly unpalatable to American consumers. In 2007, Tom Pirko, president of Bevmark, a food and beverage consulting firm, called healthy marketing pitches for artificial sweeteners a "joke." Most people, he explained, understood that they were, in fact, "putting something synthetic and not natural into their bodies when they consume diet colas." One report, from 2006, put the percentage of American adults concerned about the safety of artificial sweeteners at 60. These are significant numbers. As Pirko bluntly put it, consumer attitudes about sweeteners "ain't good."[8]

Still, the news may not be so dire for the industry. While consumers are increasingly articulating their reservations about artificial sweeteners, the overall amount of artificial sweetener consumed in the United States continues to rise. Recent studies find that roughly 45 percent of American households purchase artificially sweetened products on a regular basis. The number of Americans using artificially sweetened foods and beverages has climbed from 101 million in 1991 to 163 million in 2001 and 194 million in 2007. Although the two older brands of sweetener, saccharin/Sweet'N Low and aspartame/Equal/NutraSweet, have seen significant declines in sales (12 percent for saccharin and 93 percent for aspartame between 2004 and 2007), sucralose/Splenda saw its yearly sales increase during this same time from 119 million to 226 million, annually, a rise of nearly 90 percent.[9]

Evidence strongly suggests that consumers are less trusting of artificial sweetener, as a category, now than they have been since before World War II. At the same time, they are more likely to point to sucralose/ Splenda as a relatively safe product by explaining that the other sweeteners are the real unsafe ones. This is, of course, precisely what Johnson and Johnson encouraged through its advertising campaigns touting a close relationship between its product and sugar and suggesting that Splenda was, in fact, more natural than other options. The same approach was used for aspartame before it. The modern sweetener industry has thrived by regularly providing consumers with a new option and actively vilifying those that came before it as unnatural and very likely unsafe. The result of this approach, for consumers, is confusion. Obscured are the commonalities between these sweeteners that are, in the end, far more significant than the differences. All are chemicals. None has a closer connection to nature, in either origins or processing, than any other. And all are safe, if used in moderation. Were that not the case, certainly industry-driven scientists would have discovered their competitors' weaknesses and publicized them to consumers well before Internet activists and independent filmmakers.

Yet it is possible that artificial sweeteners have finally met their match. Stevia, a sweetener derived from the extract produced by boiling the leaves of the stevia plant, appears uniquely positioned to make good on many of the promises made but not delivered by the producers of artificial sweeteners. Stevia is, in fact, from nature. It has few calories. It can be used in processed foods, as an added sweetener, and by home cooks. And its sales are on the rise. It is too early to tell what will happen, given stevia's relatively recent introduction on the American market and low sales relative to Splenda ($3.1 million compared to Splenda's $226 million in sales in 2007). Yet the 287 percent rise in market share between 2003 and 2007 suggests that it is quickly catching on with American consumers.[10] In the midst of our current craze for local foods, natural ingredients, and organics, stevia may well break the grip artificial sweeteners have had on the low-calorie market since its inception. There would indeed be a bit of irony if stevia proved triumphant. After all, it was artificial-sweetener companies that taught consumers to demand low-calorie, safe, "like nature" alternatives to sugar, something that, at least at this point, appears to be better delivered via leaf than laboratory.

CODA

I have tried to present the history of artificial sweetener's invention, production, marketing, and consumption in the United States in a way that helps us see the fact that chemical sweet has long been embroiled in a three-way tug of war between food and chemical businesses that want to increase profits, diet and advice experts who want to provide formulas for health that sell and enhance their own prestige, and consumers who want more power to control their appetites without sacrificing pleasure. But I end by returning to the question I am most often asked: "Is it bad for me?" In fact, for individual consumers, artificial sweetener has often been a very good thing. This is certainly true for diabetics who have found in artificial sweeteners the only viable way to enjoy sweetness. But it has also been true for those who can consume sugar but have chosen to abstain, such as the women looking to make sweet special and separate from domestic service by using saccharin in the 1940s and 1950s. It has also been good for many of its makers, including men like Edwin Mitchell and Floyd Thayer, who transcended the limits of their professions on the coattails of a hybrid commodity. And it has certainly been good for entrepreneurs like Tillie Lewis, Jean Nidetch, and countless editors of women's pages in magazines and newspapers whose expertise was needed to bridge laboratory and pantry, and who through promotion of artificially sweetened food found money and power that was typically reserved for men in their eras. It was good for women like Martha Hurd, who in 1977 found they could, by advocating for saccharin, make the federal government pay attention to their experiences, their bodies, and their way of defining acceptable risk. Even today, women express powerful attachments to diet products, defining them as guilt-free indulgences and citing the times they are consumed as appealingly self-focused.

At the same time, acknowledging those positive individual choices should not distract us from the structural changes artificial sweetener has brought to our lives. It was the beginning of an economic and political collaboration between the food and pharmaceutical companies that went on to produce genetically modified foods and biochemical "nutraceutical" products. This is not inherently a bad thing: genetically modified foods alleviate hunger and enrich limited diets with vital nutrients across the world. Yet these interventions have made food increasingly complex and have blurred the boundaries between food and chemicals in ways that might make us nostalgic for the four-food-group "easy eating guides" from our childhoods. Witness the New Leaf potato from Monsanto, the 1995 potato that produced its own pesticide, internally.

Both artificial-sweetener companies and sugar companies have sponsored nutritional research on healthy sweets, resulting in predictable findings that seek to affect regulatory practices but, on the way, contribute to consumer confusion. In 1995, for example, the Obesity Task Force convened by the World Health Organization lowered the body mass index (BMI) at which individuals would be considered obese to 25 percent. According to the task force's website, the switch was part of a mission "to inform the world about the urgency of the problem and to persuade governments that the time to act is now." Once one realizes, as Eric Oliver points out, that the task force itself was funded by Abbott Laboratories, original makers of saccharin and current makers of the weight-loss drug Meridia, along with other manufacturers of weight-loss products, it is difficult to know just whom this advice is supposed to help.[11] Consumers are understandably perplexed when they must confront industry-generated guidelines for healthy weight, unchecked claims of NutraSweet and Splenda as natural products that are more healthful than sugar, and what Michael Pollan has referred to as the "32 billion dollar food marketing machine."[12] Even if one thinks critically about who is producing information about health and what the relationship between sugar consumption and a healthy weight might be, where does one look for trusted data? And if one could find and decipher that data, one would still wonder if the issue might be not calories, sugar, or BMI but, rather, American appetites writ large—manifest through but not originating from food?

Before we can find new ways of thinking about the relationship between health and sweet or sweet and appetite, we have to find the cracks in our popular culture's presentation of the "facts" about artificial sweetener. I hope that this book contributes to this. However, as a cultural historian, my tendency has been to see the pros and cons one finds in the human drama of what made these substances so successful in recent American life. It would be easier to say they are "always bad" or "in fact good," but a binary between "good" and "bad" isn't what the history of artificial sweetener reveals. Instead we see good people working hard to innovate, to profit, and to push the boundaries of what their bodies— often gendered and classed bodies—were thought able to accomplish. We see people wanting to control an increasingly byzantine world of food choice and nutritional knowledge. We see consumers adamant that if living is dangerous, then it had better be pleasurable, too.

If we look only at the material of sweetener—the chemical compounds—what they do to our bodies, and the ways they have enabled foods and pharmaceuticals to commingle, there is a stronger case for "bad." This may be even more obvious if new research emerging is, in fact, found to be true: that so-called diet sweet is actually causing us to pack on pounds. This theory first began percolating as a media story in March 2007 when *Glamour* published "Are Sugar Substitutes Making You Fat?" It cited a study at the University of Texas, San Antonio, that found that people who drank a can or bottle of diet soda a day were 35 percent more likely to become overweight than those who did not. The study was limited, and other details about the subjects' food choices were unknown; but the article was notable in that it asked a rather obvious question, one that few had asked or answered until that point. Sharon Fowler, the study's author, offered an insight that has emerged from a number of other studies in the last few years. It seems possible, she remarked, that "the taste makes your body think you're going to take in calories [and] when you don't get them, your body may push you to find calories elsewhere."[13]

Her theory was not actually new. As early as 1990, Harold Roberts, one of the antiaspartame crusaders, offered anecdotal evidence from his own practice that there appeared to be such a thing as "paradoxical weight gain" among people who consumed aspartame regularly. He cited one case in particular, a woman who gained fifty pounds while drinking aspartame, which she had begun using, as the label suggested, as a way of being "healthy" by losing weight. According to Roberts, his client told him she had "often" thought "my body knows that it is not sugar . . . it's not fooled," and her body sent her "looking for the real thing."[14]

Much of the claim that artificial sweeteners are healthy has been based on the fact that they have, in equal amounts, fewer calories than sugar. The problem here is the assumption that consumers are merely using artificial sweeteners to replace sugar—that the sugar is removed and the only thing that replaces it is the sweetener. Two fallacies of logic emerge from this approach: first, it fails to account for what consumers choose to do when they know they have "saved" calories through this exchange. Second, it does not acknowledge that artificial sweetener has a different impact on the body than does sugar in two important ways: it is much sweeter and it has little or no caloric component.

Even in the earliest studies on the effects of aspartame, scientists commented on the importance of looking at artificial sweetener in context to accurately gauge its effects. Katherine Porkos and Theodore Van Itallie argued in 1984 that more studies were needed on what happened when consumers were aware of what they called "the known energy savings from low-calorie products"; they hypothesized that many of them would use this savings as an "excuse" to increase their consumption of other high-calorie foods.[15] It was a variation of a question asked by C. I. Beck, the manager of research kitchens at Sara Lee, in 1978 in an article titled "Reduced Calorie Foods—Once We Create Them, Do They Help?" A survey of the available literature left Beck convinced that, in spite of the fact that artificially sweetened desserts and sodas had been mass-marketed for more than two decades, it was unclear whether these foods resulted in weight loss. Perhaps consumers simply ate two servings rather than one. "We are in critical need," he concluded, "of a major study of weight control through diet."[16]

We really have no idea whether NutraSweet and Splenda, as well as saccharin and cyclamates, do, in practice, help people to cut back on calories or sugar in their diets. While there is an alarming lack of unbiased research on the food choices made by consumers of artificial sweeteners, there is ample evidence to suggest that much of this focus on "saving calories" and having the "sweet that's good" by choosing artificial sweeteners over sugar has drawn our attention away from the real problem with sweet calories in the American diet: high-fructose corn syrup. The subject is now on the public radar, due in no small part to the success of Michael Pollan's *Omnivore's Dilemma* and its assertion that Americans now consume so much high-fructose corn syrup that, though they are unaware, they have become like "processed corn, walking."[17] Not only was corn syrup cheaper than other sweeteners; it also resisted freezer burn, helped preserve the foods in which it was used, tasted good, and browned nicely when heated, making it a miracle material for food manufacturers.[18] Its rise as a ubiquitous ingredient in the 1970s and 1980s coincided with the saccharin rebellion, the rise of NutraSweet, and the launching of the diet soda wars. Thus, we may have been too busy debating sugar versus artificial sweetener and artificial sweeteners versus each other to notice the slow creep of corn calories into our meals. And these calories may, in turn, have motivated us to consume even more "diet" sweets.

MY HOPE IS THAT THIS STORY ultimately provides a fresh vantage point from which to look at that can of Diet Coke. While the label may claim that it is "just what's good" and a slogan still lingers in our heads that we drink it "just for the taste of it," history reveals a very different story. There is little that is "just" about artificial sweetener. Cyclamates, saccharin, aspartame, and sucralose may have stories of accidental origins, but their invention, marketing, consumption, and even anticonsumption have been very intentional. They have made and lost fortunes, forged new partnerships between businesses and destroyed others, transformed the landscape of women's magazines, given birth to a food industry, made consumption without consequence a viable pursuit, and changed the meaning of the term "diet" itself. Yet they have not ultimately made our relationship with food more healthful. As we struggle to create sustainable American appetites, it is a good time to separate the potential of artificial sweeteners from the products and practices they have actually created. We may find that in spite of suggestions to the contrary, if we are going to have our cake, we must learn to eat it, too.

NOTES

ABBREVIATIONS

In addition to the abbreviations used in the text, the following appear in the notes.

CCG Archives   California Canners and Growers Archive, D-162, Special Collections, University of California Library, Davis

FDA Records   Food and Drug Administration Records, College Park, Maryland

SJHS   San Joaquin Historical Society and Museum, Lodi, California

INTRODUCTION

1 Pollan, *In Defense of Food.*
2 See Frieberg, *Fresh.*
3 Shannon, *Diet and Nutrition Sourcebook,* 152.
4 Evidence suggests, for example, whether because of a tendency to distrust science, an aversion to the artificial, an appreciation for more diverse body types, or the absence of targeted marketing, African American women have largely avoided substitutions and diet foods. See Chap. 6, n. 7.
5 Women between the ages of thirty-one and fifty who are moderately active should consume between 1,500 and 2,000 calories per day, while for men the range is 2,400 to 2,600, according to Shannon, *Diet and Nutrition Sourcebook,* 152.
6 Philosopher Susan Bordo has argued that bulimia is rooted in the "consumer culture contruction of desire as overwhelming" (*Unbearable Weight,* 201).
7 Severson, "Showdown at the Coffee Shop," *New York Times,* D1, D5.
8 See Conclusion, n. 13.
9 Oliver, *Fat Politics.*

CHAPTER ONE

1 Belasco, *Meals to Come*, 190.

2 Fahlberg, List & Co., *Saccharin*, 4, Warshaw Collection of Business Americana, National Museum of American History.

3 ⟨en.wikipedia.org/wiki/Coal_tar⟩ (accessed May 25, 2010).

4 Rydell, *All the World's a Fair*, 2.

5 Ibid., 5.

6 For more information, see Macinnis, *Bittersweet*, 169.

7 For more information on the history of saccharin innovation and regulation in Germany and Europe, see Merki, *Zuker gegen Saccharin*.

8 In 1901, the market priced saccharin at approximately $.06/lb. During hearings on the 1906 food and drug act a North Dakota senator read a letter from the president of the Western Canners Association stating that manufacturers "under the laws of the state of Wisconsin" paid $10,000 for sugar to sweeten canned peas, whereas competitors paid $750 for the equivalent in "saccharine made from a coal-tar product" (Wood, "Strategic Use of Public Policy," 416–17). Sugar tariffs would eventually cause the carbonated beverage manufacturers to launch an organized rebellion in the 1930s. For more information on the early sugar tariff, see Myrick, *American Sugar Industry*.

9 Mintz, *Sweetness and Power*.

10 Bellamy, *Looking Backward*.

11 "Army Emergency Rations," *New York Times*, December 10, 1896, 2; "Health of Athletes," *New York Times*, April 7, 1901, 3.

12 Saccharin appears not to have had much public recognition before Harvey Wiley's aggressive campaign against food impurities. One of the major U.S. sugar manufacturers, National Sugar Manufacturing of Colorado, called its company town newspaper the *Saccharin Gazette* between 1905 and 1913. One can assume that the sugar company would not have named the local paper in a manner to raise the profile of a competitor in the sweetener market. For information, see Sabin, *How Sweet It Was!*

13 It is difficult to fault Wiley's efforts. Yet the historical record suggests that he had reasons other than health concerns for assailing saccharin production in the early twentieth century. Twenty years earlier, when he had started out in the Department of Agriculture in the 1880s, his job had been to expand the domestic sugar market. According to historian Oscar Anderson Jr., Wiley turned to the sugar industry for "essential outside support for his division," and it was "to the power of this interest [that] he owed the size of his budget throughout the 80s." Wiley also grew up on a corn farm where in the winter it was his job to tap maple trees for syrup and sugar. See Anderson, *Health of a Nation*, esp. 3, 66.

14 Ibid., 209.

15 In spite of the failure of the panel to ban saccharin from the food supply at the national level, individual states did take action against the commodity. In March 1907, for instance, the Ohio state dairy and food commissioner banned saccharin in canned goods, even though its use was legal in neighboring states. See "Saccharin in Canned Goods Barred," *New York Times*, March 2, 1907, 11.

16 *New York Times*, December 30, 1906, 15.

17 "Do You Know These Foods?," *New York Times*, April 23, 1911, 14.

18 "Saccharin Lowers the Quality of Food," *New York Times*, May 4, 1911, 7.

19 *New York Times*, August 14, 1914, 8.

20 As culinary historian Laura Shapiro has argued, technology and science gained "an aura of divinity" among the women involved in the domestic science movement. Many became converts to and promoters of such new convenience products as Crisco and practices that necessitated the precise calculation of ingredients. Their motivations, however, came not from a particular celebration of technology for the sake of innovation but, rather, from the ability of technologies to perfect what Shapiro calls "the nutritive properties of food" in order to achieve "physical, social, and . . . moral growth" for American consumers. See Shapiro, *Perfection Salad*, 4–6.

21 For more information specifically on what Wendy Woloson calls the "democratization" of sugar in the nineteenth century, see her *Refined Tastes*, 5.

22 Atwater, *Foods*, 11.

23 Shapiro, *Perfection Salad*, 71.

24 Cohen, "Embellishing a Life of Labor," 289–305.

25 Earl Babst, "Demonstration of the Value of Large Business Units in Safeguarding the National Sugar Supply," reprinted in Babst, *Occasions in Sugar*, 15; Babst, *Century of Sugar Refining in the United States*, 14.

26 "Junius," Stonington, Connecticut, letter to the editor, *New York Times*, June 22, 1913, 8.

27 "Notes and Gleanings," *New York Times*, July 14, 1912, 10.

28 Thomas Beacall et al., *Dyestuffs & Coal-tar Products: Their Chemistry, Manufacture, and Application* (London: Crosby Lockwood and Son, 1915), 116a. The book is part of the Hagley Library holdings and, as such, can be assumed to be an important source of information for U.S. business and manufacturing. Further evidence that saccharin was regarded primarily as a medicine by the late 1910s can be found in a report produced by the U.S. Tariff Commission in 1918. There the authors discuss saccharin separately from other imports because it is a "medicinal" product. See United States Tariff Commission, *Dyes and Other Coal-Tar Products*, report to Congress recommending amendments to Title V of Act of September 8, 1918 (Washington, D.C.: Government Printing Office, 1918).

29 *Food and the War*, 174.

30 H. G. Pfafflin, *Suggested Bottlers Syrup Formulas Using Other Than Cane or Beet Sugar* (Santa Ana, Calif.: Hurty Peck and Co., ca. 1941), 6, A. W. Noling Hurty-Peck Collection of Beverage Literature, University of California, Davis.

31 Lulu Hunt Peters, "Diet and Health," *Los Angeles Times*, January 28, 1926.

32 Nabors and Gelardi, *Alternative Sweeteners*, 17.

33 American Sugar Refining Company annual report (New York, 1930), 29.

34 Hoover quoted in *Journal of Commerce*, centennial issue, September 29, 1927, reprinted in Babst, *Occasions in Sugar*, 113–34.

35 "Your Child's Dessert," *Good Housekeeping*, February 1927, 137.

36 Woloson, *Refined Tastes*, 187–88.

37 Vogt, *Sugar Refining Industry*, 1.

38 Woloson, *Refined Tastes*, 191–92.

39 As Woloson explains, "The rules about sugar consumption and children, while aimed mainly at the children themselves, were also directed at lower-class mothers. 'The mother who keeps her bantling 'good,' while she talks or works, by relays of candy, more surely creates a craving which can bring no benefit and may work infinite evil,' one writer admonished." See ibid., 65.

40 "Hold-Up in the Kitchen."

41 For more on sugar and early wartime rationing, see Cohen, *Consumers' Republic*, 65.

42 For more information on the consumption of sugar by soldiers, see Mintz, *Tasting Food, Tasting Freedom*, 25, 28. Soldiers appear to have had an equally high concentration of sugar in their packed meals as well. According to historian Harvey Levenstein, K-rations typically had three lumps of sugar to go with coffee for breakfast and three "cubes" of sugar with lemon powder to make lemonade; see Levenstein, *Paradox of Plenty*, 94.

43 Text from sugar purchase certificate ⟨www.americanhistoricalsociety.org/exhibits/events/rationing3.htm⟩ (accessed May 25, 2010).

44 Murphy, *War Time Meals*, 119.

45 Bentley, *Eating for Victory*, 110.

46 Ibid., 109.

47 Cohen, *Consumers' Republic*.

48 Bentley, *Eating for Victory*, 19.

49 These products were frequently recommended in wartime cookbooks as substitutes for sugar. See, for example, Murphy, *War Time Meals*.

50 Jane Holt, *New York Times*, June 1, 1943, 20.

51 Taylor, "Cheerful London."

52 Howard E. Kershner, "Defeated France Knows Only Hunger and Want," *New York Times*, June 28, 1942, E5.

53 *St Petersburg Times*, December 31, 1942, 19, ⟨http://news.google.com/newspapers?nid=888&dat=19421231&id=-rQKAAAAIBAJ&sjid=dk0DAAAAIBAJ&pg=7287,2152607⟩ (viewed July 14, 2009).

54 "Saccharin Spurt," *Business Week*, July 25, 1942.

55 Ibid.

56 Ibid.

57 *New York Times*, May 19, 1940, 54.

58 "About," *New York Times*, August 4, 1940, 85.

59 *New York Times*, August 29, 1942, 12. According to my own survey of the *New York Times*, there were more than twenty advertisements from different companies looking for saccharin surpluses in 1945, suggesting that consumers who were not diabetics were now contributing to demand. One typical ad, from Arrow Products of Buffalo printed on August 5, 1945, read, "saccharin wanted, powdered or tablet, any quantity."

CHAPTER TWO

1 LeBesco, *Revolting Bodies*, 58.

2 According to historian Hillel Schwartz, when Victor Lindlahr, "a diet personality," broadcast a radio "reducing party" in 1936, he had 26,000 people nationwide joining him. See Schwartz, *Never Satisfied*, 192.

3 Levenstein, *Paradox of Plenty*, 10.

4 Peiss, *Hope in a Jar*.

5 Promoters of artificial sweeteners did not begin to court nonwhite consumers until the late 1960s and not consistently until the 1980s (most notably with the Diet Pepsi and Diet Coke campaigns of 1983–85).

6 William Brady, "Saccharin for Reducing," *Los Angeles Times*, July 25, 1939.

7 William Brady, "Saccharin Is Saccharine," *Los Angeles Times*, May 21, 1946.

8 Mintz, *Sweetness and Power*, xxv, 122.

9 See, for example, Marchand, *Advertising the American Dream* and *Creating the Corporate Soul*, and Lears, *Fables of Abundance*.

10 Here one might fruitfully consider David Cheal's argument that in contemporary North America, gifts "symbolize social identities," asserting an image of the giver that he or she wants to reflect and inviting the receiver to accept that image as part of his or her visible values as well. The limited evidence of actual gift exchanges prevents a definitive analysis of the connection between these containers and social status. We can assume, however, that people would not have given a gift that reflected poorly upon themselves, suggesting that there was something attractive about saccharin, at least on the part of container givers. See Cheal, "Gifts in Contemporary North America," 86.

11 Author interview with Larry Kasoff.

12 E-mail correspondence between author and Larry Kasoff, July 1, 2004.

13 According to Cera, by 1949 the costume jewelry industry had reached sales of roughly $150,000 a year and was widely regarded as a means by which women of the middle and working class expressed creativity and inner beauty. See Cera, "Luxury of Freedom," 179, 149.

14 "Spreckles Presents: New Sugars—New Packages," *Pacific Coast Review*, May 1956, box 3, folder 10, Landor Design Collection, 1962–66, scrapbook 6, National Museum of American History.

15 *Short Story of Sugar*, 60.

16 Woloson, *Refined Tastes*, 222.

17 "Describing the Production of Raw Sugar in Cuba and the Refining Process in the United States," *The Spur*, July 14, 1924. One must be careful here to distinguish between the different treatment of labor involved in the production of bulk, granulated, and confectionary sugar. As historian Wendy Woloson argues, labor was, in fact, frequently erased in the presentation of confectionaries. See Woloson, *Refined Tastes*, 3.

18 *Monsanto, 1901–2001*, specific advertisement undated, ca. 1943, Hagley Museum and Library, Wilmington, Del.

19 Ibid., 1946.

20 Marchand, *Advertising the American Dream*, 238–40.

21 The Monsanto corporate magazine suggests that whites were predominant in factory production and in the laboratories of chemistry corporations. In the 1940s there is one photograph, out of hundreds, featuring a person of color. James Puckett, an African American, was honored with his photograph and a short caption when he reached thirty-four years of service in the St. Louis plant. See *Monsanto News*, March 30, 1940, 5.

22 Some consumers may have known that saccharin was one of Monsanto's first products. The company did promote its historic connection to saccharin, even though the actual commodity was bottled by pharmaceutical manufacturers like St. John's and Merck. In the 1940s one of the company's bowling teams called itself "saccharin" (other names were "caffeine" and "vanillin"). See *Monsanto News*, March 30, 1940, 5.

23 According to historian David Herzberg, these minor tranquilizers were featured in hundreds of articles in magazines and newspapers in the 1950s and 1960s. See Herzberg, *From Miltown to Prozac*, 47, 83. By 1960, ads frequently featured women consuming these pills while sitting down for the family meal, further connecting pill-sweetened cooking with pill-aided pharmaceuticals. See ibid., 75. In fact, the connection between dietary pills and psychological pills had been in place since the 1930s, when physicians began prescribing amphetamines for weight loss. According to Hillel Schwartz, physicians prescribed Dexedrine as "the drug of choice for weight-reducing" in 1938. See Schwartz, *Never Satisfied*, 197.

24 Shapiro, *Something from the Oven*, 29.

25 Freda De Knight, a popular food writer for *Ebony*, believed that such "world" recipes were popular for her readers because "food represented a way to climb up and perhaps out" (De Knight quoted in ibid., 32).

26 According to linguist Colleen Cotter, recipes can be viewed as "a story, a cultural narrative that can be shared and has been constructed by members of a community." See Cotter, "Claiming a Piece of the Pie," 51–72. Scholars frequently look to cookbooks in order to understand how food preparation has differed across regions, over time, and through community networks. Cookbooks, however, also frequently contain text that describes new recipes and places food preparation instructions in their broader contexts through introductions and epilogues.

27 For more information on the discovery of sodium cyclamate, see ⟨en.wikipedia .org/wiki/Cyclamate⟩ (accessed May 25, 2010) and Edward Matson, "Sucaryl in Dietetic Beverages," *National Bottlers' Gazette*, April 1953, 12.

28 Abbott Laboratories, *Calorie Saving Recipes*.

29 West, *Stop Dieting!*, 20.

30 Cannon, *Unforbidden Sweets*, 106, 45.

31 Koten, *Low-Calory Cookbook*, 196.

32 Miller, *Reducing Cookbook and Diet Guide*, 21.

33 Cannon, *Unforbidden Sweets*, 11–12.

34 "Cooking-school Methods in Every-day Life," *New England Kitchen Magazine*, April 1895, 14.

35 Cannon, *Unforbidden Sweets*, 11.

36 West, *Stop Dieting!*, 12.

37 Ibid., 12 (general quote on creative instincts), 24 (six recipes), 32 (hollandaise).

38 Most infamous of these was the Tuskegee experiments, begun in the 1930s and extending into the 1970s, wherein hundreds of African American men, mostly poor sharecroppers, with syphilis were not offered penicillin treatments long after they were available so that researchers could better understand the long-term impact of leaving the condition untreated. Another layer of distrust, es-

pecially for women, may have been added by the specific experience of black women within American medical practice, where reproductive health services have frequently been inferior and at times damaging for women of color. See ⟨http://en.wikipedia.org/wiki/Tuskegee_study_of_untreated_syphilis_in_the_Negro_Male⟩ (accessed May 25, 2010). For the history of scientific arguments in favor of white superiority, see Nye, *America as Second Creation*; Sinclair, *Technology and the African-American Experience*; and Keith Wailoo, *Drawing Blood*. For more on African American women and reproductive science, see Roberts, *Killing the Black Body*.

39   Levenstein, *Paradox of Plenty*, 21–23.

40   The publicity surrounding vitamin deficiencies and the importance of altering the diet to achieve health may in fact have had a very direct impact on women's willingness to see sweeteners as healthful commodities when added to American dishes in the 1950s. According to Harvey Levenstein, a Gallup poll in 1941 found that 84 percent of housewives were unable to explain the difference between calories and vitamins; see *Paradox of Plenty*, 22–23.

41   Meikle, *American Plastic*, 173.

42   These expositions in the 1950s were not a new phenomenon. Warren Belasco relays a vivid description of one such event: the dishwashing contest held at the Westinghouse House of Wonders at the 1933 World's Fair. Here a "slovenly Mrs. Drudge" went head-to-head with a "more composed and youthful Mrs. Modern (guess which one used the new appliance)." The same fair offered ticket buyers the opportunity to see young women in bathing suits "effortlessly" frying an egg in a bowl levitated by magnets. What was different about these fairs in the 1950s was that the technologies were usually available to consumers, particularly in the form of kitchen gadgets. See Belasco, *Meals to Come*, 192.

43   ⟨http://members.aol.com/_ht_a/diziago/HOTF_spiel.html⟩ (accessed August 2008).

44   Waldo, *Slenderella Cook Book*, 15. Consumers appear to have found displays of "plenty" in food promotion less appealing, in fact, as early as 1939. That was the year when, according to Eve Jochnowitz, the display of a "ton of food" consumed by the average American alongside scale models of New York skyscrapers, featured in a Department of Agriculture exhibit at the world's fair, "turned out not to be as appealing to the public as they might have wished." Similar exhibits had long been popular, suggesting that American attitudes toward food excess were changing. Jochnowitz quoted in Belasco, *Meals to Come*, 190; originally in Eve Jochnowitz, "Feasting on the Future: Serving Up the World of Tomorrow at the New York World's Fair of 1939–1940" (M.A. thesis, New York University 1997), 13.

45   Waldo, *Slenderella Cook Book*, 13. The argument that the ease of technological innovation had contributed to weight problems was also posed by Pollack and Morse in *How to Reduce Surely and Safely*.

46   West, *Stop Dieting!*, 13.

47   Woloson, *Refined Tastes*, 195; original citation found in Mary Elizabeth Hall, *Candy-Making Revolutionized: Confectionary from Vegetables* (New York: Sturgis & Walton, 1912), ii.

48 An example of this would be the success of Ernest Dichter, whose theories of psychology influenced food advertising in the 1950s. Dichter was famous for providing the rationale for the "one egg" cake mix and other products that enabled women to "prove" to themselves that they had, in fact, contributed something to dinner and thereby overcome their aversion to prepared food. For more information, see Shapiro, *Something from the Oven*, 63, 65.

49 Schwartz, *Never Satisfied*, 227; originally in Ursula Parrott, "Nice People Don't Eat," *Ladies' Home Journal*, March 1941, 58.

50 West, *Stop Dieting!*, 14–15.

CHAPTER THREE

1 Henry Schacht to Robert Gibson, November 24, 1970, cyclamates, August–December 1970, box 1315, CCG Archives. For information on the varieties of fruits canned with cyclamate by the California Canners, see plaintiff's response, 3, April 11, 1969, "cyclamate content of diet products," exhibits 1–75, box 1315, CCG Archives.

2 W. C. Gruber, deposition, 5, box 1959, CCG Archives. For figures on market share, see R. L. Gibson, deposition, 3, box 1959, CCG Archives.

3 Freidberg, *Fresh*.

4 Interview done by Sarah Rebolloso McCullough with Anne Pursell Blair, January 25, 2010 (interview in author's possession). Abbott Laboratories, *Abbott Tree*, describes the view upon entry: "You see a towering, heroic figure stretching skyward . . . taking its substance from a tree" (5).

5 The mural draws upon historical traditions in the United States of men employing technology and science in order to improve upon nature and, through that engagement, enable it to realize its full potential. In *America as Second Creation*, David Nye refers to this as the "second creation" and traces its tropes, particularly those that have enabled white Americans to claim Native lands. Joel Dinerstein, in "Technology and Its Discontents," insightfully connects such "second creations" to the "posthuman" evocations of technologically improved bodies freed from death and decay to show how persistent these scientific birth stories continue to be.

6 Greene, *Prescribing by Numbers*, 23.

7 For information on members, profits, and single-pool cooperative profit structure, see Don Toyoda, deposition, box 1959, CCG Archives.

8 A caveat is necessary here. My research does not intend to prove that all canning companies were run by men or that they engaged in relationships with pharmaceutical companies similar to the approach of the California Canners. My assertion is based on evidence that food technologists were primarily men (even at Tillie Lewis Foods, where a woman owned the company, the chief researcher in artificial sweeteners was male—see Chapter 4). Further, Abbott's promotional materials sent to the California Canners were standard and were sent to many prospective buyers in related food industries. It is likely that the Abbott/California Canners relationship was duplicated in other forums.

9 〈http://wikipedia.org/wiki/sodium_cyclamate〉 (accessesd May 25, 2010); McGrath, *Scientists, Business, and the State*, 3 (quote).

10 Herbert Ley Jr., commissioner on food and drugs, briefing paper, cyclamates, plaintiff's response to standard pretrial order on entitlement, exhibits 1–75, box 1315, CCG Archives.

11 "FDA for release," plaintiff's response to standard pretrial order on entitlement, exhibits 1–75, box 1315, CCG Archives.

12 Abbott Laboratories, *Abbott Almanac*, 141.

13 Saccharin continued to be used in many diet soda mixtures as well as in jams and jellies produced by the California Canners. It was eclipsed, however, by cyclamates during their two decades of market availability. By 1953 the industry standard ratio for diet soda was cyclamates to saccharin 10:1, with each providing roughly one-half of the sweetening power. See Havender, "Science and Politics of Cyclamate," 19.

14 Ley, plaintiff's response, box 1315, CCG Archives.

15 E. L. Mitchell, deposition, May 20, 1980, box 1959, CCG Archives.

16 Ibid.

17 E. L. Mitchell to R. Blayne McCurry, April 2, 1951, cyclamates, 1951–66, box 1922, CCG Archives.

18 Collins, *Story of Canned Foods*, 14–15.

19 Atwater quoted in Levenstein, *Paradox of Plenty*, 15.

20 Author interview with Dr. Clair Weast.

21 Levenstein, *Paradox of Plenty*, 11.

22 Edgar Carter to E. L. Mitchell, April 6, 1951, cyclamates, 1951–66, box 1922, CCG Archives.

23 Floyd Thayer to E. L. Mitchell, June 2, 1951, cyclamates, 1951–66, box 1922, CCG Archives.

24 E. L. Mitchell to Thayer, July 9, 1951, cyclamates, 1951–66, box 1922, CCG Archives. For the letter Mitchell sent to the FDA, see Mitchell to FDA, June 17, 1951, cyclamates, 1951–66, box 1922, CCG Archives.

25 Edgar Carter to J. R. Braden, October 1951, cyclamates, 1951–66, box 1922, CCG Archives.

26 Meikle, *American Plastic*, 41–43, quote from 43.

27 A. J. Paik to Edwin Mitchell, September 9, 1953, cyclamates, 1951–66, box 1922, CCG Archives.

28 Norman Lifflin to E. L. Mitchell, September 4, 1957, and Karl Beck to Edwin Mitchell, February 20, 1951, cyclamates, 1951–66, box 1922, CCG Archives.

29 Karl Beck to Ed Mitchell, February 23, 1959, cyclamates, 1951–66, box 1922, CCG Archives. Oddly, this same letter appears verbatim, dated November 3, 1959, in the CCG Archives. It seems possible that Beck did not recall sending the original letter and wanted to ensure that the diet syrup had been suggested. It may also suggest the high priority placed on promoting buyers' line extensions.

30 Beck to Mitchell, December 12, 1958, and Robert Nichols to E. L. Mitchell, n.d., cyclamates, 1951–66, box 1922, CCG Archives.

31 Karl Beck to Fischer Brokerage Company, n.d., stamped 1954, cyclamates, 1951–66, box 1922, CCG Archives.

32 Beck, "Have You Considered Artificial Sweeteners?"

33 Karl Beck to E. L. Mitchell, November 4, 1960, cyclamates, 1951–66, box 1922, CCG Archives.

34 Adrien Ringuette to E. L. Mitchell, February 1, 1962, cyclamates, 1951–66, box 1922, CCG Archives.

35 Edward Matson to E. N. Richmond, February 11, 1953, cyclamates, 1951–66, box 1922, CCG Archives. For information on the research studies done at the University of Illinois, see Herbert Kark, professor of medicine, to Arnold Osterberg, Abbott Labs, May 8, 1951, cyclamates, 1951–66, box 1922, CCG Archives.

36 Edward Matson to E. N. Richmond, February 11, 1953, cyclamates, 1951–66, box 1922, CCG Archives.

37 R. W. Nichols to E. L. Mitchell, February 22, 1956, and Karl Beck to E. L. Mitchell, April 11, 1961, cyclamates, 1951–66, box 1922, CCG Archives.

38 Unaddressed, unsigned memo, January 22, 1955, cyclamates, 1951–66, box 1922, CCG Archives.

39 Edward Matson to E. L. Mitchell, January 25, 1955, and Floyd Thayer to E. L. Mitchell, cyclamates, 1951–66, box 1922, CCG Archives.

40 Robert Nichols to E. L. Mitchell, February 22, 1956, and Karl Beck to E. L. Mitchell, April 11, 1961, cyclamates, 1951–66, box 1922, CCG Archives.

41 Internal memo, Richmond Chase, October 29, 1957, box 1922, cyclamates, 1951–66, box 1922, CCG Archives.

42 Manufacturing Chemists' Association, *Food Additives*, 14.

43 "Deposition of Edwin Lester Mitchell," May 20, 1980, box 1959, CCG Archives.

44 E. L. Mitchell, deposition, May 2, 1980, box 1959, CCG Archives.

45 Mitchell's comments taken from plaintiff's answers to defendant's first set of interrogatories, cyclamates, U.S. court of claims, box 1321, CCG Archives.

46 Marvin, *When Old Technologies Were New*, 9.

47 Historian Rayvon Fouche uses the concept of "technological assimilationism" to explain what motivated black engineer Lewis Latimer to innovate. Latimer, Fouche argues, was far more interested in social success than in technological success; as a black man he found that technological achievements admitted him to the ranks of white engineers that were otherwise closed. For Latimer, invention was a "credential . . . to enter and solidify his position within corporate electrical culture and the associated social and economic order." Like Mitchell, he pursued innovation for the personal and professional rewards. See Fouche, *Black Inventors in the Age of Segregation*, 84.

48 Nichols to Mitchell, October 29, 1957, cyclamates, 1951–66, box 1922, CCG Archives.

49 According to historian Vicki Ruiz, Freda Ehman founded an olive canning industry as a fifty-eight-year-old widow and personally managed the Oroville plant. Ruiz also discusses the history of Latina labor in California canning and the push for unionization. See Ruiz, *Cannery Women, Cannery Lives*, 23–25, 87.

50 Author interview with Dr. Clair Weast.

51 Greene, "Attention to 'Details,'" 276. According to Greene, *Detailing the Physician* devoted a full chapter to combating "doctor fright" (280).

52 Norman Lifflin to Richmond Chase, September 9, 1957, cyclamates, 1951–66, box 1922, CCG Archives.

53 Jack Brennan to E. L. Mitchell, April 2, 1964, cyclamates, 1951–66, box 1922, CCG Archives.

54 Ibid.

55 Nichols to Mitchell, February 4, 1963, cyclamates, 1951–66, box 1922, CCG Archives.

56 NRC study discussed in "Thayer Explains How Abbott Gained New Markets."

57 Edward Matson to E. L. Mitchell, February 26, 1953, cyclamates, 1951–66, box 1922, CCG Archives.

58 Food and Nutrition Board, NRC, summary statement on artificial sweeteners, December 2, 1954, cyclamates, 1951–66, box 1922, CCG Archives.

59 Lai, "Around the World," 30–31.

60 Articles quoted include Beck, "Have You Considered Artificial Sweeteners?"; Karl Beck and Norman Leffler, "How to Make Dietetic Frozen Desserts," *Ice Cream Trade Journal*, June 1958, 25; and Karl Beck, "Capture the Calorie-Counters' Coins," *Ice Cream Review*, March 1959, 88. Other articles are Edward Matson, "Sucaryl in Dietetic Beverages," *National Bottlers' Gazette*, April 1953, 12, 14, 19–20; Karl Beck, "What You Should Know about Sucaryl," *National Bottlers' Gazette*, December 1953, 15–16; Karl Beck, "Use of Sucaryl in Frozen Desserts," *Ice Cream Review*, February 1954, 47–48, 66; Karl Beck, "Basic Formulations of Special Dietary Frozen Desserts," *Ice Cream Review*, January 1957, 2644–45; Karl Beck, Robert Jones, and L. W. Murphy, "New Sweetener for Cured Meats," *Food Engineering*, May 1958, 114.

61 "Thayer Explains How Abbott Gained New Markets," 62. Most of the articles by Beck included a byline indicating his Abbott affiliation. At least one, however, does not, suggesting that at times "general news" about cyclamates was predigested by Abbott, unbeknownst to readers. See "Sucaryl 'Debate' Sparks Big Ohio Convention," *National Bottlers' Gazette*, December 1953, 4. In a bibliography provided by Abbott, a note next to this item indicates that it was contributed by Abbott personnel. See bibliography #77, Bob, western regional manager, Abbott to Ed Mitchell, September 18, 1961, cyclamates, 1951–66, box 1922, CCG Archives.

62 "1967 Annual Report: The In-Home Market for Low-Calorie Foods" and "1967 Annual Report: Low-Calorie Beverages in the Home Market," Abbott Laboratories, CCG Archives. These marketing surveys were also produced by competitors and sent to the California Canners and Growers. "Non-Nutritive Sweeteners for Low-Calorie Food and Beverages" (ca. 1966) was from Monsanto; see CCG Archives.

63 J. C. Lowey to E. L. Mitchell, December 26, 1967, cyclamates, 1967, box 1977, CCG Archives.

64 "Thayer Explains How Abbott Gained New Markets." See also "Abbott Teaches Dieters to Say Sucaryl," *Sales Management*, December 5, 1958, 62–66.

65 "Abbott Teaches Dieters to Say Sucaryl," *Sales Management*, December 5, 1958, 62.

66 Minutes of meetings, the Scientific Committee, Calorie Control Council, November 3, 1967, cyclamates, 1967, box 1977, CCG Archives.

67 "Commentary," July 1969, 7, cyclamates, 1969, January–September, box 1922, CCG Archives.

68 "Commentary," March 1969, 5, Calorie Control Council, cyclamates, 1969, January to September, box 1922, CCG Archives.

69 Lowey to Mitchell, February 16, 1968, and Mitchell to George Bradford, February 16, 1968, cyclamates, 1968, box 1922, CCG Archives.

70 Joseph Lowey to Maurice Charlat, September 20, 1968, cyclamates, 1968, box 1922, CCG Archives.

71 Henry Schacht to John Tobias, January 13, 1969, cyclamates 1969, box 1922, CCG Archives. Archival records indicate that the California Canners remained members of the CCC until 1976 or 1977 when they withdrew membership because it was too expensive to continue. Deposition of Edwin Mitchell, May 20, 1980, box 1959, pages unnumbered.

72 Hamilton to Charlat, June 3, 1969, cyclamates 1969 January–September, box 1922, CCG Archives.

73 The transition may have been facilitated by Schacht's relatively late arrival at the CCG in 1965. See Henry Schacht papers, 1941–94, D-157, Special Collections, University of California, Davis, online inventory at ⟨http://oac.cdlib.org/findaid/ark:/13030/kt500036jf⟩.

74 Robert Nichols to Ed Mitchell, June 3, 1965, cyclamates, 1951–66, box 1922, CCG Archives.

75 Ibid.

76 For information on the emerging studies, see P. O. Nees and Philip Derse, Wisconsin Alumni Research Foundation, "Effect of Feeding Calcium Cyclamate to Rats," *Nature*, March 25, 1967; Shoji Kojima, Hisashi Ichibagase, and Sado Iguchi, "Studies on Synthetic Sweetening Agents," report stamped "sugar research foundation library," January 11, 1967, cyclamates, 1967, box 1977, CCG Archives. For media coverage, see, for example, "Synthetic Sugar Peril Probed," *New York World Journal Tribune*, January 30, 1967; W. David Gardner, "Bitter News about Sweeteners," *New Republic*, September 14, 1968, and "Bitter Sweeteners," *Newsweek*, September 29, 1969, 83. Abbott responded to this press by assuring Mitchell that the flawed studies were the work of malevolent sugar interests. See J. C. Lowey to Mitchell, September 26, 1967, cyclamates, 1967, box 1977, CCG Archives.

77 Mitchell to Bradford, February 19, 1968, cyclamates, 1968, box 1922, CCG Archives.

78 Charlat to Mitchell, March 13, 1968, and Mitchell to Charlat, March 18, 1968, cyclamates, 1968, box 1922, CCG Archives.

79 Mitchell did go to other people for assurances, suggesting he never fully overcame his lack of faith in Abbott. Their assurances, however, ultimately echoed Abbott's, and Mitchell continued the California Canners' support of cyclamate sweetener. For example, Mitchell wrote to one member of the NRC committee, Emil Mrak of the University of California at Davis, and received a response suggesting that label restrictions might be likely after the committee issued its findings, but "I would be surprised if it went beyond that." See Mrak to Robert Gibson, November 19, 1968, cyclamates, 1968, box 1922, CCG Archives.

80 Lesser, "Dietetic Foods and the Pharmaceutical Industry," 611.

81 Although an eventual federal case for compensation brought roughly $10,000 per contributing farmer, the loss of nearly a year's worth of canned fruits was one that many in the co-op could not fully recover from.

82 For Mitchell's reaction, see Mitchell deposition, May 20, 1980, box 1959, CCG Archives; for an assessment of the irregularities of the ban decision, see Havender, "Science and Politics of Cyclamate," 22.

83 Havender, "Science and Politics of Cyclamate," 19. For Abbott's statement, see cyclamates, October 1969, box 1922, CCG Archives.

84 Harwood quoted in untitled paper, cyclamates, October 1969, box 1922, CCG Archives; inventory counts from Jay McFarland to Herm Zetterquist, "diet inventories," October 20, 1969, cyclamates, November/December, box 1922, CCG Archives.

85 Internal CCG memo from Memphis, Tennessee, to Jim Tobias, exhibit 351, exhibits 319–95, box 1315, CCG Archives; Ellen Speiden Parham, "Attitudes toward the Ban on Cyclamates"; John Sibley, "Housewives Take Ban on Cyclamates in Stride," *New York Times*, October 21, 1969, 49.

86 Memorandum for Mr. McCormick prepared by Mrs. Stoppello, November 10, 1969, cyclamates, November/December 1969, box 1922, CCG Archives.

87 Joseph Lowey, "Let's Clarify the Issues on Cyclamate Safety" program, seminar on nonnutritive sweeteners, October 8, 1969, box 1922, CCG Archives.

88 Burkholtz, *FDA Follies*, 39. For more information on the proceedings and their impact, see Bud, "Antibiotics, Big Business, and Consumers," 345.

CHAPTER FOUR

1 Untitled and undated article (ca. September 1953), box 1, folder 4, Lewis Collection, SJHS.

2 Historian Jennifer Scanlon's research on the *Ladies' Home Journal* of the 1920s reveals that women were first hired and given authority in consumer research departments because of their ability to get at the real desires of women and, as a result, create compelling product advertisements. See Scanlon, *Inarticulate Longings*.

3 See, for instance, Schwartz, *Never Satisfied*, and Levenstein, *Paradox of Plenty*.

4 Ken Albala points out that Flotill in fact bought an Illinois company called Dietex Foods in 1951. It is possible that Dietex Foods, flavored with sorbitol, provided a model for the early packaging and marketing of Tasti-Diet. See Albala, "Tillie Lewis," 10–11.

5 Author interview with Dr. Clair Weast.

6 "Tillie's Unpunctured Romance."

7 "Women in Business and Industry," speech, Soroptimist International of Lodi, February 5, 1979, box 1, folder 1, SJHS; Dorothy Walworth, "Tillie of the Valley," *Reader's Digest*, August 1952.

8 "Women in Business and Industry," 5, speech, Soroptimist International of Lodi, February 5, 1979, box 1, folder 1, SJHS.

9 The evidence for this relationship is explored in Albala, "Tillie Lewis."

10 See Lewis, speech before Lodi group, unpublished manuscript, 5, in Lewis Collection, SJHS, and "Tillie's Unpunctured Romance."

11 Tillie Lewis's formidable skills at turning situations to her own advantage may, in fact, have led to her second marriage, and the very name Tillie Lewis. She went by Tillie Wiesenberg, from her first marriage, until she met Meyer Lewis

when he was the organizer of a pending strike in one of her plants. According to folklore, after an hour the two had sufficiently impressed each other that the strike was called off, and he came to work for her as general manager. Seven years later, they were married. See "Tillie's Unpunctured Romance."

12　"Who Is Tillie Lewis?," *Reader's Digest*, August 1952, 102–3; Albala, "Tillie Lewis," 7.

13　Tillie Lewis brochure, box 2, folder 5, SJHS.

14　"Woman's Idea Builds Three Canneries," *PG&E Progress*, August 1953, 2, box 1, folder 5, Lewis Collection, SJHS.

15　"Who Is Tillie Lewis?," *Reader's Digest*, August 1952, 106. According to Clair Weast, the idea to bring in a steam engine had been his, and the saccharin experiments were done on his and his wife's own time, without Tillie's input.

16　Albala, "Tillie Lewis," 8.

17　Dorothy Walworth, "Tillie of the Valley," *Reader's Digest*, August 1952.

18　Untitled article, February 12, 1953, box 1, folder 6, SJHS.

19　William McCormack, "Tillie Lewis," 11–13 (unpublished senior paper, History Department, Stanislaus State College, December 1968), box 1, folder 2, SJHS.

20　"Tillie Lewis: 'First Lady of the Larder,'" *Good Packaging*, December 1975, 8, SJHS.

21　"Who Is Tillie Lewis?," unpublished manuscript, 2–3, box 1, folder 2, SJHS.

22　*Good Housekeeping*, April 1954, 137.

23　Author interview with Dr. Clair Weast. The *San Francisco Examiner*'s diet plan debuted on September 27, 1953. Lewis also had a promotional schedule in Iowa in 1953 (this seems to have been the first attempt at a nonlocal market) and on stock photo image she claims Des Moines is an active market. There is also a trade show photo in her archive from Cleveland, May 1952, box 2, folder 6, Lewis Collection, SJHS.

24　"This Is Dieting," September 1953, box 1, folder 4, SJHS. According to historian Elaine Tyler May, "One retrospective study of the attitudes and habits of over 4,000 Americans in 1957 found that reliance on expertise was one of the most striking developments of the postwar years" (*Homeward Bound*, 21).

25　"Final Week of Easy Low-Calorie Reducing," October 4, 1953, box 1, folder 4, SJHS.

26　"When You've Won the Battle of the Bulge," *Chicago American*, September 6, 1953, box 1, folder 4, SJHS.

27　Ibid.

28　September 1953, box 1, folder 4, SJHS. Katherine Parkin argues that "one of the most enduring advertising messages" in American food promotion history is "that women should show their love through food"; see her *Food Is Love*, 70.

29　"New 21 Day Diet by Tillie Lewis," box 3, folder 2, SJHS.

30　Photograph of trade show, box 2, folder 6, SJHS.

31　Operation Turnover scrapbook, box 1, folder 3, Lewis Collection, SJHS.

32　Medical brochures, miscellaneous, box 2, folder 2, Lewis Collection, SJHS. Advertisement "Obesity Correction" is also from this collection.

33　Lewis seems also to have sent product samples to a number of politically influential people. One of these was California state representative Leroy Johnson (in whose district Stockton was located), who in July 1955 advertised Lewis's products before the entire House of Representatives. He was motivated, in part, by the need to promote the wares from his district. His personal testimony that he "could not tell the difference" between Tasti-Diet chocolate ice cream and regular chocolate ice cream, however, suggests that he had been provided with a fair amount of product for taste testing. See *Congressional Record*, July 13, 1955. For the Outstanding Woman in Food prize, see article, September 25, 1952, box 1, folder 3, Lewis Collection, SJHS.

34 Greene, *Prescribing by Numbers*, 9.

35 LeBesco, *Revolting Bodies*, 1.

36 Scanlon, *Bad Girls Go Everywhere*, 78, 30.

37 Author interview with Dr. Clair Weast; Scanlon, *Bad Girls Go Everywhere*, 203–4.

38 Box 2, folder 6, Lewis Collection, SJHS.

39 See Cohen, *Consumers' Republic*. According to historian Charles McGovern, after the combined experiences of prosperity, depression, and war, by 1950 "an ideology emerged naming plenty as the distinctive feature of an exceptional American history and culture." So important was the private consumption of goods to this ideology that in fact a new form of "material nationalism" emerged whereby goods and spending were "at the center of social life." See McGovern, *Sold American*, 3.

40 *Brides* magazine quoted in Cohen, *Consumers' Republic*, 119. Lewis quotes, box 2, folder 6, Lewis Collection, SJHS.

41 Cultural geographers and sociologists have argued that this contradiction is at the heart of American neoliberalism. Julie Guthman and Melanie DuPuis assert that "the neoliberal shifts in personhood from citizen to consumer encourages (over)eating at the same time that neoliberal notions of discipline vilify it." See Guthman and DuPuis, "Embodying Neoliberalism," 329–51.

42 Scanlon, *Inarticulate Longings*.

43 "Woman Who Plans to Reduce Americans by 420 Million Pounds Tells Story," *Chicago American*, September 5, 1953, box 1, folder 4, SJHS.

44 Data from 303 consumer surveys taken randomly from thousands of postcards sent to the Flotill headquarters requesting more information on Tasti-Diet products, 1954, p. 5, box 2, folder 2, SJHS.

45 Nancy Koehn, "Estée Lauder: Self-Definition and the Modern Cosmetics Market," in Scranton, *Beauty and Business*, 232.

46 Al O'Dea, "To Our Brokers," November 21, 1966, "Food Editors Conference" folder, CCG Archives.

47 "How to Succeed in Business without Getting Fat," 1966 Newspaper Food Editors Conference, Boston, Massachusetts, September 28, 1966, box 1374, CCG Archives.

48 Al O'Dea, "To Our Brokers," November 21, 1966, "Food Editors Conference" folder, CCG Archives.

49 A sample of the articles, all from box 1374, CCG Archives, includes Katherine Harrington's "The Thin Line: How Low Calorie Foods Can Be Delicious," reporting on the meeting with recipes from the lunch, in the *Knickerbocker News*, Albany, N.Y., October 1966; "Persian Peach Chicken," in the *Arizona Republic*, Phoenix, October 7, 1966; "Low Calorie Dishes Continue to be Popular" (also with chicken recipe) and "Diet Foods Gain Favor," in "Today's Woman," *Phoenix Gazette*, October 3, 1966; Clementine Paddleford's "Low Calorie Landslide," in

the *World Journal Tribune*, October 2, 1966, sec. 2, p. 7; "Our Eating Habits Are Changing," with photo of apricot mousse, in the *Los Angeles Herald Examiner*, October 25, 1966; food editor Ann Chester's "New Pleasures for the Dieter," in the *Herald Statesman*, Yonkers, N.Y., October 1, 1966; and "Chicken Luncheon Keeps Calories Low," in the *Plain Dealer*, September 29, 1966. The *Boston Herald*, September 30, 1966, had photos of Dorothy Siez of the *Dallas Times Herald*, Camille Jilke of the *Chicago Sun Times*, and Sara Spano, food editor of the *Columbus Ledger Inquirer*, on the last day of conference. Additional articles appeared on October 27, 1966, in the *Cincinnati Inquirer*, *Long Beach Press Telegram*, *Philadelphia Inquirer*, *Jersey Journal*, *Post and Times Star* of Cincinnati, and *Moline Dispatch*. See also *Allentown Chronicle and Call*, October 13, 1966; *Boston Morning Globe*, September 28, 1966; *Sunday Oklahoman* women's news, October 2, 1966; and the *Washington Daily News*, September 29, 1966.

50 Marketing and advertising studies, folder v. 2, 4/66–5/66, newspaper coverage from 1–2e on January 20, 1966, January 29, 1968, and January 9, 1966, box 53, CCG Archives.

51 Howard, *Brides, Inc.*, 78.

52 Parkin, *Food Is Love*.

53 From the author's survey of *Ladies' Home Journal* and *Good Housekeeping* covering January, April, July, and November between 1964 and 1977.

54 One reason why one sees more alignment between advertisement and editorial content in magazines may be that magazine editors had much more control over overall content than did newspaper food editors. Poppy Cannon was actively courted by the Calorie Control Council in the 1960s, an effort that they said (without apparently irony) "had yet to bear fruit." Yet Cannon had produced her own cookbook, *Unforbidden Sweets*, using artificial sweetener in her own recipes in 1958.

55 Box 1958, CCG Archives. *Reader's Digest* had supported cyclamates in its copy since 1953. That year Dean Jennings wrote an article on Sucaryl declaring it "the result of monumental patience coupled with industrial know-how" and explaining that "it is now more than a figure of speech to say that dieters can have their cake and eat it too" ("Sucaryl Starts a Boom in Low-Calorie Food and Drink," December 1953, 118–20).

56 Cyclamates 1969, Jan.–Sept., box 1922, CCG Archives; *Reader's Digest*, June 3, 1969.

57 Cyclamates 1969, Jan.–Sept., box 1922, CCG Archives.

58 Nidetch, *Story of Weight Watchers*.

59 Schwartz, *Never Satisfied*, 191–93, 204.

60 By 1972 there were 3 million readers each month, according to *Weight Watchers* own subscription records. See *Weight Watchers*, March 1972, 53.

61 Nidetch, *Story of Weight Watchers*, 140.

62 Ibid., 27.

63 Ibid., 30.

64 "In the glove compartment of my car, I'd carry a can of asparagus and a can opener. I was always thinking that if I got stuck in traffic, I wouldn't want to die of starvation" (ibid., 194).

65 Ibid., 196.

66 Ibid., 19, 28, 30–31.

67 *Weight Watchers Magazine*, February 1968, 5 (Sweet'N Low), 30–35 (desserts).

68 "The New Weight Watchers Program: New Foods," *Weight Watchers Magazine*, March 1977, 53.

69 For the early product advertisements, see "For People Who Enjoy Eating but Can't Afford to Look Like It," *Weight Watchers Magazine*, May 1973, 1.

70 *Weight Watchers Magazine*, February 1973, 1.

71 Ibid., May 1976, 27.

72 Ibid., January 1973, 8.

73 Nidetch, *Story of Weight Watchers*, 204.

74 *Weight Watchers Magazine*, August 1982.

75 Berlant, *Female Complaint*, viii.

76 Ibid., 3.

CHAPTER FIVE

1 Belasco, *Appetite for Change*; Lappé, *Diet for a Small Planet*.

2 Mintz, *Tasting Food, Tasting Freedom*, 72, 77 (antisaccharites' compaign).

3 Actual numbers vary by account. I have verified that there are roughly 50,000 letters in the FDA archive from 1977. Historian Hillel Schwartz estimates that, in total, 100,000 letters reached Congress. Thousands of letters were received by the president. According to James Martin, representative from North Carolina, he received 6,000 letters from his constituents alone; he estimated, in his request for an extension to the saccharin ban ruling, that in 1977 "legislators have heard from a million angry citizens." If we include among these letters the thousands that were sent in protest to local newspapers and the roughly 100 separate petitions sent to the FDA (each with 20–100 signatures), this estimate appears accurate, if not an underreporting of total respondents. Martin quoted in Culliton, "Saccharin," 1179. See also Schwartz, *Never Satisfied*, 266. It is worth noting that not all of these letters were against the ban. While far less frequent, letters supporting the ban appear in the archive; see, for example, Mrs. Mullan to FDA, n.d. (#1426, cd1, f15), and E. Penny to Honorable Joseph Califano, Secretary of Department of HEW, March 15, 1977 (#3727, cd1, f40), FDA Records.

4 Rep. Barbara Mikulski, in U.S. Congress, House, *Hearings*, 6.

5 Rep. Lloyd Meeds, in ibid., 8. One letter suggests that the redesign of Weight Watchers' plan in the early 1970s in favor of more artificially sweetened foods may have influenced many letter writers to defend saccharin. "Recently the Weight Watcher's organization made modifications in their original diet to include many dietetic products which contain saccharin in an attempt to make the diet plan a more feasible one for its members who enjoy the 'fat foods,'" explained Patricia Amador from Brooklyn Center, Minnesota. "Needless to say," she continued, "the ban on saccharin would put a damper on this new enjoyable diet" (Amador to FDA, March 14, 1977 (#219, cd1, v3), FDA Records).

6 Of the 400 letters I reviewed, only 9 were from individuals supporting the ban.

7 U.S. Congress, House, *Hearings*, 42. This was, in fact, precisely what had happened in consumer reactions to the 1969 ban on cyclamates.

8 Ralph Nader's crusades to supply children with flame-retardant pajamas and outfit automobiles with seat belts were just two examples of myriad campaigns that led to legislation passed in the 1960s and 1970s, most of it with significant consumer support. See Huber, "Old-New Division in Risk Regulation."

9 The quote is taken from a study conducted by the Opinion Research Corporation in 1968 that found seven in ten Americans agreeing with that quote. Cited in Bailey and Farber, *America in the '70s*, 235.

10 A note on method: my evidentiary base here is 40,000 letters currently archived at the FDA, all of them written in the first year after the proposed ban. I have looked closely at 1 percent of these, or 400 total. I focused specifically on letters written in the first two weeks after the announcement, reasoning that the writers would be individuals with the most at stake. Also within this first week, the sample captures the "gut responses" to the action from individuals who placed an exceptionally high value on saccharin. Responses sent after the second week appear after weight-watching organizations had met and discussed the ban and saccharin manufacturers had taken out advertisements placing the ban in their own contexts. I have, with one or two exceptions, used letters from women, as they comprised the vast majority of writers. I have not used letters from individuals who specifically identified as diabetics, because their dietary restrictions made saccharin a different "necessity" than it was for nondiabetics. Within these parameters, I used relevant letters from the first 15 in each archived FDA CD "folder" (containing approximately 125–150 letters). I augmented these with other letters in each folder of notable length in order to analyze how those writers who took the time to situate saccharin in larger contexts chose to do so.

11 Nash, *Inescapable Ecologies*, 12.

12 Carson, *Silent Spring*.

13 "Chronology of Significant Events Relating to Saccharin," in U.S. Congress, House, *Hearings*, 45–46.

14 U.S. Congress, House, *Hearings*, 42.

15 Lappé, *Diet for a Small Planet*; Carson, *Silent Spring*.

16 German sociologist Ulrich Beck urged scholars to consider, some twenty years ago, the implications for a paradigm shift he called the "risk society." Arriving with advanced modernization, the risk society necessitated the continual posing and answering of the question, "How can the risks and hazards systematically produced as part of modernization be prevented, minimized, dramatized, or channeled?" Nuclear meltdowns, toxic pollution, and global warming are by-products of our particular economic, political, and technological systems. So are more local, low-level dangers such as cigarette smoke, murky waters, and even car travel. For some people with means, these risks can be overcome. For others, these risks are harder to control on an individual level. But they can be dramatized (through letter writing, for example) and channeled (by comparing one uncontrollable risk to another, controllable one). Using Beck as a lens through which to view many of these letters enables us to speculate that for those who could not control their immediate surroundings with wealth or power, saccharin offered an important way to at least control one's right to pleasurable risk. See Beck, *Risk Society*, 76.

17 Saccharin was also used in drugs, cosmetics, industrial processes, and animal feed. According to congressional testimony, 74 percent of saccharin consumed in the United States in 1976 was consumed in food and beverages, and 12 percent of it was consumed directly in the form of Sweet'N Low in coffee and tea and on cereal. See U.S. Department of Health, Education, and Welfare, "Saccharin and Its Salts: Proposed Rule Making," April 15, 1977 (included in U.S. Congress, House, *Hearings*).

18 Melmon's comments were made in 1976 at an American Academy of Sciences forum on sweeteners. See National Academy of Sciences, *Sweeteners*, 164–65.

19 See, for example, "Saccharin as Villain," unspecified newspaper article sent with Virginia Hetman's letter from Garfield Heights, Ohio, March 12, 1977 (#502, cd1, v12), and "Gone Too Far," *Houston Tribune*, sent with Irene Gaines's letter from Houston, Texas, March 16, 1977 (#1495, cd1, f15), both in FDA Records. The initial FDA press release is described in Smith, "Latest Saccharin Tests," 154.

20 Hurd to FDA, March 11, 1977 (#425, cd1, v12), FDA Records.

21 Turel to FDA, March 11, 1977 (#22, cd1, v1), FDA Records.

22 Deardorff to FDA, March 14, 1977 (#2732, cd1, v30), and O'Brien to FDA (#3129, cd1, v35), FDA Records.

23 "Nick O. Teen," from anonymous letter to FDA, n.d. (#18899, cd5, v151), and "Need I Say More?," from Robert Revell to FDA, March 22, 1977 (#4279, cd1, v45), FDA Records.

24 The sample included roughly 400 of 40,000 letters contained in the FDA Records. Of these, 200 were taken from the first six days (March 9–14) and 200 from the following nine days (March 15–24). These 400 included the first 15 letters of each folder within the archive over those days. These were then augmented by letters of notable length or descriptive content.

25 Gottlieb, *Forcing the Spring*, 244.

26 It is impossible from this limited study to conclusively analyze the demographics of saccharin rebels. Some overall patterns can be noted: most letters were written by women with Anglo surnames; many writers specifically state that they have little experience with politics and do not expect to be listened to; at least half write on flowery stationary in flowing cursive; many of the letters contain misspellings. Most importantly, the majority of letters emerge from the Midwest and Southeast regions of the United States. Particularly high concentrations of letters were sent from Allentown, Pennsylvania, and Lexington, Kentucky. These were not areas of affluence. Many were manufacturing centers hit hard by the off-shoring of factory work in the early to mid-1970s.

27 Kennedy quoted in Culliton, "Saccharin," 1183.

28 Dumm to FDA, March 10, 1977 (#573, cd1, v13), FDA Records.

29 Hoffman to FDA, March 15, 1977 (#1390, cd1, v20), FDA Records.

30 Turel to FDA, March 11, 1977 (#22, cd1, v1), and Pearlman to FDA, March 14, 1977 (#272, cd1, v4), FDA Records.

31 Starks to FDA, March 14, 1977 (#612, cd1, v13), FDA Records.

32 Greene to FDA, March 10, 1977 (#452, cd1, v12), and Duemler to FDA, Glendale, Missouri, March 15, 1977 (#17348, cd5, v151), FDA Records.

33 Wilson, "Commentary."

34 Beck, *Risk Society*, 36.

35 Windle to FDA, n.d. (#74, cd1, v1), FDA Records.

36 Keller to FDA, March 11, 1977 (#9, cd1, v1), FDA Records.

37 Gottlieb, *Forcing the Spring*, 244.

38 Hurd to FDA, March 11, 1977 (#425, cd1, v12), FDA Records.

39 Novak to FDA, March 10, 1977 (#3122, cd1, v35), FDA Records.

40 Whereas in 1966, 73 percent of individuals polled had expressed faith in such knowledge, by 1975 the figure was down to 42 percent. Quoted in Berkowitz, *Something Happened*, 6.

41 Gibbons to FDA, March 10, 1977 (#323, cd1, v4), FDA Records.

42 Bordo, *Unbearable Weight*, 149.

43 Robinson to FDA, March 10, 1977 (#2689, cd1, v30); Ormondroyd to FDA, March 20, 1977 (#4721, cd1, v40); Johnston to FDA, March 15, 1977 (#3740, cd1, v40); De-Vore to FDA, March 14, 1977 (#3739, cd1, v40); Newport to FDA, March 18, 1977 (#3796, cd1, v40), all in FDA Records.

44 Mrs. James Fallman to the FDA, n.d., Waco, Texas (#364, cd1, v4), FDA Records.

45 Appadurai, *Social Life of Things*, 41, 50.

46 Sze, *Noxious New York*. 209. See p. 109 for Sze's discussion of how asthma activists "prioritized" voices of children of color.

47 See #239, cd1, v3, FDA Records.

48 Beck, *Risk Society*, 23.

49 Bray, *Obesity*, 209.

50 Ibid., 75.

51 Jefferson Cowie, "Vigorously Left, Right, and Center," in Bailey and Farber, *America in the '70s*, 102.

52 Kessler, March 10, 1977 (#141, cd1, v4); anonymous (#10,151, cd10, v341); Haven-ker, March 11, 1977 (#236, cd1, v3); J. R. Murdock, n.d. (#1417, cd1, v20), FDA Records.

53 Schuster to FDA, n.d. (#903, cd1, v15), FDA Records. See also Mrs. Gyne Baker to Secretary Califano, March 22, 1977 (#19,043, cd12, v414), and Nancy Townsend to FDA, March 14, 1977 (#237, cd1, v3), FDA Records.

54 Smith to FDA, March 10, 1977 (#347, cd1, v4), and Martin to FDA, March 8, 1977 (#20, cd1, v1), FDA Records.

55 Morean to FDA, received April 14, 1977 (#21,794, cd6, v170), FDA Records.

56 Baker to FDA (#19,043, cd5, v151), FDA Records.

57 See, for instance, Elizabeth Shaw Plummer to FDA, n.d. (#229 cd1, v3); Patricia Amador to FDA, March 14, 1977 (#219, cd1, v3); and Homer Stephens to FDA, n.d. (#239, cd1, v3), FDA Records.

58 Culliton, "Saccharin," 1182.

59 See ⟨http://www.youtube.com/watch?v=uDBJ2ktSZpI⟩ (accessed August 2009).

60 Rogers to FDA, March 23, 1977 (#18,948, cd5, v151), FDA Records.

61 La Pointe to FDA, March 15, 1977 (#302, cd1, v4), FDA Records.

62 Sanders to FDA, March 11, 1977 (#488, cd1, v12), FDA Records.

63 Schwartz, *Never Satisfied*, 246.

64 Kew to FDA (#648, cd1, v13), FDA Records.

65 Newcombe to FDA, March 16, 1977 (#1384, cd1, v20); D'Amico to FDA, March

16, 1977 (#810, cd1, v15); Amador to FDA, March 14, 1977 (#219, cd1, v3), FDA Records.

66 McMullen to FDA, n.d. (#66, cd1, v1), FDA Records. Louisville, Kentucky, and Allentown, Pennsylvania, were the most common cities of origin for the letters in my sample. Both had strong Weight Watchers organizations, and many individual writers identified themselves as so affiliated. See also Kew to FDA, n.d. (#648, cd1, v13), FDA Records.

67 According to Schwartz, one could claim in 1924, using this data, that "half of all Americans over the age of thirty-five were overweight" (*Never Satisfied*, 157). For information on the first home scales and how they differed, with an emphasis on privacy in design and location, from earlier public penny scales, see ibid., 169 and 170, respectively.

68 Ibid., 208.

69 Wright to FDA, no address, March 16, 1977 (#284, cd1, v4); Tamarin to FDA, Newton Center, Mass., March 15, 1977 (#17431, cd45, v151); Kundert to FDA, Molalla, Ore. (#17985, cd5, v146); Sanders to FDA, Montgomery, Ala., March 11, 1977 (#488, cd1, v12), FDA Records.

70 Wright to FDA, no address, March 16, 1977 (#284, cd1, v4); Tamarin to FDA, Newton Center, Mass., March 15, 1977 (#17431, cd45, v151); Virginia Allee, Boulder, Colo., n.d. (#588, cd1, v13), FDA Records.

71 Novak to FDA, March 10, 1977 (#3122, cd1, v35), FDA Records.

72 Corbin to FDA, March 10, 1977 (#335, cd1, v4); Bold to FDA, March 11, 1977 (#71, cd1, v1); Emory to FDA, March 14, 1977 (#278, cd1, v4), FDA Records.

73 Richardson to FDA, March 16, 1977 (#815, cd1, v5); Roy to FDA, March 16, 1977 (#895, cd1, v15); Magee to FDA, March 15, 1977 (#631, cd1, v13), FDA Records.

74 U.S. Congress, Senate, *Dietary Goals for the United States*, 43.

75 Galbraith, "How Much Should a Country Consume?," 92.

76 "How to Succeed in Business without Getting Fat," September 28, 1966, box 1374, CCG Archives.

77 Plummer to FDA, March 15, 1977 (#229, cd1, v3), FDA Records; Beck, *Risk Society*, 76.

78 "Why the Proposed FDA Ban on Saccharin," *Los Angeles Times*, March 13, 1977, A22; "Let Yourself Be Heard," *Wall Street Journal*, March 14, 1977, 15.

79 77n-0085, cd15, v519, received May 11, 1977, FDA Records.

80 Smith, "Latest Saccharin Tests," 154.

81 The *Wall Street Journal* quoted the CCC's president, who called the FDA ban "an example of colossal government overregulation in disregard of science and the wants and needs of consumers" ("How Sweet It Was," *Wall Street Journal*, March 14, 1977, 16).

82 Mansfield to FDA, March 18, 1977 (#3211, cd1, v35), and Hertz to FDA, origin unclear, March 15, 1977 (#18,074, cd5, v146), FDA Records.

83 Phyllis Callahan to FDA, March 10, 1977 (#31, v1, cd1), FDA Records.

84 Nidetch features Celesta Wiley, "who lost 73 pounds," prominently in one full-page photograph. An African American woman can also be seen in one of the photographs of Nidetch with a crowd. Both of these photographs appear to have been taken in the mid- to late 1960s. See *Story of Weight Watchers*.

85 The "Like" campaign, designed by J. Walter Thompson to promote 7-Up's new diet soda in the early 1970s, featured only white women, nearly all of them blonde, in its ten advertisements. See "Like" Advertising Collection, Duke University, Duke Advertising Archives, Durham, N.C.

86 See, for example, *Ebony* advertisements from September 1986, 63; December 1985, 63; and January 1987, 116–17. For information on Michael Jackson's pitch for Pepsi (which resulted in the infamous scalp fire) and Coke's subsequent enlistment of black celebrities to sell Coke and Diet Coke, see Pamela Noel, "TV Ad Wars' Newest Weapon," *Ebony*, July 1984, 81–86. Ads for artificially sweetened products that featured African Americans in non–African American newspapers and magazines frequently featured famous African American men. See, for example, Famous Amos pitching chocolate soda in the *New York Times*, November 3, 1985, 73; Bill Cosby promoting Jell-O Instant Pudding in the *Los Angeles Times*, June 9, 1985, AJ67; and Flip and Geraldine Wilson with Diet 7-Up, *McCall's*, March 1981, 69.

87 Smith, "Latest Saccharin Tests," 154.

88 Culliton, "Saccharin," 1179.

89 Cox to FDA, March 11, 1977 (#24, cd1, v1); McDermott to FDA, March 11, 1977 (#135, cd1, v1); Kessler to FDA, March 10, 1977 (#141, cd1, v1), FDA Records. Part of the sympathy for the diet industry and its workers may have been encouraged by a conspiracy theory shared by many letter writers in which the sugar "lobby," facing shortages and price hikes in the early 1970s, organized to ban saccharin in order to ensure the forced consumption of their products. See, for example, Carole White to FDA, Edgewood, Md., March 10, 1977 (#3, cd1 v1), FDA Records.

90 Didrichsen to FDA, Cincinnati, Ohio, March 11, 1977 (#856, cd1, v15), FDA Records.

91 Barbara Wackly, Kansas City, Mo., March 16, 1977 (#18,036, cd5, v146), FDA Records.

92 Kloberdanz to FDA, n.d. (#1496, cd1, v20), FDA Records.

CHAPTER SIX

1 Lawler, *Sweet Talk*, 13.

2 ⟨http://en.wikipedia.org/wiki/Aspartame⟩ (accessed May 25, 2010).

3 Marie and Piggott, *Handbook of Sweeteners*, 132.

4 Ibid., 132–33.

5 Roberts, *Aspartame*, 1.

6 According to Belasco, food industry executives realized that the market for food consumption was limited by a "natural" 2 percent expansion in population growth. This was not a sufficient profit margin, many believed, and therefore they developed alternative messages about fun, pleasure, and excitement around packaged foods. See Belasco, *Meals to Come*, 55.

7 See Parkin, *Food Is Love*.

8 *Good Housekeeping*, April 1966, 69.

9 See, for example, the five ads for these products in the September 1980 issue of *Ladies' Home Journal* or the six in the March 1982 issue of *Good Housekeeping*.

10 NutraSweet advertisements frequently featured comments from individuals

who had tried the gumballs. See *McCall's*, July 1984, 2–3, and *Newsweek*, January 9, 1984, 60–61.

11 *Newsweek*, January 9, 1984, 61.

12 McCann, *Sweet Success*, viii, and William Robbins, "Rumsfeld's Remedy for Searle," *New York Times*, March 16, 1979, D1.

13 McCann, *Sweet Success*, 6.

14 ⟨http://wikipedia.org/wiki/Aspartame_controversy⟩ (accessed May 25, 2010).

15 McCann, *Sweet Success*, 55–56.

16 Ibid., 78.

17 *Newsweek*, June 11, 1984, 4–5.

18 Lawler, *Sweet Talk*, 44.

19 Norris, "Ingredient Branding," 20.

20 *Good Housekeeping*, October 1984, 292–93.

21 Brock, "Midwest Marketer of the Year."

22 *Newsweek*, November 18, 1985, 76–77.

23 Wendy Wall, "Marketing NutraSweet in Leaner Times," *Wall Street Journal*, May 7, 1987, 32. Originally quoted in McCann, *Sweet Success*, 59.

24 Gregory Gordon, "Putting on the Blitz: The Selling of a Sweetener," *United Press International, Washington News*, October 14, 1987, n.p., online, and Brock, "Nutra-Sweet Ads Sweet on Nature."

25 Brock, "NutraSweet Ads Sweet on Nature."

26 "Label Says It Does," *New York Times*, December 14, 1984, B11; "Check the Facts," *New York Times*, December 9, 1984, B9; "An Open Letter," *New York Times*, December 24, 1984, 20.

27 *Good Housekeeping*, May 1985, 64.

28 Ibid., 213.

29 See also "Something Sweet You and Your Child Can Agree On," *Newsweek*, June 11, 1984, 4–5.

30 Lawler, *Sweet Talk*, 17.

31 Michael McCarthy, *Wall Street Journal*, January 24, 1989, 1.

32 McCann, *Sweet Success*, 3.

33 Nabors and Gelardi, *Alternative Sweeteners*, 60.

34 Bailey and Farber, *America in the '70s*, 65.

35 Ibid., 127.

36 Appadurai, "Consumption, Duration, and History," 31.

37 Austin, "Commodity Knowledge," 162.

38 Crawford, "Cultural Account of 'Health,'" 67–68.

39 Ibid., 75.

40 Ibid., 93.

41 Lippert, "Reality Check."

42 Biltekoff, "Terror Within," 6; Oliver, *Fat Politics*.

43 Weaver, Gaines, and Ebron, *Slim Down Sister*, 11. Quoted in Biltekoff, "Terror Within," 18.

44 Thomas, *Improving America's Diet and Health*, 25, 211.

45 Whitney, Sizer, and Hamilton, *Understanding Nutrition*; see p. 54 in 1981 edition and pp. 82–83 in the 1984 edition.

46 Grenby, Parker, and Lindley, *Developments in Sweeteners*, v.

47 Frank Prial, "Secrets of a Chocoholic," *New York Times*, May 16, 1979, c1, c3.

48 Scarpa, Kiefer, and Tatum, *Sourcebook on Food and Nutrition*, 3.

49 Yudkin, *Sweet and Dangerous*, front matter.

50 Ibid., 183.

51 Ibid.

52 Ellen Ruppel Shell, "Fear of Sugar: Has It Gotten out of Hand?," *Atlantic Monthly*, reprinted in *San Francisco Chronicle*, October 6, 1985, n.p., online.

53 American Council on Science and Health, *Diet and Behavior*, 15.

54 Wolraich, Lindgren, Stumbo, Stegink, and Kiritsy, "Effects of Diets High in Sucrose or Aspartame," 301.

55 Lawler, *Sweet Talk*, 36.

56 Feldman, *Essentials of Clinical Nutrition*, 138.

57 The exact figure cited was 62 percent of readers. See *Weight Watchers Magazine*, Spring 1989, letter from Kathleen Parmenter, Vice President of Advertising.

58 Gussow and Jacobson quoted in Robert Johnson, "Nutritionists Detect a Dark Side in New World of Food Substitutes," *Wall Street Journal*, February 3, 1988, 25.

59 Roberts, *Aspartame*, 5.

60 Ibid., 4; Blaylock, *Excitotoxins*, 220; Mercola and Pearsall, *Sweet Deception*, 36.

61 Roberts, *Aspartame*, 5.

62 ⟨http://www.aspartamesafety.com/FAQ.htm⟩ (accessed August 2008).

63 ⟨http://www.aspartamesafety.com/mary_nash_stoddard.htm⟩. In her website description of events, it is Stoddard who has had the courage to reveal the "hidden epidemic" and the "government cover-up" and who is now helping hundreds of other people diagnose their own symptoms as aspartame-related. She mentions the crowds who gather on her tours, signaling the respect she is accorded by her many followers. Yet a closer look at the photo gallery shows that Stoddard's speaking engagements appear to have taken place mostly within the United States (Florida, Ohio, Arkansas, Texas, Wyoming, and Minnesota), with one in Canada and one in Puerto Rico (sponsored by the sugar industry). In addition to advising pilots about the risks of aspartame, she makes presentations before "D.C. brain tumor panels." She does not claim to have trained medical professionals or saved airline passengers from death at the hands of pilots who consumed too many diet sodas. These are, however, conclusions that one could reach after a quick reading of the anecdotal evidence on her site.

64 See, for instance, DuPuis, *Nature's Perfect Food*, and Griffith, *Born Again Bodies*. Gwen Shamblin's "Weigh Down Diet" website can be found at ⟨http://www.wdworkshop.com/⟩.

65 ⟨http://www.sweetpoison.com/about-janet-hull.html⟩ (accessed August 2008).

66 According to H. R. Roberts, Roth reported to him that more than 800 "aspartame victims" had called on the hotline she established after "discovering" that her blindness in one eye was caused by heavy aspartame consumption. See Roberts, *Aspartame*, 11; Harrington, *Cure Within*, 17.

67 It is also possible that the rumors about the sweetener's health risk simply carried more weight among black than white customers. As early as the 1950s, cyclamate cookbooks addressed the "misperception" that sweeteners were unsafe.

Again the rumors circulated in 1977, only to be dismissed by most. And they recirculated in the 1980s with saccharin. Patricia Turner has documented the particular power of rumor in the black community. When saccharin fears first circulated, they may have had far more traction for African Americans. For more information on African American rumor and the differences between white and black rumor practices, see Turner, *I Heard It through the Grapevine*, and Turner and Fine, *Whispers on the Color Line*.

68 In 2007, the York, Pa., parish featured three films as part of their Vespers emphasis on "health-related information." One of them was an interview with Blaylock. Another was Brackett's *Sweet Misery*. Blaylock has also been hosted by the African American City Temple Adventist Church in Dallas, ⟨http://dallascitytemple.org/ ministries_music_total.htm⟩ (accessed May 29, 2010). See Bull and Lockhart, *Seeking a Sanctuary*, esp. 146–49, 164. For information on the York Vespers film series, see ⟨http://www.yorksdachurch.org/article.php?id=23⟩ (viewed July 5, 2009).

69 Villarosa, *Body and Soul*, 51, 309.

70 Harris, "Celebrating Our Cuisine," 305–9. In a survey of eight cookbooks written in the 2000s aimed at African Americans, including two texts focused on weight loss, only one used artificial sweetener in a recipe. That book, *The New Soul Food Cookbook for People with Diabetes*, was published by the American Diabetes Association, and even the three recipes that called for sugar-free gelatin also included sugar.

71 Labelle quoted in Nettles, "Saving Soul Food," 111. See also Jones, *New Soul Food Cookbook*. For an extensive list of African American cookbooks, including titles aimed at controlling diabetes or facilitating weight loss, see Nettles, "Saving Soul Food," 106–13.

72 Lawler, *Sweet Talk*, 35.

73 According to Lawler, the FDA did studies on humans replicating the amount of aspartame that would be ingested by the top 1 percent of heavy users and "invariably those results were negative." There are roughly 1 in 15,000 people who suffer from phenylketonuria (PKU), for whom aspartame can be fatal, and warning labels on aspartame-containing products signal this possible danger. See ibid., 31, 33.

74 Jain, *Injury*, 4.

75 Nash, *Inescapable Ecologies*, 213. Nash's own research compared what she called the "disputed disease of multiple chemical sensitivity" of the late twentieth century to the Victorian-era concerns about "miasma and locally produced fevers" (ibid., 5). Also useful in thinking about the connection between disease and place is Susan Sontag, who has argued that "modern metaphors" of disease ultimately reveal more about what she terms a "profound disequilibrium between individuals and society" than they do about the objective condition of a body. See Sontag, *Illness as Metaphor and AIDS and Its Metaphors*, 137.

76 Roberts noted that among the individuals he saw in his practice suffering from this syndrome, "some . . . consume extraordinary quantities of aspartame products." One explanation for this, he believed, was that such products could induce "intense thirst" that was not easily satisfied. See Roberts, *Aspartame*, 21.

77 Gregory Gordin, United Press International, Washington News, "Seizure, Blindness Victims Point to NutraSweet," October 12, 1987, n.p.

78 Alli and Crapo, "Sweetener Safety," 37.

79 McNamara, "Sweeteners Plateau," and Lindley, "Non-Nutritive Sweeteners," 13.

80 In March 2000, Monsanto sold NutraSweet to the private equity firm J. W. Childs, which continues to own the brand today. It has lost market share to sucralose (Splenda) but continues to have strong sales. See ⟨http://en.wikipedia.org/wiki/NutraSweet⟩ (accessed August 2009).

81 McNamara, "Sweeteners Plateau."

82 Rogers, Carlyle, Hill, and Blundell, "Uncoupling Sweet Taste and Calories," 549.

83 Lawler, *Sweet Talk*, 18.

84 Gaull and Goldbert, *New Technologies and the Future of Food and Nutrition*, 4, 7, 9. This point of view was supported by journalist Joseph McCann, who saw the NutraSweet Company as remarkable not for creating diet foods but for becoming "the vanguard of the emerging 'high tech' food companies" that were "changing the very way we relate to food" (McCann, *Sweet Success*, vii).

CONCLUSION

1 Kobus and Shannon, "Splenda Not 'Equal' to Real Sugar."

2 "Top That; Sweeteners," *Economist*, July 12, 2008, online edition.

3 Advertising using the same slogans continued in the United States after the settled suit, and even after rulings in France, Australia, and New Zealand forced a change in what was ruled to be deceptive advertising practices. See "Judge Sets Date for Splenda Trial: Johnson and Johnson Stands Accused of False Advertising the Artificial Sweetener," *PR Newswire, U.S.*, August 11, 2008.

4 ⟨http://www.splenda.com/index.jhtml⟩ (accessed August 2008).

5 "Judge Sets Date for Splenda Trial: Johnson and Johnson Stands Accused of False Advertising the Artificial Sweetener," *PR Newswire, U.S.*, August 11, 2008.

6 "McNeil Nutritionals and Sugar Association Settle Splenda Suit," *Philadelphia Business Journal*, November 17, 2008, ⟨http://www.bizjournals.com/philadelphia/stories/2008/11/17/daily13.html⟩ (accessed August 2009).

7 Lawler, *Sweet Talk*, 43. For an example of how this has continued in later years, see Rogers, Carlyle, Hill, and Blundell, "Uncoupling Sweet Taste and Calories," 547–52. In the acknowledgments, the authors explain that although they "gratefully acknowledge" the study's "partial funding by the Sugar Bureau," that support did not affect the study's outcome, which found that artificial sweetener did not effectively contribute to weight loss.

8 Andrew Martin, "Makers of Sodas Try a New Pitch: They're Healthy," *New York Times*, March 7, 2007 (accessed online, August 9, 2009); "More Than 60 Percent of Americans Wary of Artificial Sweeteners," *FoodProcessing.com*, ⟨http://www.foodprocessing.com/industrynews/2006/095.html⟩ (accessed August 10, 2009).

9 "Artificial Sweeteners Market to Change," *ICIS Chemical Business*, May 19, 2009, ⟨ICIS.com⟩ (accessed August 19, 2009).

10 Ibid.

11 Oliver, *Fat Politics*, 29.

12 Pollan, *In Defense of Food*, 4.

13 "Are Sugar Substitutes Making you Fat?," *Glamour*, March 2007, 146. This ques-

tion of "satiety" in artificial-sweetener consumption is just beginning to be explored. One early study is David Benton's "Can Artificial Sweeteners Help Control Body Weight and Prevent Obesity?" which found that people did tend to consume more sweet calories after artificial sweeteners unless they were making a conscious decision to engage in "dietary restraint."

14 Roberts, *Aspartame*, 147–48.
15 Quoted in Stegink and Filer, *Aspartame*, 284–85.
16 Beck, "Reduced Calorie Foods."
17 Pollan, *Omnivore's Dilemma*, 22–23.
18 Chen, *Taste of Sweet*, 125–26.

BIBLIOGRAPHY

ARCHIVAL COLLECTIONS
College Park, Maryland
  Park Lawn Building
    Food and Drug Administration Records
Davis, California
  University of California Library, Special Collections
    A. W. Noling Hurty-Peck Collection of Beverage Literature
    California Canners and Growers Archives, D-162
Durham, North Carolina
  Duke University, Duke Advertising Archives
    "Like" Advertising Collection
Lodi, California
  San Joaquin Historical Society and Museum
    Tillie Lewis Foods Collection, 1935–1978, MS52
Washington, D.C.
  Library of Congress
    Weight Watchers Magazine Collection, LC#90650575, RM222.2.W32,
      February 1968 to present
  National Museum of American History
    Landor Design Collection, ca. 1930–1994
    N W Ayer Advertising Agency Records
    Warshaw Collection of Business Americana
      Sugar Collection
        Fahlberg, List & Co. *Saccharin.* #60, box 1, folder 12

INTERVIEWS DONE BY AUTHOR
Kasoff, Larry. August 30, 2004, San Francisco, California.
Weast, Dr. Clair. April 6, 2009, Manteca, California.

PUBLISHED AND UNPUBLISHED SOURCES

Abbott, Elizabeth. *Sugar: A Bittersweet History*. Toronto: Penguin, 2008.

Abbott Laboratories. *The Abbott Almanac: 100 Years of Commitment to Quality Health Care*. New York: Benjamin Company, 1987.

———. *The Abbott Tree*. North Chicago, 1955.

———. *Calorie Saving Recipes for Foods Sweetened without Sugar Using Sucaryl, the New Non-caloric Sweetener for Diabetic and Reducing Diets*. North Chicago, 1952.

Albala, Ken. "Tillie Lewis: The Tomato Queen of San Joaquin." Unpublished manuscript, November 2008.

Alli, Cynthia, and Phyllis Crapo. "Sweetener Safety: The Bitter Debate." *Diabetes Forecast*, September–October 1985, 34–37.

American Council on Science and Health. *Diet and Behavior: A Report by the American Council on Science and Health*. New York, 1987.

Anderson, Jr., Oscar E. *The Health of a Nation: Harvey W. Wiley and the Fight for Pure Food*. Chicago: University of Chicago Press, 1958.

Appadurai, Arjun. "Consumption, Duration, and History." *Stanford Literature Review* 10, no. 1–2 (1993): 11–33.

———, ed. *The Social Life of Things*. Cambridge: Cambridge University Press, 1986.

Aspartame Consumer Safety Network. *Aspartame Consumer Safety Network*. ⟨http://www.aspartamesafety.com⟩.

Atwater, W. O. *Foods: Nutritive Value and Cost*. U.S. Department of Agriculture. Washington, D.C.: Government Printing Office, 1894.

Austin, S. Bryan. "Commodity Knowledge in Consumer Culture: The Role of Nutritional Health Promotion in the Making of the Diet Industry." In *Weighty Issues: Fatness and Thinness as Social Problems*, edited by Donna Maurer and Jeffrey Sobal, 159–71. New York: Aldine Transactions, 1999.

Avila, Eric. *Popular Culture in the Age of White Flight: Fear and Fantasy in Suburban Los Angeles*. Berkeley: University of California Press, 2004.

Babst, Earl. *A Century of Sugar Refining in the United States*. New York: American Sugar Refining Company, 1918.

———. *Occasions in Sugar*. Privately printed, 1915.

Bailey, Beth, and David Farber, eds. *America in the '70s*. Lawrence: University Press of Kansas, 2006.

Beck, C. I. "Reduced Calorie Foods—Once We Create Them, Do They Help?" *Food Product Development* 12, no. 2 (1978): 70, 72, 74.

Beck, Karl. "Have You Considered Artificial Sweeteners for Special Purpose Desserts and Puddings?" *Food Processing* 16 (1955): 42–44.

Beck, Ulrich. *Risk Society: Towards a New Modernity*. Translated by Mark Ritter. London: Sage Publications, 1992.

Belasco, Warren. *Appetite for Change: How the Counterculture Took on the Food Industry*. Ithaca: Cornell University Press, 1993.

———. "Food and the Counterculture: A Story of Bread and Politics." In *The Cultural Politics of Food and Eating: A Reader*, edited by James L. Watson and Melissa L. Caldwell, 217–34. San Francisco: Wiley-Blackwell, 2005.

———. "'Lite' Economics: Less Food, More Profit." *Radical History Review* 28–30 (1984): 270.

———. *Meals to Come: A History of the Future of Food*. Berkeley: University of California Press, 2006.

Bellamy, Edward. *Looking Backward*. 1888. New York: Oxford University Press, 2007.

Bentley, Amy. *Eating for Victory: Food Rationing and the Politics of Domesticity*. Champaign: University of Illinois Press, 1998.

Benton, David. "Can Artificial Sweeteners Help Control Body Weight and Prevent Obesity?" *Nutrition Research Reviews* 18, no. 1 (June 2005): 63–76.

Berkowitz, Edward. *Something Happened: A Political and Cultural Overview of the Seventies*. New York: Columbia University Press, 2006.

Berlant, Lauren. *The Female Complaint: The Unfinished Business of Sentimentality in American Culture*. Durham: Duke University Press, 2008.

Biltekoff, Charlotte, "The Terror Within: Obesity in Post 9/11 U.S. Life." *American Studies* 48, no. 3 (Fall 2008): 5–30.

Birch, G. G. *Low-Calorie Products*. Edited by M. G. Lindley. London: Elsevier Applied Science, 1987.

Blaylock, Russell L. *Excitotoxins: The Taste That Kills*. Santa Fe, N.M.: Health Press, 1994.

Bordo, Susan. *Unbearable Weight: Feminism, Western Culture, and the Body*. Berkeley: University of California Press, 1993.

———. *Unbearable Weight*. 2nd ed. Berkeley: University of California Press, 2003.

Bray, George, ed. *Obesity in America*. Department of Health, Education and Welfare, Public Health Service, National Institutes of Health, May 1980. Original conference held in 1977.

Brock, Fran. "Midwest Marketer of Year: G. D. Searle." *Adweek*, March 6, 1985, n.p.

———. "NutraSweet Ads Sweet on Nature." *Adweek*, February 3, 1986, n.p.

Brown, Helen Gurley. *Sex and the Single Girl*. New York: Random House, 1962.

Brumberg, Joan Jacobs. *The Body Project: An Intimate History of American Girls*. New York: Random House, 1997.

Bud, Robert. "Antibiotics, Big Business, and Consumers: The Context of Government Investigations into the Postwar American Drug Industry." *Technology and Culture* 46 (April 2005): 329–49.

Bull, Malcolm, and Keith Lockhart, eds. *Seeking a Sanctuary: Seventh-day Adventism and the American Dream*. Indianapolis: Indiana University Press, 2006.

Burkholtz, Herbert. *The FDA Follies*. New York: Basic Books, 1994.

Cannon, Poppy. *Unforbidden Sweets: Delicious Desserts of 100 Calories or Less*. New York: Crowell, 1958.

Carson, Rachel. *Silent Spring*. Cambridge, Mass.: Houghton Mifflin, 1962.

A Century of Sugar Refining in the United States. New York: American Sugar Refining, 1918.

Cera, Deanna Farnei. "The Luxury of Freedom, the Freedom of Luxury in the United States, 1935–1968." In *Jewels of Fantasy: Costume Jewelry of the 20th Century*, 147–219. New York: Harry N. Abrams, 1991.

Chandler, Jr., Alfred D. *Shaping the Industrial Century: The Remarkable Story of the Evolution of the Modern Chemical and Pharmaceutical Industries*. Cambridge, Mass.: Harvard University Press, 2005.

Cheal, David. "Gifts in Contemporary North America." In *Gift Giving: A Research*

Anthology, edited by Cele Otnes and Richard Beltramini, 85–98. Bowling Green, Ky.: Bowling Green State University Press, 1996.

Chen, Joanne. *The Taste of Sweet: Our Complicated Love Affair with our Favorite Treats*. New York: Crown Books, 2008.

Cohen, Lizabeth. *A Consumers' Republic: The Politics of Mass Consumption in Postwar America*. New York: Vintage, 2003.

———. "Embellishing a Life of Labor: An Interpretation of the Material Culture of American Working-Class Homes, 1885–1915." In *Material Culture Studies in America*, edited by Thomas Schlereth, 289–305. New York: Rowman Altamira, 1995.

Collins, James H. *The Story of Canned Foods*. New York: Dutton, 1924.

Cotter, Colleen. "Claiming a Piece of the Pie: How the Language of Recipes Defines Community." In *Recipes for Reading: Community Cookbooks, Stories, Histories*, edited by Anne L. Bower, 51–72. Amherst: University of Massachusetts Press, 1997.

Counihan, Carole. "Food Rules in the U.S.: Individualism Control and Hierarchy." In *The Anthropology of Food and Body*, 113–27. New York: Routledge, 1999.

Cowan, Ruth Schwartz. *More Work for Mother: The Ironies of Household Technology from the Open Hearth to the Microwave*. New York: Basic Books, 1983.

Crawford, Robert. "A Cultural Account of 'Health': Control, Release, and the Social Body." In *Issues in the Political Economy of Health Care*, edited by John B. McKinlay, 60–103. New York: Tavistock Publications, 1984.

Culliton, Barbara J. "Saccharin: A Chemical in Search of an Identity." *Science*, n.s., 196, no. 4295 (June 10, 1977): 1179–83.

Dinerstein, Joel. "Technology and Its Discontents." In *Rewiring the "Nation": The Place of Technology in American Studies*, edited by Siva Vaidhyanathan and Carolyn de la Peña, 15–41. Baltimore: Johns Hopkins University Press, 2007.

Dumit, Joe. *Picturing Personhood: Brainscans and Biomedical Identities*. Princeton, N.J.: Princeton University Press, 2003.

DuPuis, E. Melanie. *Nature's Perfect Food*. New York: New York University Press, 2003.

Dusselier, Jane. "Bonbons, Lemon Drops, and Oh Henry! Bars: Candy, Consumer Culture, and the Construction of Gender, 1895–1920." In *Kitchen Culture in America: Proper Representations of Food, Gender, and Race*, edited by Sherrie Inness, 13–50. Philadelphia: University of Pennsylvania Press, 2001.

Ellenbogen, Leon, ed. *Controversies in Nutrition*. New York: Churchill Livingstone, 1981.

Farrell, Amy. "The Narrowing of American Bodies: Christian Fitness Culture and the Politics of Size Reduction." *American Quarterly* 58, no. 2 (2006): 517–22.

Feldman, Elaine B. *Essentials of Clinical Nutrition*. Philadelphia: F. A. Davis Company, 1988.

Feudtner, Chris. *Bittersweet: Diabetes, Insulin, and the Transformation of Illness*. Chapel Hill: University of North Carolina Press, 2003.

Fine, Ben, Michael Heasman, and Judith Wright. *Consumption in the Age of Affluence: The World of Food*. London: Routledge, 1996.

"First Aspartame-Sweetened Cereal." *Chilton's Food Engineering International* 7, no. 11 (1982): 11.

Food and the War: A Textbook for College Classes. New York: Houghton Mifflin, 1918.

Forrestal, Dan. *Faith, Hope and $5000: The Trials and Triumphs of the First 75 Years, the Story of Monsanto*. New York: Simon and Schuster, 1977.

Fouche, Rayvon. *Black Inventors in the Age of Segregation: Granville T. Woods, Lewis H. Latimer, and Shelby J. Davidson*. Baltimore: Johns Hopkins University Press, 2003.

Freidberg, Susanne. *Fresh: A Perishable History*. Cambridge, Mass.: Harvard University Press, 2009.

Friedan, Betty. *The Feminine Mystique*. New York: Dell, 1963.

Galbraith, John Kenneth. "How Much Should a Country Consume?" In *Perspectives on Conservation: Essays on America's Natural Resources*, edited by Henry Jarrett, 89–99. Baltimore: Johns Hopkins University Press, 1958.

Gaull, Gerald, and Ray Goldbert, eds. *New Technologies and the Future of Food and Nutrition: Proceedings of the First Ceres Conference*. Williamsburg, Va., October 1989. New York: John Wiley and Sons, 1991.

Gibbons, Barbara. *Equal Delicious Recipes*. N.p.: G. D. Searle & Co., 1983.

Gibson, G. G., and R. Walker, eds. *Food Toxicology — Real or Imaginary Problems?* London: Taylor and Francis, 1985.

Gottlieb, Robert. *Forcing the Spring: The Transformation of the American Environmental Movement*. Washington, D.C.: Island Press, 2005.

Greene, Jeremy. "Attention to 'Details': Etiquette and the Pharmaceutical Salesman in Postwar American" [*sic*]. *Social Studies of Science* 34, no. 2 (April 2004): 271–92.

———. *Prescribing by Numbers: Drugs and the Definition of Disease*. Baltimore: Johns Hopkins University Press, 2007.

Grenby, T. H., K. J. Parker, and M. G. Lindley, eds. *Developments in Sweeteners — 2*. London: Applied Science Publishers, 1983.

Griffith, R. Marie. *Born Again Bodies: Flesh and Spirit in American Christianity*. Berkeley: University of California Press, 2004.

Guthman, Julie. "Eating Risk: The Politics of Labeling Genetically Engineered Foods." In *Engineering Trouble: Biotechnology and Its Discontents*, edited by Rachel A. Schurman and Dennis Doyle Takahashi Kelso, 130–51. Berkeley: University of California Press, 2003.

Guthman, Julie, and Melanie DuPuis, "Embodying Neoliberalism: Economy, Culture, and the Politics of Fat." *Environment and Planning D: Society and Space* 24 (2006): 427–48.

Harrington, Anne. *The Cure Within: A History of Mind-Body Medicine*. New York: Norton, 2008.

Harris, Ellen, and Alvin Nowverl. "What's Happening to Soul Food? Regional and Income Differences in the African American Diet." *Ecology of Food and Nutrition* 38 (2000): 587–603.

Harris, Jessica B. "Celebrating Our Cuisine." In *The Black Women's Health Book*, edited by Evelyn C. White, 305–9. 1990. Seattle: Seal, 1994.

Havender, William. "The Science and Politics of Cyclamate." *Public Interest* 71 (Spring 1983): 17–32.

Hawthorne, Fran. *Inside the FDA: The Business and Politics behind the Drugs We Take and the Foods We Eat*. Hoboken, N.J.: Wiley, 2005.

Henkel, John. "Sugar Substitutes: Americans Opt for Sweetness and Lite." *FDA Consumer Magazine* (November–December 1999). ⟨http://www.fda.gov/FDAC/features/1999/699_sugar.html⟩.

Herzbert, David. *From Miltown to Prozac: Happy Pills in America*. Baltimore: Johns Hopkins University Press, 2009.

"The Hold-Up in the Kitchen." *New York World*, April 14, 1929. Reprinted in American Bottlers of Carbonated Beverages, *What Price Sugar*. Washington, D.C., 1929.

Horowitz, Roger, ed. *Boys and Their Toys? Masculinity, Technology, and Class in America*. New York: Routledge, 2001.

Howard, Vicki. *Brides, Inc.: American Weddings and the Business of Tradition*. Philadelphia: University of Pennsylvania Press, 2006.

Howe, Louise Kapp. *The White Majority: Between Poverty and Affluence*. New York: Random House, 1970.

Huber, Peter. "The Old-New Division in Risk Regulation." *Virginia Law Review* 69, no. 6 (September 1983): 1035–1107.

Hull, Janet Starr. *Sweet Poison: How the World's Most Popular Artificial Sweetener Is Killing Us*. Far Hills, N.J.: New Horizon Press, 1999.

———. *Sweet Poison*. ⟨http://www.sweetpoison.com⟩.

Jain, Sarah Lochlann. *Injury: The Politics of Product Design and Safety Law in the United States*. Princeton, N.J.: Princeton University Press, 2006.

Jones, Wilbert, *The New Soul Food Cookbook: Healthier Recipes for Traditional Favorites*. New York: Kensington Publishing, 2005.

Kearns, Robin, and Graham Moon. "From Medical to Health Geography: Novelty, Place and Theory after a Decade of Change." *Progress in Human Geography* 226, no. 5 (2002): 5–25.

Kee, Ed. *Saving Our Harvest: The Story of the Mid-Atlantic Region's Canning and Freezing Industry*. Baltimore: CTI Publications, 2006.

Kobayashi, Audrey, and Linda Peake. "Racism out of Place: Thoughts on Whiteness and an Antiracist Geography in the New Millennium." *Annals of the Association of American Geographers* 90, no. 2 (2000): 392–403.

Kobus, Theodore, and David J. Shannon. "Splenda Not 'Equal' to Real Sugar in Lanham Act False Advertising Suit; Claim against Splenda for False and Misleading Advertising Discussed." *New Jersey Law Journal*, April 11, 2008, 1–2.

Koten, Bernard. *The Low-Calory Cookbook: Non-Fattening Recipes for People who Love Good Food*. New York: Random House, 1951.

LaBelle, Patti. *Lite Cuisine: Over 100 Dishes with To-Die-For Taste Made with To-Live-For Recipes*. New York: Gotham Books, 2003.

La Follette, Marcel. *Making Science Our Own: Public Images of Science, 1910–1955*. Chicago: University of Chicago Press, 1990.

Lai, C. "Around the World: An Introduction to Pentothal Advertising Postcards from Abbott Laboratories, 1956–1968." *Proceedings of the History of Anesthesia Society* 31 (2002): 29–31.

Lappé, Frances Moore. *Diet for a Small Planet*. New York: Ballentine Books, 1972.

Lasch, Christopher. *The Culture of Narcissism*. New York: Norton, 1978.

Lawler, Philip. *Sweet Talk: Media Coverage of Artificial Sweeteners*. Washington, D.C.: The Media Institute, 1986.

Lears, Jackson. *Fables of Abundance: A Cultural History of Advertising in America*. New York: Basic Books, 1994.

LeBesco, Kathleen. *Revolting Bodies: The Struggle to Redefine Fat Identity*. Boston: University of Massachusetts Press, 2004.

———. "There's Always Room for Resistance: Jell-O, Gender, and Social Class." In *Cooking Lessons: The Politics of Gender and Food*, edited by Sherrie A. Inness, 129–49. New York: Rowman & Littlefield, 2001.

Lesser, Milton. "Dietetic Foods and the Pharmaceutical Industry." *Drug and Cosmetic Industry* 73, no. 5 (November 1953): 610–11, 690–92.

Levenstein, Harvey. *Paradox of Plenty: A Social History of Eating in Modern America*. Berkeley: University of California Press, 2003.

———. *Revolution at the Table: The Transformation of the American Diet*. Berkeley: University of California Press, 2003.

Liesse, Julie. "Bitter Future for NutraSweet." *Advertising Age*, May 1991, 33.

Lindley, Michael. "Non-Nutritive Sweeteners; Markets and Marketing." *International Food Ingredients* 6 (1993): 11–14.

Lippert, Barbara. "Reality Check." *Adweek*, March 14, 1994, 32.

Macinnis, Peter. *Bittersweet: The Story of Sugar*. New York: Allen and Unwin, 2007.

Manufacturing Chemists' Association. *Food Additives: What They Are and How They Are Used*. Washington, D.C., 1961.

Marchand, Roland. *Advertising the American Dream*. Berkeley: University of California Press, 1985.

———. *Creating the Corporate Soul*. Berkeley: University of California Press, 2001.

Marie, S., and J. R. Piggott, eds. *Handbook of Sweeteners*. Glasgow: Blackie Academic and Professional, 1991.

Marvin, Carolyn. *When Old Technologies Were New: Thinking about Electric Communication in the Late Nineteenth Century*. New York: Oxford University Press, 1988.

May, Earl Chapin. *The Canning Clan: A Pageant of Pioneering Americans*. New York: Macmillan, 1937.

May, Elaine Tyler. *Homeward Bound: American Families in the Cold War Era*. New York: Basic Books, 1988.

McCann, Joseph. *Sweet Success: How NutraSweet Created a Billion Dollar Business*. Homewood, Ill.: Business One Irwin, 1990.

McGovern, Charles. *Sold American: Consumption and Citizenship, 1890–1945*. Chapel Hill: University of North Carolina Press, 2006.

McGrath, Patrick J. *Scientists, Business, and the State, 1890–1960*. Chapel Hill: University of North Carolina Press, 2002.

McKinlay, John B., ed. *Issues in the Political Economy of Health Care*. New York: Tavistock Publications, 1984.

McNamara, Damian. "Sweeteners Plateau." *Chemical Marketing Reporter* 247, no. 22 (March 29, 1995): 16–17.

Meikle, Jeffrey. *American Plastic: A Cultural History*. New Brunswick, N.J.: Rutgers University Press, 1997.

Mercola, Joseph, and Kendra Degen Pearsall. *Sweet Deception: Why Splenda, Nutra-Sweet, and the FDA May Be Hazardous to Your Health*. New York: Nelson Books, 2006.

Merki, Christoph Maria. *Zuker gegen Saccharin: Zur Geschichte der Künstichlen Süßtoffe*. Frankfurt: Campus Verlag, 1993.

Milburn, Colin. *Nanovision: Engineering the Future*. Durham, N.C.: Duke University Press, 2008,

Miller, Llewellyn. *Reducing Cookbook and Diet Guide*. New York: Crowell, 1951.

Mintz, Sidney. *Sweetness and Power: The Place of Sugar in Modern History*. New York: Penguin, 1986.

———. *Tasting Food, Tasting Freedom: Excursions into Eating, Culture, and the Past*. Boston: Beacon, 1996.

———. "Time, Sugar, and Sweetness." In *Food and Culture: A Reader*, edited by Carole Counihan and Penny Van Esterik, 357–69. New York: Routledge, 1997.

Munro, Daniel Colin. *Slenderizing for New Beauty*. New York: Bartholomew House, 1953.

Murphy, Margot. *War Time Meals*. New York: Greenberg, 1942.

Myrick, Herbert. *The American Sugar Industry*. Springfield, Mass.: Orange Judd Company, 1899.

Nabors, Lyn O'Brien, and Robert C. Gelardi. *Alternative Sweeteners*. New York: Marcel Dekker, 1986.

Nash, Linda. *Inescapable Ecologies: A History of Environment, Disease, and Knowledge*. Berkeley: University of California Press, 2006.

National Academy of Sciences. *Sweeteners: Issues and Uncertainties*. Washington, D.C., 1975.

Nestle, Marion. *Food Politics: How the Food Industry Influences Nutrition and Health*. Berkeley: University of California Press, 2002.

Nettles, Kimberly. "'Saving' Soul Food." *Gastronomica*, Summer 2007, 106–13.

Nichter, Mimi. *Fat Talk*. Cambridge, Mass.: Harvard University Press, 2000.

Nidetch, Jean. *The Story of Weight Watchers*. New York: W/W Twentyfirst Corporation, 1970.

———. *Weight Watchers Food Plan Diet Cookbook*. New York: New American Library Books, 1982.

Norris, Donald. "Ingredient Branding: A Strategy Option with Multiple Beneficiaries." *Journal of Consumer Marketing* 9, no. 3 (Summer 1992): 19–20.

Nye, David. *America as Second Creation: Technology and Narratives of New Beginnings*. Boston: MIT Press, 2003.

Oliver, J. Eric. *Fat Politics: The Real Story behind America's Obesity Epidemic*. New York: Oxford University Press, 2006.

Parham, Ellen Speiden. "Attitudes toward the Ban on Cyclamates." *Journal of the American Dietetic Association* 56 (June 1970): 525.

Parkin, Katherine. *Food Is Love: Food Advertising and Gender Roles in Modern America*. Philadelphia: University of Pennsylvania Press, 2006.

Peiss, Kathy. *Hope in a Jar: The Making of America's Beauty Culture*. New York: Holt Paperbacks, 1999.

Plante, Ellen. *The American Kitchen, 1700 to the Present: From Hearth to Highrise*. New York: Facts on File, 1995.

Pollack, Herbert, and Arthur Morse. *How to Reduce Surely and Safely*. New York: McGraw-Hill, 1955.

Pollan, Michael. *In Defense of Food: An Eater's Manifesto*. New York: Penguin, 2008.

———. *The Omnivore's Dilemma: A Natural History of Four Meals*. New York: Penguin, 2006.

Pratt, William D. *The Abbott Almanac: 100 Years of Commitment to Quality Health Care*. New York: Benjamin Company, 1987.

Probyn, Elspeth. *Carnal Appetites: FoodSexIdentities*. London: Routledge, 2000.

Roberts, Dorothy. *Killing the Black Body: Race, Reproduction, and the Meaning of Liberty*. New York: Vintage, 1998.

Roberts, H. J. *Aspartame (NutraSweet): Is It Safe?* Philadelphia: Charles Press, 1990.

Rogers, Peter J., J. A. Carlyle, A. J. Hill, and J. E. Blundell. "Uncoupling Sweet Taste and Calories." *Physiology and Behavior* 43, no. 5 (1988): 547–52.

Rose, Nikolas, and Peter Miller. "Political Power beyond the State: Problematics of Government." *British Journal of Sociology* 43, no. 2 (1992): 173–205.

Rosner, Lisa, ed. *The Technological Fix: How People Use Technology to Create and Solve Problems*. New York: Routledge, 2004.

Rubin, Lawrence. "Merchandising Madness: Pills, Promises, and Better Living through Chemistry." *Journal of Popular Culture* 28, no. 2 (November 2004): 369–84.

Ruiz, Vicki. *Cannery Women, Cannery Lives*. Albuquerque: University of New Mexico Press, 1987.

Rydell, Robert. *All the World's a Fair: Visions of Empire at American International Expositions, 1876–1916*. Chicago: University of Chicago Press, 1984.

Sabin, Deana Markoff. *How Sweet It Was! The Beet Sugar Industry in Microcosm*. New York: Garland, 1986.

Scanlon, Jennifer. *Bad Girls Go Everywhere: The Life of Helen Gurley Brown*. New York: Oxford University Press, 2009.

———. *Inarticulate Longings: The Ladies' Home Journal, Gender, and the Promises of Consumer Culture*. New York: Routledge, 1995.

Scarpa, Ioannis S., Helen Chilton Kiefer, and Rita Tatum, eds. *Sourcebook on Food and Nutrition*. 2nd ed. Chicago: Marquis Academic Media, 1980.

Schoenthaler, S. J. "Sugar and Children's Behavior." *New England Journal of Medicine* 330, no. 26 (June 30, 1994): 1901–4.

Schwartz, Hillel. *Never Satisfied: A Cultural History of Diets, Fantasies, and Fat*. New York: Free Press, 1986.

Scranton, Philip, ed. *Beauty and Business: Commerce, Gender, and Culture in Modern America*. New York: Routledge, 2001.

Seely, Stephen, David Freed, Gerald Silverstone, and Vicky Rippere. *Diet-Related Diseases: The Modern Epidemic*. London: Croom Helm, 1985.

Shannon, Joyce Breenfleck. *Diet and Nutrition Sourcebook*. 3rd ed. Health Reference Series. New York: Omnigraphics, 2006.

Shapiro, Laura. *Perfection Salad: Women and Cooking at the Turn of the Century*. New York: Modern Library, 2001.

———. *Something from the Oven: Reinventing Dinner in 1950s America*. New York: Viking, 2004.

A Short Story of Sugar: Worthwhile Facts about a Valuable Food. Chicago: W. A. Havermeyer, 1923.

Sims, Laura. *The Politics of Fat: Food and Nutrition Policy in America*. New York: M. E. Sharpe, 1998.

Sinclair, Bruce. *Technology and the African-American Experience*. Boston: MIT Press, 2004.

Slocum, Rachel. "Whiteness, Space, and Alternative Food Practice." *Geoforum* 38, no. 3 (2006): 520–33.

Smith, Mark M. "Producing Sense, Consuming Sense, Making Sense: Perils and Prospects for Sensory History." *Journal of Social History* 40, no. 4 (Summer 2007): 841–58.

Smith, R. Jeffrey. "Latest Saccharin Tests Kill FDA Proposal." *Science*, n.s., 208, no. 4440 (April 11, 1980): 154–56.

Sontag, Susan. *Illness as Metaphor and AIDS and Its Metaphors*. New York: Anchor Books, 1990.

Stacey, Michelle. *Consumed: Why Americans Love, Hate, and Fear Food*. New York: Simon and Schuster, 1994.

Stearns, Peter N. "Fat in America." In *Cultures of the Abdomen: Diet, Digestion, and Fat in the Modern World*, edited by Christopher Forth and Ana Carden-Coyne, 239–58. New York: Palgrave, 2005.

Steginck, Lewis D., and Lloyd J. Filer Jr., eds. *Aspartame: Physiology and Biochemistry*. New York: Marcel Dekker, 1984.

Stumpf, Samuel Enoch. "Culture, Values, and Food Safety." *Bioscience* 28, no. 3 (1978): 186–90.

Suitor, Carol West, and Merrily Forbes Hunter. *Nutrition: Principles and Application in Health Promotion*. Philadelphia: Lippincott, 1980.

Sze, Julie. *Noxious New York: The Racial Politics of Urban Health and Environmental Justice*. Boston: MIT Press, 2006.

Taylor, Henry J. "Cheerful London; Sullen Berlin." *New York Times*, February 15, 1942, SM 11.

"Thayer Explains How Abbott Gained New Markets." *Drug Trade News* 33, no. 37 (November 3, 1958).

Thomas, Paul, ed. *Improving America's Diet and Health: From Recommendations to Action, a Report of the Committee on Dietary Guidelines and Implementation*. Washington, D.C.: National Academy Press, 1991.

"Tillie Lewis: 'First Lady of the Larder.'" *Good Packaging* 36, no. 12 (December 1975): 6–8.

"Tillie's Unpunctured Romance." *Time*, November 19, 1951.

Tone, Andrea, and Elizabeth Siegel Watkins. *Medicating Modern America: Prescription Drugs in History*. New York: New York University Press, 2007.

Trager, James. *The Enriched, Fortified, Concentrated, Country-Fresh, Lip-Smacking, Finger-Licking, International, Unexpurgated Foodbook*. New York: Grossman, 1970.

Traweek, Sharon. *Beamtimes and Lifetimes: The World of High Energy Physics*. Cambridge, Mass.: Harvard University Press, 1992.

Turner, Patricia. *I Heard It through the Grapevine: Rumor and African-American Culture*. Berkeley: University of California Press, 1994.

Turner, Patricia, and Gary Allen Fine. *Whispers on the Color Line: Rumor and Race in America*. Berkeley: University of California Press, 2004.

U.S. Congress. House of Representatives. *Hearings before the Subcommittee on Health* and the Environment of the Committee on Interstate and Foreign Commerce (HSHE). 95th Cong., 1st sess., March 21, 22, 1977.

———. Senate. Select Committee on Nutrition and Human Needs. *Dietary Goals of the United States*. 95th Cong., 1st sess., February 1977, Washington, D.C.

U.S. Department of Health and Human Services. *The Surgeon General's Call to Action to Prevent and Decrease Overweight and Obesity*. Rockland, Md.: U.S. Department of Human Services, Public Health Service, Office of the Surgeon General, 2001.

Valentine, Gill. "A Corporeal Geography of Consumption." *Environment and Planning D: Society and Space* 17 (1999): 329–51.

Villarosa, Linda, ed. *Body and Soul: The Black Women's Guide to Physical Health and Emotional Well-Being*. New York: Harper Collins, 1994.

Vogt, Paul. *The Sugar Refining Industry in the United States: Its Development and Present Condition*. Philadelphia: University of Pennsylvania, 1908.

Wagner, Mahlon W. "Cyclamate Acceptance." *Science*, n.s., 169, no. 3939 (June 1970): 1605.

Wailoo, Keith. *Drawing Blood*. Baltimore: Johns Hopkins University Press, 1997.

Waldo, Myra. *The Slenderella Cook Book*. New York: G. P. Putnam's Sons, 1957.

Walker, Nancy. *Shaping Our Mother's World: American Women's Magazines*. Jackson: University Press of Mississippi, 2000.

Wansink, Brian, Koert Van Ittersum, and James E. Painter. "Ice Cream Illusions: Bowls, Spoons, and Self-Served Portion Sizes." *American Journal of Preventative Medicine* 31, no. 3 (2006): 240–43.

Warner, Deborah Jean. "How Sweet It Is: Sugar, Science, and the State." *Annals of Science* 64, no. 2 (April 2007): 147–70.

Warnes, Andrew. *Hunger Overcome: Food and Resistance in Twentieth-Century Literature*. Athens: University of Georgia Press, 2004.

Watts, Sara Hervey. *The Sucaryl Cookbook of Sugar-Free Recipes*. New York: Random House, 1968.

Weaver, Ronice, Fabiola D. Gaines, and Angela Ebron. *Slim Down Sister: The African American Woman's Guide to Healthy, Permanent Weight Loss*. New York: Dutton, 2000.

West, Ruth. *Stop Dieting! Start Losing!* New York: Dutton, 1956.

Whitney, Eleanor Noss, and Frances Sienkeiwicz Sizer. *Nutrition: Concepts and Controversies*. 1st–4th eds. St. Paul: West Publishing, 1979.

Whitney, Eleanor Noss, Frances Sienkeiwicz Sizer, and Eva May Nunnelly Hamilton. *Understanding Nutrition*. 2nd ed. St. Paul: West Publishing, 1981.

———. *Understanding Nutrition*. 3rd ed. St. Paul: West Publishing, 1984.

Williams-Forson, Psyche A. *Building Houses out of Chicken Legs: Black Women, Food, and Power*. Chapel Hill: University of North Carolina Press, 2006.

Wilson, Richard. "Commentary: Risks and Their Acceptability." *Science Technology and Human Values*, 9, no. 2 (Spring 1984): 11–22.

Winslow, Thyra Samter. *Think Yourself Thin: The New Mental Outlook to Help you Lose Weight*. New York: Abelard Press, 1951.

Woloson, Wendy. *Refined Tastes: Sugar, Confectionary, and Consumers in Nineteenth-Century America*. Baltimore: Johns Hopkins University Press, 2002.

Wolraich, Mark L., Scott D. Lindgren, Phyllis J. Stumbo, Lewis D. Stegink, Mark I. Appelbaum, and Mary C. Kiritsy. "Effects of Diets High in Sucrose or Aspartame on the Behavior and Cognitive Performance of Children." *New England Journal of Medicine* 330, no. 5 (February 3, 1994): 301–7.

Wood, Donna. "The Strategic Use of Public Policy: Business Support for the 1906 Food and Drug Act." *Business History Review* 59, no. 3 (Autumn 1985): 403–32.

Yudkin, John. *Pure, White, and Deadly*. New York: Viking, 1986.

———. *Sweet and Dangerous*. New York: Bantam Books, 1972.

ACKNOWLEDGMENTS

This is a better book because of the efforts of a number of people, and it is a pleasure to be able to thank them permanently in print. As historians well know, books turn on the knowledge of archivists. I was fortunate to be hanging out with Axel Borg, archivist at the University of California at Davis, several years ago when this project was just beginning. I mentioned my interest in artificial sweetener, and he pointed me toward the treasures I would find in the California Canners and Growers files in the Shields Library Special Collections. Once I arrived, John Skarsdad, university archivist, proved an ideal guide. Leigh Johnsen at the San Joaquin County Historical Museum's library and Kimberly Bowden at the Haggin Museum helped me find my way through their Tillie Lewis collections. I also owe a special debt to several staff members whose names I don't know at the Food and Drug Administration who, some years ago, made the decision to scan thousands of public letters written in response to the proposed saccharin ban before they were thrown away.

I received funding assistance from the Chemical Heritage Foundation Library and from the Hagley Center for Business and Industry. While in Philadelphia and Wilmington, Ronald Bradshear and Roger Horowitz kept me plied with useful documents and provided good company. I also received support from the University of California through the Washington, D.C., center's short-term faculty research grant and a systemwide Humanities Research Institute residential fellowship, and from the University of California at Davis through yearly faculty grants in aid of research, a Humanities Institute fellowship, a Professional Development Award, and a Chancellor's Fellowship. I owe a special debt to Georges Van den Abbeele for convening a fabulous group of scholars in

2005 to work on food and culture at the Davis Humanities Institute and to Melanie DuPuis for assembling an inspired assortment of UC faculty (with culinary talent, too) in 2006 for our semester in residence on food and race. This book is much better for the hard questions asked by my colleagues that quarter: DuPuis, Julie Guthman, Roberto Alvarez, Kimberly Nettles, Parama Roy, Michael Owen Jones, and Sarita Gaytan. I also want to thank David Theo Goldberg, UCHRI director, for his steadfast support for these interdisciplinary humanities collaborations.

Many of the chapters benefited from forums where I was able to share work in progress with colleagues who sharpened my thinking. Thank you to Roger Horowitz of the Hagley Center for Business and Industry, to Lauren Rabinowitz at the University of Iowa, to Steven Hoelscher and the graduate students of the American Studies program at the University of Texas at Austin, to Rayvon Fouche and the Center for Advanced Study at the University of Illinois Urbana-Champaign, to Ken Albala at the University of the Pacific, to David Serlin of UC San Diego's Science Studies Program, and to Caren Kaplan and the Cultural Studies graduate students at UC Davis as well as the members of the TechnoScience, Culture, and the Arts research cluster at UC Davis.

I owe a special debt to a set of phenomenal research assistants over the years who never tired of my random requests, late-night e-mails, and lost page numbers for quotes. Megan Neves, Alison Hilman, Sivan Kovnator, Rebecca Chamow, Kristine Vandenberg, Elise Chatelian, Lauren Agatstein, Anne-Marie Litak, and especially Emily Laurel Smith, Ami Sommariva, and Sarah Rebolloso McCullough exceeded expectations at every turn.

Every person writing a book should have an opportunity to assemble a dream team of scholars and graduate students with deep interdisciplinary knowledge of their field. This for me was the Studies of Food and the Body multicampus research group founded in 2007. They provided a model of careful critique and interdisciplinary exchange and continually reminded me of the merits of studying culture through the lens of food. Thanks especially to Alie Alkon, Charlotte Biltekoff, Michelle Branch, Lissa Caldwell, Glenda Drew, Melanie DuPuis, Ryan Galt, Julie Guthman, Stacy Jameson, David Michalski, Daniel Nemser, Kimberly Nettles, Alia Pan, Erika Rappaport, and Mike Ziser, without whom none of it would have happened in the first place and who always kept us on track and made us smarter. We are all fortunate to be working at the University of California, where the administrators value food studies and its cross-disciplinary scholars.

Several friends and colleagues, while not responsible for the errors and omissions in the final project, gave me leads, editorial tough love, and moral support along the way that improved it and its author. Thank you to Joel Dinerstein, Siva Vaidhyanathan, Christina Cogdell, Maureen Reed, Lara Downes, Cary Cordova, Ari Y. Kelman, Joe Dumit, Colin Milburn, Caren Kaplan, Laura Grindstaff, Ryken Grattet, Laurie San Martin, Sam Nichols, Kent Ono, Sarah Projansky, Leslie Madsen-Brooks, Eric Smoodin, Julie Sze, Grace Wang, Jay Mechling, Michael Smith, Seeta Chaganti, Benjamin Lawrance, Cathy Kudlick, Sophie Volpp, Regina Canegan, jesikah maria ross, Elliott Pollard, Darra Goldstein, Lucy Bunch, Amy Kautzman, Kim Nalder, Jackie Hausman, Robert Irwin, Rafel Diaz Escamilla, Jessie Ann Owens, Jeffrey Meikle, Elizabeth Engelhardt, Warren Belasco, Sidney Mintz, Amy Bentley, Laura Shapiro, Ken Albala, Edie Sparks, Kyle Tobin-Williams, Susanne Freidberg, Patricia Turner, Psyche Williams-Forson, Doris Witt, and Sharon McDonough. Staci Della-Rocco taught me lessons about perseverance that made this a better book, and me a better person. I am grateful to Jennifer Langdon, Amy Farrell, and an anonymous reviewer for their close readings and insightful comments on full drafts.

My editor at UNC Press, Sian Hunter, is smart and funny and possesses a superior critical eye. Working with her and Stephanie Wenzel, my copyeditor, has been a stress-free and enjoyable publishing process.

And finally a few words of gratitude to those who have been in it for the long haul. Charlotte Biltekoff, colleague and friend, has impacted my thinking about food and culture, and my sense of mission, more than she knows. My in-laws Joe and Ardith de la Peña provided a home away from home where the cupboards now stock more sugar than sweetener. My sister- and brother-in-law Jodi and Gary de la Peña Vanderpol made things fun Costa Rican style at a critical moment. My mother, Catherine Vade Bon Coeur, encouraged me, entertained my children, and reminded me of the virtues of Diet Pepsi. And for my husband, David de la Peña, who tolerates my tendency to say, "I'm almost done," when I'm not and who, when it counts, is almost always right, I reserve the biggest thanks of all. Along with our kids, Sofia and Eva, he has built for me a world so great that I almost always, eventually, want to stop working and go play.

INDEX